USE OF HEALTH CARE RESOURCES

A Comparative Study of Two Health Plans

**health
administration
press**

*Health Administration Press was
established in 1972 with the support
of the W.K. Kellogg Foundation and
is a nonprofit endeavor of The
University of Michigan Program
and Bureau of Hospital
Administration.*

USE OF HEALTH CARE RESOURCES

A Comparative Study of Two Health Plans

Edited by

Donald C. Riedel
Daniel C. Walden
Samuel M. Meyers
Renate Wilson

Health Administration Press
Ann Arbor, Michigan
1984

Library of Congress Cataloging in Publication Data
Main entry under title:

Use of health care resources.

Bibliography: p.
Includes index
1. Insurance, Government employees' health —
Washington (D.C.) 2. Blue Cross and Blue Shield
Association. 3. Group Health Association (Washington,
D.C.) 4. Hospital utilization — Washington (D.C.)
5. Medical care — Washington (D.C.) 6. Health surveys —
Washington (D.C.) 7. Washington, (D.C.) — Statistics,
Medical. I. Riedel, Donald C., 1934-   . [DNLM:
1. Expenditures, Health — United States. 2. Insurance,
Health — United States. 3. Hospitals — Utilization —
United States. W 275 AA1 U8]
RA413.5.U6W288   1984   353.001'234   84-4616
ISBN 0-914904-96-5

Health Administration Press
The University of Michigan
1021 East Huron
Ann Arbor, Michigan 48109
(313) 764-1380

Contents

List of Tables and Figures

Tables are presented at the conclusion of each chapter.

TABLES

Forewords

In the late 1960s, there was considerable speculation about variations in health service use, cost and quality between prepaid group practices and more typical patterns of service delivery. Were the lower hospital admission rates associated with prepaid group practice a sign of greater effectiveness or of lower quality of care? These and related questions were a source of discomfort for many, particularly those providing care in conventional settings. Lack of definitive data did little either to cool the often heated debate over delivery arrangements or to guide improvements. During this period, I felt that the Blue Cross Association and Plans, as major financers of community health services, had a responsibility to their subscribers to look further into the subject of utilization and other differences across alternative forms of medical practice. Were there systematic variations in use, cost, or quality? If so, what were associated factors? And what were the consequences for consumers? The Federal Employee Health Benefits Program appeared to offer the best opportunity for study. Specifically, it presented the possibility of comparing two contrasting delivery systems under one administration in one geographical area and with enough volume to control age, sex and other key variables. Based on the need and opportunity, the Blue Cross Association research staff was instructed to initiate a study—a study that shortly involved many others in public and private service, beyond the confines of the Association.

In promoting research into questions about use, cost and quality variations, we were aware of the potential consequences. Specifically, if methodologically sound research found no justifiable basis for differences in use, we would face the imposing challenge of bringing higher use rates into line. This, of course, could involve significant changes in ways of doing business, and such change is rarely easy.

The complexities of this research subject were underestimated by many involved. The study which is described in the following—thorough as it was—raised more questions than it answered about differences and similarities between the Group Health Association and the Blue Cross-Blue Shield Federal Employees Program. Straightforward explanations for hospital use variations do not emerge from the data, that is, from either measured differences among consumers or providers or differences in the appropriateness of hospitalization decisions. Utilization variations, despite much study, continue to be a perplexing issue for researchers and decision makers. Further research of the kind seen here, even if limited to a single site, is enormously costly in time and money. New approaches to reduce the time and money commitments must be developed.

Some of the data reported in this study are now over a decade old. Alternative delivery systems, such as HMOs, have grown although not to the extent that many advocates had hoped. And evidence of real cost savings to the community is more elusive than some of us had anticipated. In addition, new research has focused attention on pre-existing differences in the preferences and use patterns of people who select HMOs rather than conventional medical service arrangements. It seems these differences can be substantial. Also, we have seen for all Blue Cross Plan subscribers an 18-percent decline in hospital use rates over the last dozen or so years. The gap between HMOs and traditional practice forms is narrowing. One reason is that new cost containment programs have been designed to make sure that inpatient hospital services are appropriately used. Undoubtedly, the competitive impact of HMOs continues to be another reason. In many areas, however, we know that more must be done, and we continue to seek the knowledge base for effective action. There is much in this book to instruct us in this quest.

In the 1980s we can anticipate further reductions in public budgets devoted to health and other areas of the American economy. New opportunities are unfolding for private sector creativity and initiative. These opportunities demand new scrutiny of private sector performance. I believe that the sort of examination of consumer and producer behavior exemplified in this research has merit for other enterprises. Good information can help head off wasteful debate and can promote high quality decision-making in a less or, at least, a differently regulated environment.

One implication of this study is that a facile "which delivery system is better" mentality is not very helpful. It is likely that there is no inherently "best" structure for health care delivery. Organizational performance is too complex for that, too contingent upon the particular dynamics generated by specific clients, staffs, communities and political/economic circumstances. Absent simple answers, we must focus instead on improving and developing a variety of health services options because people differ in what they want and need from the health system. The last dozen years have seen considerable progress toward this objective, with the HMO providing a useful standard for the use of hospital services. The current decade offers even greater opportunities, if we have the patience to avoid simplistic and precipitous action, the foresight to promote full debate over alternatives, and the wit to forge constructive public and private action from the resulting clash of views.

September 1982

WALTER J. MCNERNEY

Professor of Health Policy
Graduate School of Management
Northwestern University
and former President,
Blue Cross and Blue Shield Associations

By the end of the 1960s, the inappropriate use and rising cost of medical care had become critical issues in the health field. One of the strategies proposed for dealing with these problems was expanding the number of prepaid group practice plans. There was some evidence by 1970 that this organizational arrangement might be a more effective and efficient way to deliver health services than the traditional fee-for-service approach. But no definitive study had been undertaken to resolve the matter and many questions remained to be answered. The National Center for Health Services Research (NCHSR) and the Blue Cross Association therefore initiated a study in 1970 to compare the use and cost of services under these two alternative approaches to delivering health care. The Federal Employees Health Benefits Program provided the basis for a natural experiment that made such a study possible. The findings from this study are presented here.

Despite the fact that the data on which the analyses are based were collected prior to 1975, the findings are relevant today. There are two reasons why this is the case. First, the two systems that form the basis for this study appear not to have changed significantly in the intervening years. Second, the study was designed and carried out in such a manner that it has been possible to reach some general conclusions about consumer, professional, and organizational behavior. The analyses reported here go beyond mere comparisons of how medicine is practiced under these different plans.

Only a few health services research projects underway today can be compared with this study in terms of scope and complexity. This is the case not because we could not benefit from such projects. Rather, it is a consequence of not making available the resources required to support them. The loss is real and should be of great concern to those involved in formulating health policy and administering health programs. Many questions cannot be addressed by analyzing data that have been assembled to deal with other problems or serve other ends. Ingenious use of such data can only take us so far. This study is, therefore, a tribute not only to those who planned and directed it, but also to a period when, if one were to judge by the funds available for these studies, there was a better understanding of the value of such research.

Washington, D.C., January 1983

DONALD GOLDSTONE, M.D.
Associate Deputy Director for Medical and Scientific Affairs
and Acting Director,
National Center for Health Services Research

Preface

When we began this study, the questions it posed and the design employed reflected both the national health policy issues of the 1970s and the state of knowledge about factors associated with variations in use and expenditures for health services. Even then, these questions were prompted by continuing increases in health expenditures, especially those associated with inpatient services. Should the federal government encourage further growth in prepaid group practice plans? How could such plans be integrated into the Medicare and Medicaid programs and could they be included in some form of national health insurance?

Though differences in hospital admission rates between beneficiaries of prepaid group practice plans or HMOs and those covered by health insurance and who received their care in fee-for-service settings had been recognized for some years, particularly from the experience of federal employees covered by the various types of plans in the Federal Employees Health Benefits Program, little was known about what accounted for these differences. There was concern that they may have been more an artifact of the data systems upon which the reports of hospital admission rates were based than true differences between these two approaches to providing health insurance coverage and delivering health care.

Thus, an early goal of our research was the careful construction of a data base from which differences, if any, in hospital admission rates could be established with certainty. Drawing from the experience of researchers before us, we developed a study that we believed would clearly demonstrate the factors associated with any true differences in hospital admission rates between the two types of plans. Hence, we gave emphasis to the collection of data on those characteristics of members and patients believed to be associated with differences in both ambulatory and inpatient use, on provider characteristics and behavior, and on characteristics of the plans *per se* and of the specific health insurance benefits they provided. We also drew from the then new and growing field of research on clinical factors associated with appropriate hospital use, with the expectation that it would provide a key element in our understanding of these phenomena. Though we recognized that our research design could not incorporate a study of health outcomes, our assessment of the care provided to inpatients tried to respond to the concern about any differences in the quality of health care provided under the two plans.

These and related concerns were reflected in the continued support of this study by the National Center for Health Services Research (NCHSR). Through contract 110-70-416 with Health Services Foundation, it has funded the research for this project by Blue Cross Association, Group Health Association, Inc., Group Hospitalization, Inc., Yale University and the Bureau of Social Science Research, Inc. for Phase I, and under NCHSR contract 110-72-271 with the Bureau of Social Science Research, Inc., funds were provided for Phases II and III. Also, much of the final analyses of which this book is a summary were conducted at the Division of Intramural Research of this Center, where detailed tables and the study instruments are available upon request.

The editors wish to take this opportunity to thank Dr. Gerald Rosenthal, former Director, NCHSR, and Dr. Donald Goldstone, Acting Director, NCHSR, for their continued interest and support and to acknowledge in particular the initiative and support of Walter J. McNerney, who proposed the original study and who, in his foreword to this volume, expresses the concerns and interest of the Blue Cross and Blue Shield Associations in the questions addressed. We also thank Group Health Association, Inc., the United States Civil Service Commission (now the Office of Personnel Management), and Group Hospitalization, Inc. (GHI) (the Washington, D.C. Blue Cross plan) for their continued interest and support. The editors are particularly indebted in this respect to Mrs. Goldie Krantz, who did not live to see this study completed, and to Mrs. Marie Henderson, formerly of the United States Civil Service Commission; to Alan F. Ridgway and his staff at GHI; and to the research and field staff of the Bureau of Social Science Research, Inc., for the endless and painstaking technical work that is the foundation of all studies of this kind.

Since the beginning of our study, there has been some change in national health policy issues, and researchers concerned with the factors associated with variations in health care use and expenditures can benefit from the findings and methods employed in a variety of studies that have taken place in the interim. However, many of these issues remain essentially unchanged, and our capacity to explain the fundamental question, variations in use of health services, has likewise not grown significantly. Costs of health care, and particularly the efficient use of the hospital, remain intractable policy issues.

Our comparison of one prepaid group practice plan with a Blue

Cross–Blue Shield plan in Washington, D.C. clearly indicates, as have similar studies since the early 1970s, that hospital admission rates are indeed substantially lower under HMOs than in fee-for-service settings. Our analyses suggest no simple and direct explanation for these differences, but they do not appear related to out-of-plan use, demographic characteristics, or the illness levels of the populations studied. Thus, the potential for further understanding of variations in hospital use, we believe, will not evolve from more population based studies but rather from studies of medical decisions as to who is and who is not hospitalized; these decisions must be examined in the context of professional and organizational incentives and disincentives and of the structure within which they are made.

THE EDITORS

1

Introduction

Donald C. Riedel

Students of health care have long held that the manner in which the delivery of care is organized and financed affects the use of available services by both providers and consumers. And it is the belief of many that some forms of organization, especially prepaid group practice, are superior to the more traditional fee-for-service arrangement by solo practitioners. Well controlled studies in support of this proposition are few, however, and true experiments even fewer, the Rand Health Insurance Experiment being the current exception. Nonetheless, the findings of several comprehensive reviews (Luft, 1981, 1980a,b, 1978; Donabedian, 1969, 1965; and Klarman, 1963) consistently and clearly demonstrate that the use of the hospital, the most expensive tool in the medical care workshop, is lower under prepaid group practice than under the fee-for-service arrangements of solo practice.

Observers of these differences have postulated various explanations, often in the absence of definitive proof; these can be summarized as follows: Prepaid group practice plans frequently offer a greater range of benefits, allowing a more rational consumption of services; they emphasize comprehensive ambulatory care, including prevention of illness and early detection and treatment; they might select more qualified physicians who make more prudent decisions on the use of resources; patients in such plans are likely to be routed to modal specialists, whose decisions on use of services are more likely to be correct; their physicians have limited access to hospital beds (a factor cited especially in earlier studies of differential hospital use where group physicians had a limited choice of facilities offering admitting privileges); there is a lack of financial incentives under prepaid group practice to hospitalize patients. On the one hand, the failure of providers in such prepaid plans to diagnose and treat illnesses has been argued; on the other hand, more extensive peer review of the decision-making process leading to hospitalization has been assumed. Finally, it has been proposed that subscribers to prepaid group practices may make use of hospital services outside the plan, thereby deflating the rates of use attributable to the plan. To this list might be added an assumed gravitation of providers and/or patients to prepaid group practices who tend to a lower use of hospital inpatient facilities; in other words, the characteristics of the participants who choose this organizational form determine the pattern of utilization rather than it being a product of the organization of delivery. Thus, the lower rates of hospital use are variously seen as attributable to a reduction in need for hospitalization in populations served by prepaid group practice plans (by primary prevention and early detection and treatment); to a lower level of need consistent with the characteristics of the subpopulations selecting that form of practice; and to differences in decision making by which hospital resources are allocated by providers.

Although this pattern of difference in hospital inpatient use is fairly consistent from study to study, the relative volume of ambulatory care received by the subscribers to prepaid group practices as compared to patients in the fee-for-service, principally solo practice sector is not as constant. In some cases, the consumption of ambulatory services is similar under the two forms of practice, and in some instances the pattern is reversed, with both higher hospital *and* ambulatory use observed for patients cared for in service benefit settings, partly negating the hypothesis that there is a substitution of ambulatory care for expensive inpatient care in prepaid group practice plans. Furthermore, there are methodological flaws in some of these comparative studies which restrict generalizations. These include major differences between plans in available benefits; lack of information on important membership characteristics; and differences in geographic location of the plans compared, where known variations in modes of medical practice exist.

In view of the importance of the relationship between the organization and the cost of care for national policy making, the Federal Employees Health Benefits program, a national program for federal employees and their dependents that allowed choice among several different arrangements with identifiable differences in benefit structure and the organization of medical care, offered a unique opportunity for a detailed study of use and costs of service. The purpose of this study was twofold. It documented the nature and magnitude of differences in use of and expenditures for health services between a prepaid group practice plan and a service benefit plan and attempted to determine the influence of both subscriber and provider characteristics on variations in this respect. The findings presented in this volume are the result of a large, interdisciplinary effort spanning several years and focusing on two of the health insurance plans offered to federal employees and their dependents.

THE FEDERAL EMPLOYEES
HEALTH BENEFITS PROGRAM

The Federal Employees Health Benefits Program (FEHBP) is the largest employer sponsored, contributory health insurance program in the United States. It is completely voluntary; at the time this study began in 1970, approximately 80 percent of those eligible were covered — 8.8 million persons, including 2.8 million employees and annuitants and 6 million dependents. It was established under an Act of Congress, began operation in July of 1960, and is administered by the United States Civil Service Commission (now the Office of Personnel Management).

At the time of the study, federal employees enjoyed a wider range of choice of health plans under this program than had ever been offered in a comparable program. The options included two government-wide plans: a service benefit plan administered by Blue Cross and Blue Shield, and an indemnity benefit plan offered by the insurance industry through Aetna Life Insurance Company. In addition, a number of employee organizations offered indemnity-type plans to their members. A further choice was available to employees residing in certain geographic areas where comprehensive medical plans, including group practice and individual practice prepayment plans, were in operation. At the time, seven individual practice plans and fourteen group practice plans participated in the FEHBP. Most plans also offered employees a choice between two options or levels of benefits, i.e., a more expensive high option that offered greater benefits and a less expensive low option.

Although all served federal employees, the several types of plans have varied consistently and sizeably since the beginning of the program in the proportions of beneficiaries who received particular benefits during a given year. Some of these variations appear to reflect differences in benefit structure, since the first dollar coverage of out-of-hospital care by the prepaid group practice plans is much more extensive than that of the other plans. However, one of the most significant areas of difference among the plans has been in hospital use and expenditures, for which differences in coverage were relatively small. This variation in use has been documented by Perrott (1966) and Perrott and Chase (1968), who found that the highest rates of use occurred in the service benefit plan (BC-BS) and the lowest in the prepaid group practice plans. Josephson (1966, 1964) also showed wide variation in rates of hospital use by geographic region of the country within the service benefit plan. Perrott has presented findings which indicated lower rates of hospital use in prepaid group practice plans for conditions in which admission to the hospital and/or the procedure employed is more discretionary in nature (e.g., tonsillectomies and adenoidectomies; acute respiratory infections).

Background

Through the collaboration of a number of organizations and agencies, an opportunity was created to conduct an in-depth study of the factors related to use of services and expenditures by families enrolled in a prepaid group practice plan in contrast with the experience of families covered under the service benefits of Blue Cross and Blue Shield.

The study focused on federal employees and their families in the Washington, D.C. area who were enrolled in the FEHBP high-option plans of either Group Health Association, Inc. (GHA), a prepaid group practice plan, or the government-wide service benefit plan of the Blue Cross Association and the National Association of Blue Shield Plans (BC-BS). The high-option plans represented about 90 percent of all enrolled persons at that time. Although this comparative study could have been conducted in any of several locations across the country where federal employees could choose a prepaid group practice as their health plan, the Washington, D.C. area was selected for two reasons. First, since GHA did not operate its own hospitals and its patients were admitted to hospitals in the Washington area, it was possible to control, at least in part, the effect of hospital characteristics on patterns of utilization. Second, GHA used Group Hospitalization, Inc. (the local Blue Cross plan) as a fiscal agent for the payment of all hospital bills. Hence, comparable hospital claims data for both plans were available from a central source. Choice of a particular community for this comparative study also offered the advantage of controlling any differences in rates of use noted in earlier research that might have been attributable to varying patterns of medical practice in different regions of the country. In other words, the populations studied were constrained in their use of medical services by the same external factors, and these services were administered by physicians who were members of the same professional community. Another important factor in deciding on this geographic area was the willingness of the two plans involved to cooperate actively in this self-evaluation.

However, there are several limitations inherent in the focus on one pair of plans at one point in time. First, of course, is the simple observation that the particular ways in which services are organized and provided in the prepaid group practice plan might be different from the form employed in other prepaid group practices. Second, the plans are not static, but change over time through enactment of new policies and procedures, by virtue of membership growth and attenuation, and by the infusion of new professionals responsible for the delivery of care. Third, there are known differences in the mode, or style, of patient care in various regions of the country; these differences might affect the distinction between types of plans in levels of use of service. Fourth, the majority of hospitalized GHA patients were cared for in teaching hospitals in the D.C. area, a relationship not necessarily observed in other prepaid group practice plans. These and other obvious limitations should be kept in mind when examining the findings of this study. In essence, it offers a cross-sectional view of two plans (one of which was quite heterogeneous in terms of physician practice arrangements) at a single point in time.

The following descriptions of the two plans, including administrative practice, the characteristics of providers, premiums for coverage, and the population served by each, are based on data covered by the study period, which extended from roughly 1970 to 1975. Various changes have occurred since that time, but they are not pertinent to analysis and interpretation of the data in this book.

A Summary Description
of Two Plans

Group Health Association

The Group Health Association, Incorporated, of Washington, D.C. (GHA), is a consumer owned, prepaid health care organization that in 1970 provided comprehensive services to some 75,500 members. Seventy-five percent of these were federal employees, annuitants, and their dependents covered under FEHBP, 12 percent were covered under a contract with Local 689 Transit Workers Health and Welfare Fund (bus drivers), and the remaining 13 percent were general members employed by embassies or small businesses, or were private entrepreneurs and the like. Fifty percent of the members lived in the District of Columbia, 35 percent in the Maryland suburbs, and 15 percent in the Virginia suburbs of the Washington metropolitan area.

The oldest urban prepaid group practice in the United States, GHA was formed in 1937 by a group of federal employees working in the Home Owners Loan Corporation. It made medical and legal history in the late 1930s and early 1940s when the District of Columbia Medical Society and the American Medical Association tried to enjoin GHA physicians from having hospital privileges in the local hospitals. The U.S. Supreme Court found the Medical Society in restraint of trade and ruled that it was legal for GHA to provide comprehensive care for its membership.

At the time of this study, ambulatory care was provided at four health centers operated by GHA in the District of Columbia and in the suburban sections of Maryland and Virginia. Inpatient care was provided at local community hospitals; most admissions, however, were to several teaching hospitals where many of the GHA professional staff held faculty appointments.

In 1970, the GHA medical staff had the equivalent of 75 full-time physicians, who were paid in several ways. The full-time physician staff were organized into a group with whom the GHA Board of Trustees had a contract providing for a capitation fee for every enrolled member. The group included those in the specialties of pediatrics, internal medicine, and obstetrics-gynecology, as well as several other specialties. Physicians who were not full-time members of the group, principally those practicing in surgery and highly specialized areas such as neurology, were paid on a per-capita, fee-for-time, or retainer basis. In addition to the usual complement of health care professionals, GHA used various other paramedical personnel, including nurse practitioners, corpsmen, and midwife counselors, to provide a range of services to its members.

Blue Cross and Blue Shield

From the start of the FEHBP in 1960, the majority of all federal employees and annuitants have chosen BC-BS; in 1973, more than 60 percent of the total were so enrolled. To provide the authorized high-option and low-option programs of the government-wide service benefit plan, the Civil Service Commission contracted jointly with the Blue Cross Association and the National Association of Blue Shield Plans. At the time of this study, these had as members the 75 U.S. Blue Cross Plans and the 71 U.S. Blue Shield Plans. The Associations acted as agents for the plans, who agreed to underwrite and provide the benefits specified in the master contract through local contracts with hospitals and physicians throughout the nation. Although the program for federal employees was contracted to and directed by the national Associations of the plans, the individual plans shared proportionally in the total expense. The plans were separately incorporated in the several states but tied together for FEHBP and other common operating purposes through their national Associations. Federal employee subscribers were not enrolled in any particular Blue Cross or Blue Shield Plan on the basis of residence or place of employment, but were served by the entire system of plans, with claims usually processed by whatever plan had an arrangement in effect with the hospital or physician actually providing care. Basic payments were almost always made directly to the provider of the care, but supplemental benefits were paid to the subscriber when applicable. Centralized records of enrollments and claim histories were maintained in Washington, D.C., to which every Blue Cross and Blue Shield Plan had direct access for claims adjudication purposes.

Comparison of Premiums and Benefits

Premiums

Premium costs under the FEHBP were shared by the federal government and the employees, with employee contributions withheld by payroll deductions. The 1970 GHA premium was one of the highest in the country among FEHBP plans of this type, making this contrast between a prepaid group practice and a BC-BS plan greater than would have been found had the study been conducted in another community. The 1970 high-option premium levels are compared in this context because the Phase I findings, reported in Chapter 2, are based on hospital utilization during the 1967–1970 period. However, GHA premiums were found higher also during Phase II (see Chapter 7). The GHA biweekly premium for a high-option single contract was $9.74, compared with $7.25 for BC-BS; premiums for family contracts were $24.85 and $17.69, respectively. Total GHA premiums for both types of contracts being higher than those for BC-BS, the proportion of the government's contribution to premiums paid by BC-BS subscribers was greater, since in the period from July 1966 through December 1970 it was fixed at $1.68 every two weeks for all FEHBP single contracts and $4.10 for all family contracts. For family contracts, for example, the government paid 23 percent of the BC-BS premium and 16 percent of the GHA premium.

Benefits

Although many of the BC-BS and GHA high-option benefits were essentially identical, there were major differences in coverage for specific types of services.

Local Hospital Services. Coverage for those admitted to local hospitals was in large part the same under both plans. Charges to BC-BS beneficiaries for semiprivate accommodations and other ancillary hospital services in member hospitals were covered in full for up to 365 days of care. If a hospital admission was authorized by a GHA physician, the same charges were paid in full for GHA patients for an unlimited number of days. For family contracts in both plans, the benefits for maternity admissions were the same as those for other types of admissions, with the exception under GHA of a $50 deductible for each maternity admission. Maternity admissions were not covered under the single contracts of either plan, although the BC-BS single contract included hospital benefits for legally performed therapeutic abortions. No distinction in hospital benefits was made in the BC-BS plan for patients admitted to member hospitals with nervous and mental diseases, while benefits ceased for GHA members when a final diagnosis of nervous and mental disorder requiring long-term care was made. Hospital charges for inpatient admissions for diagnostic tests were not covered as basic benefits in BC-BS if x-ray and laboratory procedures could have been performed on an outpatient basis without prejudicing the patient's physical condition or adversely affecting the quality of medical care received. Hospital charges for inpatient admissions under GHA for diagnostic tests were paid in full if the admission was authorized by a GHA physician.

Local Physician Services. It was in this area that the greatest differences in coverage existed between the two plans. Nearly all types of physician services were covered in full for GHA members if they were rendered and/or authorized by a GHA physician, with the exception of home visits and psychotherapy services. Eye refractions were included in GHA services, and this service accounted for a sizeable volume of ambulatory visits (see Chapter 5).

Blue Cross and Blue Shield covered physician services under the provisions for both basic and supplemental benefits. First, under basic and supplemental benefits provisions, benefits for physician services provided to hospital inpatients and for emergency ambulatory treatment of illness or injury were governed by a schedule of fees for specific services. Such fees represented payment in full only when (1) a family contract holder's income was less than $10,000 (if single, less than $6,500) and (2) services were rendered by a participating physician. (Prior to August 1969, the income limits for family and single contracts were $7,500 and $5,000, respectively.) If the contract holder's annual income was over these limits or services were rendered by a nonparticipating physician, the same allowances were paid; the physician, however, was not required to accept this allowance as full payment but could charge the usual fee for service. In such cases, if the patient's $100 annual deductible for the range of benefits covered by the supplemental benefits provisions had been met, 80 percent of the difference was paid, up to the usual, customary, and reasonable charge. During the course of the study, the income provision was dropped, as was the fee schedule. BC-BS participating physicians were paid their usual customary or reasonable fees.

Second, under the supplemental benefits provision, 80 percent of the charges for most other out-of-hospital physician services were covered by BC-BS if the deductible had been satisfied. (Under a family enrollment covering three or more persons, only two deductibles had to be satisfied during any calendar year. Prior to 1969, there were no maternity benefits for pre- and postnatal care.) Excluded from any BC-BS coverage, but covered by GHA, were routine physical examinations, well-baby care, and immunizations.

Drugs and Diagnostic Services. Both plans included benefits for prescribed medicines. In BC-BS, after the annual $100 deductible for supplemental benefits had been met, 80 percent of such charges were paid. GHA also paid 80 percent of charges for prescription drugs and medicines prescribed by a GHA physician, with an annual individual member deductible of $50 for such charges. Charges for diagnostic x-ray and laboratory services to BC-BS beneficiaries on an outpatient basis were paid in full, regardless of income. In GHA, such charges were paid in full if services were rendered or authorized by a GHA physician.

Out-of-Area Coverage. Under BC-BS, services were covered by the same scope of benefits regardless of where care was received, while care obtained by GHA members outside the service area was covered much less comprehensively, with the exception of reciprocal agreements for emergency outpatient medical care with other comprehensive group practice plans and for services specifically authorized by a GHA physician. GHA members away from home were covered only for emergency services, accidental injury, and acute illness; in such cases, hospital charges were paid in full only after the first $75 and only up to 180 days of care. Surgical services were paid according to a fee schedule with a $250 ceiling; medical services were limited to $5 per day for inpatient and $15 per visit for outpatient services.

In concert, there were no differences in benefits between the plans that might be expected to influence admissions to short-term general hospitals for other than psychiatric care. However, the GHA benefits for ambulatory care were sufficiently more comprehensive to warrant the expectation of a higher rate of ambulatory use.

THE STUDY DESIGN

As stated earlier, the purpose of the Federal Employees Health Benefits Program Utilization Study (FEHBPUS) was to document the nature and magnitude of differences in use of, and expenditures for, health services in a prepaid group practice plan and a service benefit plan. The study had three phases and employed three distinct data bases.

Phase I was designed to collect data under controlled conditions to document the rates of hospital use in GHA and BC-BS. This phase was based on a sample of individual and family contracts selected from each of the two plans (see Chapter 2). Characteristics of the BC-BS members covered under each contract were verified through mail questionnaire and telephone interview. Data on hospital admissions and lengths of stay were obtained from hospital and physician claims files for the two plans for the period from January 1, 1967 to September 30, 1970, with the discharge diagnosis verified by examination of the hospital medical record. Provider characteristics were obtained from published sources and files. Thus, Phase I permitted a comparison of hospital admission rates with accurate data on denominators, or populations at risk; previous studies of the Federal Employees Health Benefits Program were based on health insurance plan data which relied on estimates of family size per contract for the population denominator. This phase was also designed to determine the age–sex composition of the patient populations and the nature and magnitude of differences in hospital admission rates and length of stay by diagnostic category.

Phase II was based on a 12-month survey of households drawn from single and family high option subscribers to the two plans (updated subsamples of those units chosen for Phase I). The specific aim of this part of the study was to examine the following questions:

— What were the sociodemographic characteristics of the members of the two plans that might influence their use of health services?

— What was the reported health status of members in each plan, including chronic illness and days of disability?

— To what extent were physicians and other health care personnel contacted when illness or injury was experienced by members of each plan, and how long did it take to obtain care?

— What were the rates of use of various types of health services by members of the two plans, and how did they differ?

— Were differences in rates of use associated with the variables listed above and with differences in various administrative and structural characteristics of the two plans (such as length of time necessary to obtain an appointment)?

— Did patterns of care and patient behavior vary between plans within episodes of illness involving a particular health problem?

— How much out-of-plan use existed among GHA members, and what were the reasons for such use?

— To what extent did total out-of-pocket expenditure for health care by members of the two plans differ?

Most of the data for Phase II, as reported in Chapters 3 to 7, were obtained in interviews with a responsible representative of each family unit in the sample during October 1, 1972 to April 30, 1974. In order to maximize recall and ensure sufficient data for analysis, use and expenditure information was collected each month for a year from each sampled household.

Phase III documents patterns of care received by members of the two plans in specific episodes of illness leading to hospitalization. The sampling frame for this phase was the population of patients in GHA and BC-BS who had been discharged from hospital within a twelve-month period (August 1973 to July 1974) in one of a group of selected primary discharge diagnoses. Selection of these diagnostic categories was based on several factors: differences between the plans in admission rates observed in Phase I; availability of criteria for the evaluation of appropriateness of care and of standardized medical record abstract forms; expected differences in patterns of ambulatory care between prepaid group practice and service benefit plans according to findings from earlier studies; and the involvement of a variety of medical specialties as well as generalists in care and treatment.

Some of the data in Phase III were obtained from interviews with eligible patients in the sample shortly after their discharge from the hospital. In order to document the clinical aspects of care related to the hospitalization, the hospital medical records of the interviewed patients were abstracted on forms specifically designed for each of the selected diagnoses. Interviews with the physicians responsible for the care of the hospitalized patients elicited information on both inpatient and ambulatory care provided (see Chapter 8). In this as in other phases of the study, strict rules of confidentiality were observed, and the permission of respondents for the use of information relating to them was secured prior to data collection.

In addition to brief descriptions of differences among provider characteristics and among patient behavior in the two plans (Chapters 9 and 10), evaluations were also performed of the hospital stage of the care, yielding estimates of appropriateness of admission and validity of diagnosis, of the severity of illness at the time of admission, and of the appropriateness of inpatient management (Chapters 11 to 13). Chapter 14 provides an overview of the major findings of the study, together with an integrated interpretation, conclusions reached and recommendations emanating from them.

In broad strokes, then, the overall study design can be likened to a funnel approach: beginning with rather gross comparisons of patterns of hospital use primarily based on centrally available data in the GHA and local BC-BS files; relating these patterns of utilization to the benefit structure of the two plans; moving on to a more detailed analysis of social and demographic characteristics of the family units in each plan; comparing patterns of ambulatory use and expenditures experienced by a cross-section of members of the two plans over a year's time; isolating the amount and reasons for out-of-plan use by members of GHA; determining the length and content of pre- and post-admission episodes of illness experienced by those in each plan who were discharged with one of several specific diagnoses; securing information on the reasons for choice of alternative modalities of care and specific services provided on an ambulatory basis directly from the physicians responsible for the care of these persons; evaluating the appropriateness of admission for these patients in each plan and of the care received while in the hospital, and the relative severity of their illness at the time of admission to the hospital; and finally, obtaining a detailed specification from the hospital medical record of the diagnostic and therapeutic procedures administered to a sample of patients in specific diagnostic categories so as to examine the influence of physician characteristics and plan structure on quality and type of care.

Although the study was mainly designed to identify the factors associated with differences in hospital admission rates between the two plans, data obtained from each of the sources of information listed above provides a basis for analysis in its own right. In concert, they provided an unparalleled opportunity to examine patterns of care and some of the factors influencing variation in these patterns, using patients with known characteristics as the referent.

2

Rates of Hospital Use in Two Plans

Donald C. Riedel

The principal objective of the initial phase of the study was to accurately document differences in the hospital admission rates and lengths of stay for members of two health insurance plans, and to determine if variations in these rates were attributable to differences in the distributions of selected characteristics in the two plan populations and the providers of care to these populations. Admissions and length of stay were documented in terms of both total and nonobstetrical rates as well as in terms of diagnostic-specific groupings, adjusted for age and sex, so as to provide a more detailed basis of comparison than gross admission totals and length of stay undifferentiated by discharge diagnoses (see also Riedel et al., 1975). The diagnostic categories developed for this purpose were based on a regrouping of ICDA–8 categories, with a view to obtaining clinically distinct entities that would permit specific analyses of patterns of hospital use. Observed differences between the plans in rates of admission and lengths of stay for selected discharge diagnoses were then used to design more detailed analyses of patterns of hospital use in the two plans, which are described in Chapters 8 to 13.

The two populations for this phase of the study were defined as all nonannuitant, high-option contract holders and their families under the Federal Employees Health Benefits Program who were enrolled in either GHA or BC-BS on September 30, 1970, and resided in the greater Washington, D.C. area. This study area was defined as the GHA service area and included the District of Columbia; the towns of Alexandria and Falls Church and the counties of Arlington and Fairfax in Virginia; and the counties of Montgomery and Prince George in Maryland. Admission and length-of-stay data for a sample drawn from this population were obtained from plan hospital claims and verified on the basis of hospital record abstracts for the period from January 1, 1967, to September 30, 1970.

Although it would have been of interest to examine patterns of hospital use by members of each plan and their dependents over several years, the population of contract holders could only be obtained for a given point in time. As in most insurance plans, the membership roster is continuously modified to include new enrollees, transfers, and terminations of various kinds. It was not possible, therefore, to reconstruct the population at risk for the entire study period, and it was decided to sample only current contracts and verify the accuracy of the membership characteristics for that sample. Excluded from the sampling frame, therefore, are contract holders who were members during the study period but who terminated their membership (i.e., died, retired, or transferred to another plan) before the date of sample selection. Although this exclusion undoubtedly biased the estimates of total rates of use for each plan to some degree, there is no evidence that it seriously affected the estimates of differences between the two plans. A prospective design would have allowed collection of use data for those who left the plans, but at the expense of extending the project for several years.

SAMPLE DESIGN

The size of the sample to be drawn from the two plan populations was determined by the requirement of obtaining a sufficient number of hospital admissions for diagnostic specific analysis of the most frequent causes of admission. On the basis of previous findings (McNerney et al., 1962), it was estimated that this would require at least 6,000 admissions for each plan during the study period (January 1, 1967, to September 30, 1970), to be allocated between single contracts and family contracts on the basis of the ratio of total expected single contract claims to total expected family contract claims. The target of 6,000 admissions per plan was derived from estimates of diagnostic-specific annual admission rates under the two plans, ranked as a percent of total admissions. Forty-five categories, estimated to represent about 60 percent of all admissions, were selected for detailed analysis, based on the requirement that the least frequent of these categories would have to contain at least 30 cases, or about 0.5 of all admissions for both plans (Hess, Riedel, and Fitzpatrick, 1975).

A systematic technique was employed to select a sample of necessary size from both the BC-BS and GHA membership files as of September 30, 1970. The sample design is presented in Table 2.1. For GHA, 11,949 contracts were sampled, representing about 75.4 percent of the total high-option, nonannuitant contracts in that plan. For BC-BS, the actual number of contract holders in the study area was not known because the computerized membership files identified only the state of residence. It was estimated that approximately two-thirds of contract holders in Maryland and Virginia actually lived in the Greater Washington Metropolitan area. Accordingly, the BC-BS sampling fraction was increased to about 5.0 percent of total

BC-BS high option, nonannuitant contracts of Maryland, Virginia, and the District of Columbia, for a total of 11,830 contracts. Original FEHBP registration forms were then examined for enrollment addresses, and all BC-BS contract holders residing outside the Washington, D.C. area were dropped from the sample, leaving 6,974 contracts with enrollment addresses in the study area. It should be noted that the disproportion in sample sizes between the two plans (nearly 2:1) was dictated by substantially lower estimates of admission rates per 1,000 members in GHA, which required a larger number of contracts to be drawn from GHA than from BC-BS so as to obtain the required number of admissions in each plan for study.

DATA COLLECTION AND
METHODS OF ANALYSIS

The Plan Populations

Since sampling for this phase of the study was confined to enrollment contracts, data on characteristics of the two populations were limited to those available on the FEHBP registration form, i.e., age, sex, and number of members covered at the time of enrollment. While GHA membership files also contained current information on residential address, age, and sex of the contract holder and, in the case of family contracts, of family members covered under the contract, BC-BS membership files did not contain current information on persons covered by family contracts. A survey contractor, the Bureau of Social Science Research, Inc. (BSSR), attempted to contact all sampled BC-BS contract holders either by telephone interview or mail questionnaire to verify this information. Despite difficulties in reaching contract holders due to the considerable mobility of the population within the metropolitan area, the lack of forwarding addresses, and a sizeable number of subscribers with unlisted telephone numbers, the overall response rate was 76 percent; 12 percent refused to participate in the study, and for another 12 percent of the sample, useable data were not available, largely because the contract holder could not be located during the available time. Estimates were made of the age, sex, and number of dependents of nonresponding family contract holders (1,093 of the 1,655 contract holders who either refused to provide information or could not be contacted) so as to permit use of all hospital claims associated with the sampled contracts. Age and sex of all contract holders (and their families at time of enrollment) were available from BC-BS membership records; inasmuch as the number of dependents and the age and sex composition of responding and nonresponding contract holders at the time of enrollment were essentially the same, it was assumed that changes in the age and sex composition of dependents of nonresponding contract holders from the time of enrollment to the time of sample selection were the same as for the rest of the sample. Adjustments for dependents by sex and age of family contract holders were made accordingly, utilizing the ratio observed for responding contract holders.

Providers of Care

To determine if a relationship existed between provider characteristics in each plan and rates of hospital use, selected characteristics of both the hospitals and physicians who provided care to members of the hospitalized populations during the study period were compared.

Hospitals

The characteristics of Washington metropolitan area hospitals identified from BC-BS and GHA hospital claims data and as described in the Guide Issue of *Hospitals* (American Hospital Association, 1971) were examined to determine the feasibility of grouping these hospitals according to characteristics known to affect length of stay, i.e., accreditation, for-profit status, and teaching programs. Of the 28 short-term nonfederal hospitals in the Washington area, one was not accredited, and three were proprietary hospitals, together representing less than 6 percent of the short-term nonfederal hospital beds in the Washington area. Bed size for the 28 hospitals ranged from 33 to 983 beds; groupings based on hospital bed size, however, were not homogeneous with respect to approved physician teaching programs. Hence, for purposes of analysis it was decided to group the hospitals according to the characteristics of these teaching programs; during a parallel, unpublished analysis of the data, this aspect was found to explain more variance in length of stay than groupings based on other available hospital characteristics.

Data from both the Guide Issue of *Hospitals* (American Hospital Association, 1971) and the *Directory of Approved Internships and Residencies* (AMA, 1969, 1967) were used to combine hospitals into the following five groups:

- Hospitals operated by the three Washington area university medical schools

- Hospitals with a major unit of a medical school teaching program

- Hospitals used to a limited extent by a medical school teaching program and used by medical school graduate training programs only or with other teaching programs

- Hospitals without teaching programs

— Hospitals outside the Washington area, the characteristics of which could not be determined from local BC-BS and GHA claims files

Physicians

Board certification and years in practice since graduation from medical school were selected as two major physician characteristics known to be related to differential patterns of hospital use. Board certification status was obtained by three categories: physicians board certified in any specialty; physicians who declared themselves general practitioners; and physicians who were not board certified but declared their practice limited to a particular specialty. Years in practice were calculated as of 1970. Physicians were identified by matching BC hospital claims to BS physician billing claims and, in the case of GHA, with medical records. Primary physicians were identified for each admission to the extent possible, and their characteristics were obtained either from the *Medical Directory* (AMA, 1969, 1967) or a bibliographic data file of the American Medical Association. The inability to obtain these data for 29.4 percent of physicians in BC-BS and 33.4 percent in GHA was due largely to the fact that for some admissions there was no associated claim for care provided by a primary physician in the Blue Shield file; also, for many out-of-area admissions the name of the primary physician was not available. In a number of instances, the required information could not be found in either the American Medical Directory or the AMA biographic file.

Hospital Use Data

Data on hospital admissions and length of stay for the period from January 1, 1967, to September 30, 1970 were obtained from five sources:

— The computerized claims files of the local Blue Cross plan

— Copies of individual hospital claims

— Tape files from the local Blue Shield plan

— Abstracts of hospital medical records

— Abstracts of GHA records

These data sources were linked by the unique identification number of each sampled contract. As the hospital claims files of the local Blue Cross plan were the principal data source for both BC-BS and GHA (GHA used GHI as a fiscal agent for the payment of hospital claims), comparable inpatient claims information was obtained for all sample contracts with admission dates for the period January 1, 1967, through September 30, 1970. This information consisted of patient age and sex, hospital identification number, admission and discharge dates, length of stay, a two-digit diagnostic code, and total hospital charges, as well as the unique contract identification number and a unique hospital claim number for each admission.

Copies of claims for BC-BS admissions outside the study area (805 or 12.3 percent of all BC-BS admissions) were not available. (Out-of-area hospitalizations of members of Blue Cross plans are handled administratively through an arrangement known as the Inter-Plan Bank Transfer Agreement, where the hospitals are reimbursed by the local Blue Cross plans and the "home" plan billed by means of a claim mechanism with standardized data.) For GHA admissions to hospitals outside the metropolitan area, copies of hospital claims were obtained from GHA.

To take into account possible discrepancies between discharge diagnoses available from copies of hospital claims and the first-listed diagnosis in the hospital medical records (Doyle, 1966), the discharge diagnosis was verified against the hospital record for BC-BS admissions and against the GHA medical record for admissions under that plan, which in most instances contained hospital discharge summaries. At this time, patient age and sex were also verified. For the small number of cases in which neither the hospital nor the plan medical record was found, the diagnosis entered on the claim form was used. All discharge diagnoses were then uniformly coded into the first four digits of the ICDA–8 codes (International Classification of Diseases, Adapted, Eighth Revision; National Center for Health Statistics, 1967). All data on a given admission were combined into an analytical file containing the four-digit ICDA–8 discharge diagnostic code as well as a three-digit diagnostic code developed for this analysis and permitting the grouping of four-digit ICDA–8 codes into 48 discrete diagnostic categories, with subgroups for certain diagnostic categories (see Table 2.2). This categorization had been developed at Yale on the basis of a detailed analysis of utilization of hospital services associated with individual diagnoses, supplemented by intensive clinical review by physicians associated with Yale–New Haven Hospital (see also Fetter et al., 1980). The objective was a set of mutually exclusive categories of homogeneous conditions in terms of expected utilization which could be converted from the traditional ICDA designations. The diagnostic specific hospital utilization data reported in the following are based on this three-digit code, with the exception of the aforementioned out-of-area admissions under BC-BS. For these, the only diagnostic data available were the first two digits of ICDA–8 codes recorded in the claims process established for out-of-area hospitalizations. They are combined in Tables 2.4 and 2.6 in a category designated "All other diagnoses."

Methods of Analysis

As already discussed, members of the sample population had been subscribers to their respective plans for varying lengths of time. In addition, for many contracts the number of members covered changed during the study period because of marriages, births, and deaths. To account for these variations, the denominator for admission rates was expressed as 1,000 membership years, rather than as the traditional 1,000 persons. Age and age/sex-specific rates were determined according to patient age at the time the sample was drawn and the age and sex composition of the plan populations as ascertained through the verification procedures previously described. Because of aging of this population over the 45-month period of observation, individual admissions were associated with the age group of the person at the time the sample was drawn, instead of the age group at the time of hospital admission. Total rates were then adjusted for age and sex on the basis of the direct method of adjustment (Remington and Schork, 1970).

To test the statistical significance of differences in admission rates per 1,000 membership years for selected diagnostic categories, all rates were converted to membership weeks so as to obtain a sufficiently short time period in which the admission rate could be considered a binomial variable, since it was assumed that no member of the study population had more than one admission in any particular week. Since the number of membership weeks for both plans was relatively large, the sampling distribution of the difference between proportions was approximately normal, with mean zero and standard deviation (Blalock, 1972). For length-of-stay estimates, the null hypothesis (no difference between mean lengths of stay in the two plans) was tested, with no assumptions made about variances. One-tailed tests of statistical significance were used for comparisons of admission rates because of the known direction of differences between the plans. The statistical significance of differences of a combined measure of use of hospital services (patient days) was not assessed because of the direct effect on this measure of its components, admissions and average length of stay.

FINDINGS

No major differences were found in the age and sex composition of the membership of the two plans, although the GHA population had a somewhat greater proportion of members under age 25 (53.0 percent as compared to 47.7 percent of BC-BS members). Also, while there was no difference in the male to female ratio overall (males in BC-BS, 49.1 percent; in GHA, 49.3 percent), there were proportionately more female contract holders in GHA (27.9 percent vs. 21.1 percent in BC-BS). The two samples also differed in family size, with families enrolled in BC-BS generally smaller. In GHA, 56.7 percent of family contracts covered four or more persons, as compared with 45.7 percent in BC-BS. Roughly half of current BC-BS contract holders had been members of their plan since the beginning of FEHBP (July 1960), as compared to a third in GHA, while only 13.4 percent in BC-BS had joined after January 1970, compared to 22.9 in GHA. Also, although the mean age of all contract holders in both plans was statistically indistinguishable (BC-BS, 40.8 years; GHA, 40.5 years), within tenure categories GHA contract holders were roughly two years older than BC-BS contract holders. In this study, contract tenure is defined as the number of months contract holders belonged to a particular plan under their current FEHBP contract, although they might have been members of the plan under other auspices for a longer period of time. Hence, under this definition the longest possible membership for any member would have been 123 months, from the inception of FEHBP in July 1960 to September 1970, the eligibility date for the sample.

A clear and large difference between the plans was found in the teaching status of hospitals to which plan members were admitted in 1967–1970. Almost all GHA admissions were to hospitals with at least some teaching program, and almost two-thirds were to university teaching hospitals, reflecting the pattern of appointments of GHA physicians in the D.C. area. A much larger proportion of BC-BS admissions (21.1 percent) was to non-teaching hospitals and, as expected, to out-of-area hospitals (12.3 percent).

This difference did not appear to extend to the physicians, however, at least to the limited extent to which it was possible to establish their characteristics in this phase of the study. Of the primary physicians attending the admissions examined, 48.1 were board certified specialists in BC-BS and 51.4 percent in GHA. While a somewhat greater proportion of GHA admissions was associated with physicians who had been in practice a shorter length of time than was observed for BC-BS (in 1970, 23.5 percent of primary GHA physicians had been in practice less than 15 years since medical school, compared with 18 percent of BC-BS physicians), caution should be exercised in interpreting these figures because of the large proportion of admissions (roughly a third in each plan) for which either the identity of the physician or their characteristics could not be ascertained from the available data.

The hospital admission rates in this study confirmed previous findings based on U.S. Civil Service Commission data of substantially lower hospital admission rates for members of a prepaid group practice plan than under fee-for-service plans (Perrott and Chase, 1968; Perrott, 1966). Both unadjusted and age/sex-adjusted admission rates per 1,000 membership years showed an almost twofold difference (roughly 121 admissions in BC-BS and 69 in GHA; Table 2.3), and this difference was maintained when single and family contracts were considered separately and obstetrical admissions excluded. For single contracts, the BC-BS admission rate was again two times the GHA rate (135.5 versus 66.3), and for family contracts, the ratio was 1:7. The total annual nonobstetrical hospital admission rate was 99.8 per 1,000 membership years for BC-BS and 51.3 for GHA. In both plans, females had the expected higher admission rates than males for all admissions combined, but in BC-BS this difference was considerably greater (79.4 for males and 155.5 for females, compared with 53.6 and 85.3 admissions, respectively, in GHA); also, there was no difference between males and females for nonobstetrical admissions in GHA, but a 30-percent difference in BC-BS. Further, the relationship by sex of admission rates under single and family contracts was reversed in the two plans. In BC-BS, males covered under family contracts had higher rates than single male contract holders, and single females had higher rates than females under family contracts. The opposite was found in GHA. Likewise, while the age/sex-adjusted nonobstetrical rates by type of contract (see Table 2.3) showed more admissions under single contracts than under family contracts in each plan, the proportionate difference was considerably smaller in GHA (43 percent in BC-BS and 13.8 percent in GHA).

Differences in admission rates persisted to varying degrees in most of the selected diagnostic categories. Admissions per 1,000 membership years in these categories are shown in Table 2.4, listed in descending order of the ratio of differences between BC-BS and GHA. While it could be argued that the largest difference (which was sixfold and observed for diseases of the oral cavity, salivary glands, and jaw) was at least in part due to different benefit structures in the two plans (see Riedel et al., 1975), this cannot be assumed for such diagnoses as disorders of menstruation, hypertrophy of tonsils and adenoids, or pneumonia, where differences in admission rates were also substantial but benefits in each plan were similar. Again, adjustment for age and sex did not affect this pattern. In only 4 of the 45 categories examined — birth injuries and diseases of early infancy, other diseases of the male genital organs, adverse effects of chemical substances and other trauma, and wounds and burns — did GHA admission rates exceed those in BC-BS; the difference was statistically significant in only the last category.

In contrast, there was little overall difference in length of stay; for all admissions, both the unadjusted and age/sex-adjusted average length of stay was roughly 6.5 days in both plans (Table 2.5). Again in both plans, the average hospital stay was longer for single than for family contracts, and adjustments for age and sex did not significantly alter these findings. Males had longer average hospital stays than females for all admissions, and relatively large differences in average length of stay for nonobstetrical admissions were observed between males and females under single contracts. Thus, the variability between the plans in unadjusted and age/sex-adjusted average lengths of stay by diagnostic category (Table 2.6) does not follow the pattern observed for admission rates. Differences were generally small and statistically significant in only 11 instances. Three of these involved longer stays by BC-BS patients (infectious diseases caused by viruses, psychotic and psychoneurotic disorders, and diseases of the gall-bladder and biliary duct); while stays by GHA patients were longer for diseases of the oral cavity, salivary glands, and jaw; diseases of the ear; hyperplasia of prostate and prostatitis; arteriosclerotic and other heart disease; fractures, dislocations, and sprains of selected sites; diseases of the eye; delivery; hypertrophy of tonsils and adenoids; and chronic tonsillitis. As observed previously, in two of the categories (diseases of the oral cavity and psychotic disorders) differences may be attributable to plan benefit structures, resulting in case mixes of different severity; but elsewhere there is little indication of a consistent pattern.

The unambiguous and substantial differences between the plans in their rate of hospital admission thus had no equivalent in average lengths of stay. It is clear, therefore, that the large differences found in patient days per 1,000 membership years (Table 2.7) were almost entirely a function of differential admission rates. For all admissions, the unadjusted rates were 804.2 patient days in BC-BS and 452.8 days in GHA. Age-adjusted patient day rates by sex and type of contract again indicated considerably higher total rates for single contracts than for family contracts, and total age/sex-adjusted patient day rates showed an 81 percent higher rate in nonobstetrical admissions for BC-BS, with differences in rates between type of contract again greater in BC-BS than in GHA (by 76 percent in BC-BS and by 64 percent in GHA).

SUMMARY

Phase I of this study can be summarized as follows:

— There were few differences in the age and sex composition of the memberships in each of the two plans. The mean number of persons covered by family contracts in BC-BS was 3.55; it was 4.06 in GHA. Sampled BC-BS contract holders had been members of this plan longer than GHA contract holders had been members of GHA.

— While a larger percentage of GHA patients was admitted to teaching hospitals, reflecting the pattern of hospital appointments of physicians in the two plans in 1970, there were no differences in the proportion of patients attended by board certified specialists. A somewhat greater percentage of GHA patients was cared for by physicians with fewer years of practice, but the value of this finding is limited by the large proportion of missing data.

— On the other hand, differences between plans in rates of hospital admission were substantial. Overall, the hospital admission rate per 1,000 membership years was 121 for BC-BS and 69 for GHA, and large differences remained even after correction for the small demographic differences found in the two plan populations.

— Females experienced higher rates of nonobstetrical hospital admission than males in BC-BS. Although in GHA there also was a higher admission rate for males than for females, the magnitude of this difference was considerably smaller than in BC-BS. Also, the difference in nonobstetrical admission rates between female members of the two plans was greater than for males. In both plans a higher hospital admission rate was observed for members covered under single contracts than for those under family contracts.

— An examination of diagnostic-specific admission rates indicated that in most diagnostic categories examined, BC-BS rates exceeded GHA rates by statistically significant margins. In only one category was the GHA admission rate significantly higher. Among the largest of these differences were admissions for disorders of menstruation, acute respiratory infections, hypertrophy of tonsils and adenoids, and chronic tonsillitis. None of these could be attributed to the benefit structure of the two plans.

— Length of stay was the same overall for members of both plans, and differences in specific diagnostic categories were of a smaller order of magnitude than those found for admission rates. Statistically significant differences indicated longer stays by BC-BS patients in three diagnostic categories; in eight categories, longer stays were found for GHA patients.

— The substantial differences in patient day rates between the two plans (804 patient days in BC-BS per 1,000 membership years and 453 days in GHA) reflected the general patterns of differences by age, sex, and type of contract found for hospital admission rates.

These findings were derived from a determination of characteristics of the two sampled populations and of hospital claims under carefully controlled conditions. The age, sex, and family size of the sampled BC-BS population were verified through telephone and mail questionnaires; corresponding data for the GHS sample were obtained from plan records which were considered of sufficient reliability for the purposes of this analysis. All hospital claims of the two sampled populations for the period January 1, 1967 to September 30, 1970 were obtained from the local Blue

Cross plan. Discharge diagnosis and the age and sex of hospitalized patients were verified through abstracts of hospital medical records for BC-BS members and through plan records for GHA members. The hospitals providing care to the sampled populations were identified from hospital claims and grouped according to hospital teaching status and other medical education programs. The primary physicians providing inpatient care to the sampled populations were grouped according to years in practice and board certification status on the basis of information obtained from Blue Shield claims and from GHA plan records and professional registers.

In general, Phase I confirmed that hospital use by members of prepaid group practice plans differs from that of members of more traditional service benefit plans. However, although based on carefully collected and verified data from a variety of sources, these estimates can provide only a dim reflection of the impact of the plan characteristics on the use of resources. They do not in themselves afford a precise understanding of the influence of personal, professional, and organizational factors on providers and consumers in each system of care. Specifically lacking is information on the decisional processes by which members in each plan elect to seek care; the use of ambulatory care services associated with episodes of illness occasioning admission to the hospital; use of services outside the plan or benefit structure; the reasons for choice of treatment on the part of the responsible physician; and most important, the clinical appropriateness of this use. Phases II and III of this study, which are described in the following chapters, were designed to address these and other issues.

Table 2.1 Sample design—Phase I: High option nonannuitant contracts in Blue Cross-Blue Shield (BC-BS) and Group Health Association (GHA) active as of September 30, 1970

	BC-BS			GHA		
	Family	Single	Total	Family	Single	Total
All contracts, DC, VA, MD	169,168	69,637	238,805	––	––	––
Sampled contracts, DC, VA, MD	8,836	2,994	11,830	––	––	––
All contracts, DC–Metro area	––	––	––	10,040	5,804	15,040
Sampled contracts, DC–Metro area	4,903	2,071	6,974	8,083	3,866	11,949
Ineligible contracts	35	0	35	0	0	0
Eligible contracts	4,868	2,071	6,939	8,083	3,866	11,949
Members covered by eligible contracts	17,331[a]	2,071	19,402	32,763	3,866	36,629
Hospital admissions[b]	5,872	655	6,527	6,361	608	6,969

[a]Includes estimate of family members in 1,093 family contracts where family contract holder could not be located.

[b]From January 1, 1967, to September 30, 1970.

––Not applicable.

Table 2.2   Diagnostic categories used in Phase I analyses of hospital use

Category	ICDA-8 codes included[a]
Infections caused by viruses	040-079
Spirochetal, parasitic, and other infectious diseases	006-009, 080-097, 100-136, 390, 392.9
Malignant neoplasms	140-199
Allergic disorders	493, 507, 692, 708
Diabetes mellitus[b]	250, 962.3
Diseases of thyroid and other endocrine glands	226, 240-246, 251-258
Psychotic and psychoneurotic disorders	295-300
Other mental disorders	301-315
Inflammatory and other diseases of the central nervous system	225, 320-349
Diseases of the eye	224, 360-379
Diseases of the ear	380-389
Selected diseases of the heart	391-392.0, 393-398, 420-429
Arteriosclerotic and other heart disease	400-414
Other diseases of the circulatory system	227, 289, 403-404, 440-444.1, 444.3-458, 734.1
Acute respiratory infections	460-474
Pneumonia[b]	480-486
Selected diseases of upper respiratory tract	212.0-212.1, 501-506, 508
Hypertrophy of tonsils and adenoids[b]	500
Bronchitis, emphysema, and other diseases	212.2-212.9, 490-492, 510-519
Diseases of the oral cavity, salivary glands, and jaws	210, 520-529
Diseases of upper gastrointestinal system	211.0-211.2, 530-537
Appendicitis[b]	540-542
Other diseases of appendix, hernia, and intestinal obstruction	444.2, 543, 550-560
Other diseases of intestines and peritoneum	211.3, 561-569, 685
Diseases of liver and pancreas	211.6, 570-573, 577
Diseases of gall bladder and biliary ducts[b]	211.5, 574-574.1, 575-576
Selected diseases of urinary tract	223, 580-584, 590-599
Other diseases of male genital organs	214.1, 222, 602-607
Hyperplasia of prostate and prostatitis	600-601
Other diseases of breast and female genital system	217, 219-221, 611-625, 627-629
Chronic cystic breast disease[b]	610
Disorders of menstruation[b]	626
Fibromyoma of uterus[b]	218

Table 2.2 (Continued)

Category	ICDA-8 codes included[a]
Complications of puerperium	670-678
Delivery	650-661, 764-768, Y20, Y22, Y23, Y26, Y27
Diseases of skin and subcutaneous tissue	214, 214.9, 216, 232.2, 680-691, 693-707, 709, 757.1
Arthritis, rheumatism, and gout	274, 710-718
Osteomyelitis and other diseases of bone and joint	213, 720-725, 725.8-729
Displacement of lumbar and lumbosacral intervertebral disc	725.1, 726, 846
Others diseases of musculoskeletal system	215, 730-734, 734.9
Congenital anomalies	735-759
Birth injuries and diseases of early infancy	771-778, Y21, Y24-Y25, Y28-Y29
No classifiable diagnosis or no illness	228, 230-232.1, 233-239, 780-796, Y00-Y13
Fractures, dislocations, and sprains of selected sites	800-848
Injury to internal organs	850-854, 860-869, 920-939, 950-959, E914-E915
Wounds and burns	870-918, 940-949
Adverse effects of chemical and other trauma	960-962.2, 962.4-999, E800-E999
Infectious diseases caused by bacteria	000-005, 010-027, 030-039, 098-099
Neoplasms of lymphatic and hematopoietic systems	200-207
Nutritional and other metabolic diseases	260-273, 275-279
Anemia	209, 208-285
Other diseases of blood and blood-forming organs	208, 286-289
Organic brain disorders	290-294, 309
Cerebrovascular disease	430-438
Diseases of nerves and peripheral ganglia	350-358, 574.9
Complications of pregnancy	630-645, 760-763, 769-770

[a]National Center for Health Statistics. 1967. *International Classification of Diseases, Adapted for Use in the United States.* Eighth Revision. DHEW Publication no. (PHS) 1693. Washington: Government Printing Office.

[b]Corresponds directly to a diagnostic category also selected for Phase III (see Table 8.1).

Use of Health Care Resources

Table 2.3   Annual hospital admissions under two plans: Unadjusted and age and age-sex adjusted rates per 1,000 membership years by type of contract

		All admissions		Nonobstetrical admissions	
			(per 1000 membership years)		
Type of contract		BC–BS	GHA	BC–BS	GHA
			Unadjusted		
	Total	121.2	* 69.3	99.8	* 51.3
	Single	135.5	* 66.3	133.6	* 62.4
	Family	119.8	* 69.6	96.6	* 50.1
			Age adjusted		
Males	Total	79.4	* 53.6	79.4	* 53.6
	Single	78.2	* 67.0	78.2	* 67.0
	Family	87.5	* 52.4	87.5	* 52.4
Females	Total	155.5	* 85.3	111.0	* 51.0
	Single	204.7	* 66.2	197.8	* 64.1
	Family	150.1	* 88.0	103.0	* 49.4
			Age-sex adjusted		
	Total	121.8	* 69.6	99.0	* 52.6
	Single	138.7	* 66.2	138.3	* 64.6
	Family	119.9	* 70.0	95.3	* 50.8

*P ≤ .05.

Table 2.4 Hospital admissions in selected diagnostic categories[a] under two plans: Unadjusted and age-sex adjusted rates per 1,000 membership years

Diagnostic categories	Unadjusted		Age-sex adjusted		Ratio of adjusted rates[b]
	BC–BS	GHA	BC–BS	GHA	
1. Diseases of oral cavity, salivary glands and jaw[c]	1.8 *	0.2	2.1	0.2	10.5
2. Disorders of menstruation	2.5 *	0.3	2.4	0.3	8.0
3. Acute respiratory infections	1.7 *	0.3	1.7	0.3	5.7
4. Hypertrophy of tonsils and adenoids, chronic tonsillitis	5.6 *	1.6	5.9	1.5	3.9
5. Arthritis, rheumatism, gout	1.0 *	0.3	0.9	0.3	3.0
6. Pneumonia	1.3 *	0.4	1.2	0.4	3.0
7. Bronchitis, emphysema, and other diseases of the respiratory system	1.4 *	0.5	1.4	0.5	2.8
8. Spirochetal, parasitic, and other infectious diseases	1.2 *	0.4	1.1	0.4	2.8
9. Other diseases of breast and female genital system	8.9 *	3.4	8.9	3.4	2.6
10. Selected diseases of urinary tract	7.6 *	2.9	7.5	2.9	2.6
11. Diseases of skin and subcutaneous tissue	2.3 *	1.0	2.4	1.0	2.4
12. Diseases of liver and pancreas	0.7 *	0.3	0.7	0.3	2.3
13. Diseases of thyroid and other endocrine glands	0.9 *	0.4	0.9	0.4	2.3
14. Chronic cystic breast disease	1.2 *	0.4	1.1	0.5	2.2
15. Psychotic and psychoneurotic disorders[c]	1.3 *	0.6	1.3	0.6	2.1
16. Other diseases of circulatory system	3.3 *	1.5	3.3	1.6	2.1
17. Diabetes mellitus	1.1 *	0.5	1.0	0.5	2.0
18. Selected diseases of upper respiratory tract	1.0 *	0.5	1.0	0.5	2.0
19. Selected diseases of the heart	1.4 *	0.7	1.3	0.7	1.9
20. Diseases of upper gastrointestinal system	2.2 *	1.1	2.1	1.1	1.9
21. Diseases of gall bladder and biliary ducts	1.1 *	0.6	1.1	0.6	1.8
22. Other diseases of intestines and peritoneum	2.0 *	1.1	2.0	1.1	1.8
23. Hyperplasia of prostate and prostatitis	0.7 *	0.4	0.7	0.4	1.8

Table 2.4 (Continued)

Diagnostic categories	Unadjusted		Age-sex adjusted		Ratio of adjusted rates[b]
	BC–BS	GHA	BC–BS	GHA	
24. Diseases of the eye	1.7 *	1.0	1.8	1.0	1.8
25. Infections caused by viruses	0.8 *	0.5	0.9	0.5	1.8
26. No classifiable diagnosis or no illness	4.1 *	2.4	4.0	2.4	1.7
27. Osteomyelitis and other diseases of bone and joint	1.7 *	1.0	1.7	1.0	1.7
28. Other diseases of musculo-skeletal system	1.0 *	0.7	1.0	0.6	1.7
29. Arteriosclerotic and other heart disease	1.7 *	0.9	1.6	1.0	1.6
30. Injury to internal organs	1.7 *	1.1	1.8	1.1	1.6
31. Appendicitis	1.0 *	0.7	1.1	0.7	1.6
32. Fibromyoma of uterus	1.9	1.1	1.8	1.2	1.5
33. Delivery	16.0 *	13.4	17.9	13.0	1.4
34. Allergic disorders	0.8	0.6	0.8	0.6	1.3
35. Fractures, dislocations, and sprains of selected sites	3.3 *	2.7	3.4	2.6	1.3
36. Diseases of the ear	1.1 *	0.8	1.0	0.8	1.3
37. Inflammatory and other diseases of the central nervous system	0.8 *	0.5	0.8	0.5	1.3
38. Other diseases of appendix, hernia, and intestinal obstruction	4.7 *	3.7	4.6	3.8	1.2
39. Malignant neoplasms	1.7 *	1.3	1.6	1.4	1.1
40. Complications of pregnancy	4.6	4.4	5.0	4.4	1.1
41. Congenital anomalies	1.4	1.3	1.4	1.3	1.1
42. Birth injuries and diseases of early infancy	1.1	0.9	0.9	1.0	0.9
43. Other diseases of male genital organs	1.4	1.6	1.4	1.6	0.9
44. Adverse effects of chemical substances and other trauma	0.7	0.8	0.7	0.8	0.9
45. Wounds and burns	1.0 *	1.6	1.0	1.5	0.7
46. All other diagnoses	14.0	6.9	13.6	7.3	1.9
All diagnoses	121.2	69.3	121.8	69.6	1.8

[a]Categories correspond to the discharge diagnosis as determined from the medical record; the ICDA codes included are shown in Table 2.2.

[b]BC-BS/GHA

[c]Categories with differences in benefit structures between the two plans.   *P ≤ .05.

Table 2.5   Length of stay under two plans: Unadjusted and age and age-sex adjusted mean days of stay per hospital admission by type of contract

Type of contract		All admissions		Nonobstetrical admissions	
			(mean days of stay)		
		BC–BS	GHA	BC–BS	GHA
		Unadjusted			
	Total	6.6	6.5	7.3	7.5
	Single	8.7	9.0	8.7	9.1
	Family	6.4	6.3	7.0	7.2
		Age adjusted			
Males	Total	7.3	7.6	7.3	7.6
	Single	9.9	10.7	9.9	10.7
	Family	6.4	7.3	6.4	7.3
Females	Total	6.4	5.9	7.5	7.3
	Single	7.5	8.0	7.7	8.2
	Family	6.2	5.8	7.4	7.2
		Age-sex adjusted			
	Total	6.5	6.6	7.1	7.4
	Single	8.4	9.1	8.4	9.3
	Family	6.2	6.3	7.0	7.2

Table 2.6 Length of stay for selected diagnostic categories[a] under two plans: Unadjusted and age-sex adjusted mean days of stay

	Unadjusted		Age-sex adjusted		Ratio of adjusted length of stay[b]
Diagnostic categories	BC–BS	GHA	BC–BS	GHA	
1. Diseases of oral cavity, salivary glands, and jaw[c]	2.1 *	4.1	2.0 *	3.4	0.59
2. Disorders of menstruation	3.2	3.0	3.2	3.1	1.03
3. Acute respiratory infections	4.3	3.9	4.0	3.0	1.33
4. Hypertrophy of tonsils and adenoids, chronic tonsillitis	1.5 *	1.7	1.5	1.6	0.94
5. Arthritis, rheumatism, gout	14.3	14.5	14.0	12.1	1.16
6. Pneumonia	7.9	7.8	7.5	7.7	0.97
7. Bronchitis, emphysema, and other diseases of the respiratory system	9.2	7.3	9.1	7.0	1.30
8. Spirochetal, parasitic and other infectious diseases	6.7	6.5	6.4	6.0	1.07
9. Other diseases of breast and female genital system	5.5	5.7	5.5	6.0	0.92
10. Selected diseases of urinary tract	5.0	4.8	5.0	5.1	0.98
11. Diseases of skin and subcutaneous tissue	5.3	6.6	5.0	6.5	0.77
12. Diseases of liver and pancreas	14.6	12.0	14.0	11.4	1.23
13. Diseases of thyroid and other endocrine glands	8.1	6.9	8.2	6.5	1.26
14. Chronic cystic breast disease	2.9	2.6	3.0	2.6	1.15
15. Psychotic and psychoneurotic disorders[c]	18.2 *	12.8	19.2 *	12.6	1.52
16. Other diseases of circulatory system	9.0	8.9	10.0	9.0	1.11
17. Diabetes mellitus	11.1	9.9	11.0	10.2	1.08
18. Selected diseases of upper respiratory tract	3.0	4.0	3.0	4.0	0.75
19. Selected diseases of the heart	11.7	13.1	12.0	11.8	1.02
20. Diseases of upper gastrointestinal system	10.3	9.2	9.3	10.1	0.92
21. Diseases of gall bladder and biliary ducts	12.6 *	9.6	12.1 *	9.4	1.29
22. Other diseases of intestines and peritoneum	7.3	7.9	7.3 *	8.0	0.91
23. Hyperplasia of prostate and prostatitis	6.3 *	10.5	7.1 *	10.0	0.71

Table 2.6 (Continued)

	Diagnostic categories	Unadjusted		Age-Sex adjusted		Ratio of adjusted length of stay[b]
		BC–BS	GHA	BC–BS	GHA	
24.	Diseases of the eye	4.0 *	5.3	4.5	5.0	0.90
25.	Infections caused by viruses	9.6 *	5.6	8.7 *	5.7	1.53
26.	No classifiable diagnosis or no illness	5.9	5.8	6.0	6.0	1.00
27.	Osteomyelitis and other diseases of bone and joint	11.5	10.0	12.0	10.00	1.20
28.	Other diseases of musculo-skeletal sytem	4.3	5.1	4.3	6.0	0.72
29.	Arteriosclerotic and other heart disease	13.1 *	17.6	13.2 *	17.2	0.77
30.	Injury to internal organs	7.1	5.2	6.4	5.0	1.28
31.	Appendicitis	5.8	6.5	5.4	6.3	0.86
32.	Fibromyoma of uterus	8.5	8.3	8.5	8.2	1.04
33.	Delivery	4.0 *	4.2	4.0 *	4.3	0.93
34.	Allergic disorders	6.6	6.1	5.5	6.0	0.92
35.	Fractures, dislocations, and sprains of selected sites	9.2 *	11.4	9.3 *	12.0	0.78
36.	Diseases of the ear	2.8 *	4.2	2.7 *	4.1	0.66
37.	Inflammatory and other diseases of the central nervous system	11.0	10.2	8.3	10.3	0.81
38.	Other diseases of appendix, hernia, and intestinal obstruction	6.1	5.4	6.0	5.5	1.09
39.	Malignant neoplasms	12.8	12.1	13.0	12.6	1.03
40.	Complications of pregnancy	3.0	3.1	3.0	3.2	0.94
41.	Congenital anomalies	7.1	6.0	7.0	6.2	1.13
42.	Birth injuries and diseases of early infancy	11.2	13.1	11.0	13.1	0.84
43.	Other diseases of male genital organs	4.2	3.5	4.0	4.0	1.00
44.	Adverse effects of chemical substances and other trauma	4.9	6.6	5.0 *	7.3	0.68
45.	Wounds and burns	6.8	5.1	7.0	5.1	1.37
46.	All other diagnoses	9.4	8.9	9.9	9.6	1.03
	All diagnoses	6.6	6.5	6.5	6.6	0.98

[a]Categories correspond to the discharge diagnosis as determined from the medical record; the ICDA codes included are shown in Table 2.2.

[b]BC–BS/GHA.

[c]Categories with differences in benefit structures between the two plans.   *P ≤ .05.

Table 2.7   Patient days under two plans: Unadjusted and age and age-sex
adjusted rates per 1,000 membership years by type of contract

		All admissions		Nonobstetrical admissions	
		(patient days per 1,000 membership years)			
Type of contract		BC–BS	GHA	BC–BS	GHA
		Unadjusted			
	Total	804.2	452.8	723.9	382.8
	Single	1,173.4	599.5	1,164.8	594.8
	Family	767.8	438.1	680.4	361.5
		Age adjusted			
Males	Total	578.1	409.6	578.1	409.6
	Single	771.7	719.9	771.7	719.9
	Family	563.2	382.4	563.2	382.4
Females	Total	997.7	501.0	834.3	375.9
	Single	1,555.4	533.8	1,525.8	526.6
	Family	936.4	507.4	761.3	356.6
		Age-sex adjusted			
	Total	792.8	459.4	707.7	390.8
	Single	1,177.8	607.7	1,165.3	603.4
	Family	754.8	444.3	663.8	367.9

3

Household Survey Design and Methods

Samuel M. Meyers

While the focus of Phase I of this study was on the use of hospital inpatient services by members of two health insurance plans, interest in Phase II centered on their use of ambulatory services. The design of Phase II was guided by the following objectives:

- To examine in more detail than possible in Phase I characteristics of the members of the two plans that might be associated with the use of health services, including (but not limited to) their reported state of health; and to gain some insight into administrative and structural characteristics of the providers of care under the two plans as reflected in appointment patterns

- To determine the extent to which the services of physicians and other health care personnel were used by members of the two plans, both for reasons of illness or injury or for preventive care; whether and how differences in rates of use were associated with the independent variables examined; and whether differences existed in the behavior of members of the plans within specific episodes of illness

- To examine out-of-plan use by members of GHA

- To determine differences in out-of-pocket expenditures and in the components of these expenditures

A MODEL OF USE

With regard to these objectives, this study adopted in its general outlines the model of determinants of health services use proposed by Andersen (1968) and by Andersen and Newman (1973), although some modifications should be noted. Since the major purpose of Phase II was a comparison of use and patient behavior under two health insurance plans, the technological and manpower resources in the systems component of this model could not be specifically addressed; however, it was hoped that an analysis of patterns of use of the resources available to the members of the two plans would provide some indirect evidence of the effect of differences in access and in administrative structure. The following population characteristics were elicited in the survey:

PREDISPOSING FACTORS

Sociodemographic

Age
Sex
Race
Marital status
Religion
Prior hospitalizations

Socioeconomic

Education
Occupation
Income
Family size
Parent work status

Attitudes

Tendency to use physician services
Attitudes to use of preventive services
   (physical examinations)
Satisfaction with medical care
Satisfaction with plan

ENABLING FACTORS

Type of health insurance (plan)
Length of plan membership
Knowledge of plan benefits
Regular source of care
Type of regular source of care
Accessibility of care
   (time to obtain services)

PERCEIVED ILLNESS LEVELS

Health status
Chronic problems
Treated chronic problems

Bed and restricted activity days
Pain and worry days
Episodes of illness

In contrast to the Andersen and Newman approach, income was treated as a predisposing variable, similar to education and occupation, rather than as an enabling variable. The comprehensive health benefits coverage offered by both plans, and the fact that the populations studied were by definition employed and generally above the poverty level, were assumed to reduce the effect of income on the ability to obtain services. This is equally true for health insurance, where plan membership was used as an enabling factor indicative mainly of differences in benefits (see Chapter 1) and of relative accessibility of services. On the other hand, the use of race as a sociodemographic indicator among predisposing variables was considered to be of special interest. Should one expect the differences in use by race which were consistently observed in the literature at the time of the study (Andersen and Newman, 1973; Aday and Eichhorn, 1972) to be maintained or decreased in populations at the same level of health insurance coverage and with a common employer? Was there a differential effect in this respect between the service benefit and the prepaid group practice plan?

As in most large household surveys, the cost of matching medical records to reports of illness would have been prohibitive. The data on estimates of health and illness in the study population are therefore based on reports of perceived morbidity and do not indicate actual levels of clinical disease and severity. However, the lack of clinical evaluation should not affect comparison of the illness behavior of the two populations, at least at the level of initial contact with their providers of care.

Finally, the structure of the utilization component should be mentioned. Analysis of type of service was restricted to the ambulatory medical services described in Chapter 5, although hospitalizations during the survey reference period were determined and the multivariate analysis in that chapter includes prior hospitalizations as a predictor variable. The purpose of contacts was determined by a relatively simple division of visits into those for treatment, diagnosis, or prevention, without regard to levels of care. Both the percentage of persons with specific types of contacts in the study population and the volume of contacts were determined. Episodes of illness constituted an additional unit of analysis, employing a somewhat different construct from those developed by Richardson (1971) and Solon et al. (1967). Specific definitions of each variable used and its derivation are provided in context in Chapters 4–7.

SURVEY PROCEDURES

Data Sources

The primary data sources for Phase II of the study were household survey interviews with a sample of subscribers from each plan. Plan records, although an alternative, were considered inadequate to meet the objectives of the study, in particular with regard to detailed characteristics of the members of the two plans and to aspects of the use of health services that are not captured by insurance or prepaid group plan records. The survey information was collected in 12 monthly interviews, as a year's worth of data was believed likely to furnish sufficient instances for analysis of even relatively rare events, such as hospitalizations or use of preventive services. A monthly interview schedule was considered necessary to avoid long recall periods and resulting under- or over-reporting (Cannell, Fisher, and Baker, 1965; Cannell and Fowler, 1965; and Cannell and Fowler, 1963).

A second source of data, hospital claims for the year prior to the survey and the year of data collection, might have afforded a measure of past illness predictive of current ambulatory use and a check on the validity of household data. However, while claims data were collected, they were excluded from analysis because of unresolved discrepancies between reported and recorded hospitalizations. Similarly, since information analogous to that in Phase I on the providers of care could not be obtained for all physicians seen by household respondents during the survey year, the Phase II analysis does not include individual provider characteristics.

Sampling Design and
Completion Rates

The sampling frame for Phase II was the sample used in Phase I (see Chapter 2); it was updated to include those who joined either plan between September 30, 1970, the date of the original sample draw, and March 14, 1972, and to exclude those who were no longer active federal employees as of the latter date. The updated sampling of new federal employees followed the procedure used in Phase I, and the Phase II sample was drawn by means of a systematic procedure.

The sample size considered necessary for the analyses planned in this phase of the study was about 1,250 persons in each plan, comprising both single and family contracts in proportion to their estimated number in the total GHA and BC-BS populations in the Washington, D.C. metropolitan area. Based on an estimate of 2.5 persons per contract, the sampling plan required 666 GHA and 669 BC-BS contracts to be drawn, from which 500 contract holders in each plan were expected to be eligible and available for interview. The oversampling was to compensate for losses of eligible contract holders because of refusal to participate in the survey or because, prior to the start of interviewing, they ceased to be covered by the respective plan, had retired from government employment or terminated employment for other reasons, no longer lived in the Washington Metropolitan area, or had died. In fact, there were further increases in ineligibility among the sample because of an unanticipated open-enrollment season permitting federal employees to change health plans just before the start of the fieldwork, and because of changes in early retirement regulations. As a result, those contract holders were declared ineligible who, on the first contact by an interviewer, indicated that retirement or a change in health plan was contemplated. In all, of the original household sample, 12.4 percent in BC-BS and 19.3 percent in GHA were found ineligible between the time of sampling and the first contact (6 to 12 months).

Of those eligible, 81.9 percent in BC-BS and 84.4 percent in GHA completed the first interview. Refusals to participate in the survey, which were more frequent in BC-BS than in GHA (14.2 and 11.1 percent, respectively), accounted for most of this nonresponse rate. Of the households who participated in the first interview (480 in BC-BS and 454 in GHA), 91.1 percent in BC-BS and 87.8 percent in GHA completed all monthly interviews. The overall response rate for both plans was similar (74.6 percent, BC-BS; 74 percent, GHA).

Survey Instruments

The household survey questionnaire included both newly developed items as well as questions used previously in the Health Interview Survey of the National Center for Health Statistics (1970, 1966) and the health surveys of the National Opinion Research Center (1969, 1967), as well as by Anderson and Andersen (1970), Andersen (1968), Metzner and Bashshur (1967) and McNerney et al. (1962). In developing questionnaire items, the model for analyzing individual determinants of health care use developed by Andersen and Newman (1973) was especially useful, as it provided both a framework for variable classification and a point of reference for examining whether specific questions would yield suitable data for analysis in the light of the study objectives.

The questionnaire used in the initial interview inquired into the following:

— Demographic and socioeconomic characteristics of family members

— Health insurance coverage additional to that provided by BC-BS or GHA, respectively

— Overall health status and the presence of chronic complaints

— Attitudes toward seeking health care

— Satisfaction with care and with the health insurance plan

— Reasons for having joined either plan

— The respondent's usual source of care

— Knowledge of plan benefits

In addition, a set of core questions was used in this and the subsequent 11 interviews so as to elicit, for each monthly interview period:

— Instances of illness and injury associated with days of bed rest, restricted activity, and/or pain and worry

— Use of various types of ambulatory services

— Hospitalizations

— Selected indicators of access to care (length of time to obtain an appointment, waiting time in the provider's office, delay in seeking care, and whether visits were by appointment or walk-in)

— Out-of-pocket expenditures for health care

The questionnaires were generally alike for both plans, with the exception of a number of plan-specific questions and changes in wording. For example, GHA respondents were additionally asked about out-of-plan use, by which was meant any use of services not covered by plan benefits or without the approval of the plan, and BC-BS respondents were queried about supplemental benefits available and obtained under their plan.

Fieldwork

A number of data collection strategies were considered; i.e., face-to-face household interviews, diaries, mail questionnaires, telephone interviews, or combinations of these. In view of the personal nature of the data to be collected, and in order to gain the respondent's cooperation for 11 additional contacts, at least the first interview was conducted in the contract holder's home. Also, even though earlier studies had indicated that a diary is a reliable survey tool for obtaining instances of use and illness, a decrease in the quality and quantity of the reported data over time was expected. Moreover, it was assumed that an unacceptably high number of respondents would be unwilling to complete a diary through an 11-month period without personal follow-up (Roghmann and Haggerty, 1972; Alpert, Kosa, and Haggerty, 1967; Mooney, 1962; Allen et al., 1954; Muller, Waybur, and

Weinerman, 1952; Peart, 1952). This concern for continued respondent cooperation originally led to the decision to adopt an alternating interview pattern of two monthly telephone interviews after the initial interview, followed by a face-to-face interview in the home of the contract holder, until completion of the 12-month survey. However, the first two months of telephone follow-ups proved so successful with regard to data collection and in maintaining respondent interest in the study that it was decided to conduct all subsequent interviews by telephone.

Each contract holder in the sample received a letter from the Director of the Bureau of Retirement, Insurance and Occupational Health, U.S. Civil Service Commission, outlining the purpose of the study, assuring recipients of the confidentiality of the data and that participation in the survey was voluntary, and alerting them to expect a visit from a field interviewer. This approach helped to obtain current addresses through the postal service for those who had moved from the address of record. When the field staff was assured that the letter had been delivered, each case was assigned to professional interviewers who had received special training. Appointments for interviews were made by telephone or through personal contact at the contract holder's home.

Current addresses for contract holders who could not be located through the postal service were established by means of inquiries at their former address; personnel locator files in the agency where the employee, according to plan records, was employed; and checks for addresses in recent BC-BS claims or GHA enrollment or medical records. Where all else failed, a commercial locator service was used.

Because of the anticipated difficulty of completing all initial interviews within the first month of the survey (October 1972), and in order to make more efficient use of the interviewing staff, the sample was divided into three parts, with initial interviews held over a three-month period. However, locating and contacting respondents proved to be more difficult than foreseen, and the initial interview phase required seven months; the total data collection period therefore extended from October 1, 1972 through April 30, 1974. Although each household was interviewed over a 12-month period, the survey reference period differed accordingly. Since respondents were asked to recall events that occurred during the calendar month prior to the interview, interviewers were instructed to make appointments for each follow-up interview during the first two weeks of the month to maximize accuracy of recall. The recall period was longer where respondents were not available during the scheduled time period, and in some cases interviews covered two months.

During the initial interview in the contract holder's home, the contract holder and his spouse, or the female contract holder, were asked to participate. In general, responses were accepted from the person who appeared most knowledgeable, although the contract holder was asked to answer questions on attitudes to medical care. Older children, if present, were permitted to answer questions for themselves. This interview required an average of 1 hour and 25 minutes, ranging from 30 minutes to over 3 hours dependent upon family size and reporting of instances of illness and medical use. Since almost all subsequent interviews were conducted by telephoning the home of the contract holder, the most knowledgeable person about family illness and expenditures, usually the spouse of a male contract holder or a female contract holder, was asked to act as respondent. These follow-up interviews, which inquired mainly into instances of illness, use of services, and out-of-pocket expenditures, required substantially less time than the initial interview; they averaged 25 minutes, with a range from 10 to 90 minutes.

Fifteen percent of each interviewer's records were verified by the field supervisor for both initial and follow-up interviews, and additional training was given if the work was not up to standards. Continued substandard work was a ground for dismissal. In addition to supervisory monitoring, all interviews were edited by trained editors. Problems were routed back to supervisors and then to the interviewers for correction.

METHODS OF ANALYSIS

For purposes of data processing and analysis, the data obtained in the household interview survey were aggregated into files representing different units of analysis or measurement. Code books were prepared for each file and the data were edited, coded, and cleaned.

The basic analytic technique used was a cross-tabulation of variables. A variance reduction technique employing an automated grouping program (AUTOGRP, Mills et al., 1976) was used to assess the relative importance of specific variables as predictors of use (see Chapter 5 for a detailed discussion of this technique). Also, to control for the large differences in the racial composition of the two plans (the black-to-white ratio being 1:2 in BC-BS and 2:1 in GHA; see Chapter 4) and the lower rates of use among the black as compared to the white groups in both plans, data on the use of services and on episodes of illness were adjusted for race. In Chapter 7, data on expenditures are additionally adjusted for contract type. The race adjustment was made by creating a standard population consisting of the combined GHA and BC-BS population, determining the black-to-white ratio in the standard population and then using that ratio in each of the plans to create two standard populations with the same black-to-white ratio. The race-adjusted mean or percent was calculated in the following manner (GHA being used as an example):

$$\overline{X}_G = W_{GB}\overline{X}_{GB} + W_{GW}\overline{X}_{GW}$$

where

$\overline{X}_G$ = the race-adjusted mean or percent for GHA,

and

W_{GB} = proportion of blacks in the GHA standard population,
$\overline{X}_{GB}$ = the observed mean or percent of GHA blacks,
W_{GW} = proportion of whites in the GHA standard population,
$\overline{X}_{GW}$ = the observed mean or percent of GHA whites,

and where

$W_{GB} + W_{GW} = 1.$

For those eligible but not remaining in the survey the entire year (roughly a tenth of households), data for the period of nonresponse were imputed by extrapolating previously reported rates of use to the entire year. A comparison of rates for those in the study the entire year and the total rates for each variable, including those for whom the particular values were imputed, showed few statistically significant differences.

Tests of significance included t-tests, the z-test, the chi square test, and Fisher's exact test of probabilities when the numbers in a fourfold table were small. Differences between groups are considered statistically significant at $p \leq .05$ throughout. While these tests were performed for all comparisons between plans and statistically significant differences are indicated in the tabular presentations, exclusive reliance on statistical differences is not appropriate in interpreting the findings. There are inherent limitations in significance testing when many statistical tests are performed on the same data, as is the case here, since this increases the probability that some statistically significant results may be due solely to chance. Also, such tests lose power when subgroups smaller in number than the whole sample are compared.

Other factors to be considered in this context are the difference in variability within groups, as well as the likelihood that intrafamily correlations, resulting from the collection of data from household units containing several members, may have affected some of the variables examined. Since the calculation of the standard errors used in these tests assumed observational independence, they tend to be smaller than if adjustments for intrafamily correlations had been made for the variables affected. As a result, some differences may have been judged to be statistically significant when, in fact, they were not. For these reasons, the substantive importance of differences and their pattern and consistency must also be considered in the interpretation of the data.

In the tabular presentations, percents do not always add to 100 because of rounding. It should be noted that data are shown only where the base number in a given cell is at least 25, or about 1 percent of the total sample of 2,691 persons.

Finally, while the survey was designed to minimize problems of recall, recall errors undoubtedly remain. A record check would not necessarily have resolved these errors, since records are not necessarily more accurate than survey respondent reports. An example in the present study is the search of the BC claims file for hospitalizations during the survey year, which yielded 15 percent fewer retrievable claims than the number reported by the respondents (210 versus 245). Although it could not be established whether some claims were lost and therefore never appeared in the claims file, or whether there was over-reporting by respondents, the latter type of error is not considered likely in view of the one-month recall period and of the fact that hospitalizations are usually reported accurately. Moreover, the emphasis in this study on comparisons between plans makes the problem of under- or over-reporting a moot question. There is no reason to assume that there were more reporting errors in one plan than in the other.

4

The Household Survey Population

Sarina B. Hirshfeld and Mary Helen Shortridge

One of the arguments in comparisons of prepaid group practice and service benefit plans is based on the assumption that differences in levels and types of use under such plans are related to the composition of their membership. If given the choice, this argument holds, persons with certain characteristics will opt for a prepaid group practice plan, and rates of use will at least partly reflect these characteristics (Donabedian, 1969, 1965; Klarman, 1963). This is seen in contradistinction to the influence of structural or organizational factors; for example, the characteristics of the medical staff who choose to work in a prepaid group practice and the organizational constraints on both providers and consumers that are inherent in the provision of care by one organization, as opposed to a variety of practice patterns in a fee-for-service setting.

The question of self-selection cannot be directly addressed in this study for the reasons stated in Chapter 1, and no assumptions were made about the distribution in the two plan populations of demographic and other characteristics held to be influencing the use of services (see, in particular, Andersen and Newman, 1973; Aday and Eichhorn, 1972; and Andersen, 1968). The following examination of predisposing and enabling factors, levels of perceived illness, and some measures of access to care in the two plans has a twofold purpose, therefore: to establish whether differences in this respect existed between the two plans, and to examine whether these were of sufficient magnitude to explain the differences in hospital use found in Phase I of this study.

The distributions of the two study populations by the classes of variables discussed in Chapter 3 were derived from responses to the monthly household questionnaire administered over a 12-month period (see Chapter 3 also for sampling and survey procedures). They are presented both as percentage distributions of the entire sample and of specific subgroups, and as percentages of persons in specific categories of the variables examined; the underlying numbers of persons are shown where necessary to establish the basis for these distributions. Selected indicators of illness were controlled for race, age, sex, and some measures of access to care are presented, including appointment patterns during the survey year and satisfaction with services received prior to the survey.

PREDISPOSING FACTORS

Sociodemographic Characteristics

The most obvious difference in the composition of the two study populations was their racial distribution; in GHA, two-thirds of enrollees in 1972 were black, while in BC-BS two-thirds were white (Table 4.1). To varying degrees, this difference between prepaid group practice and service benefit populations had been reported elsewhere in the literature (e.g., Bashshur, Metzner, and Worden, 1967; Wolfman, 1961). Various reasons have been suggested for this phenomenon, including the greater residential proximity of blacks to prepaid group practices and their greater emphasis on getting full coverage for health services, although it could not be determined to what extent such reasons prevailed in the present study. Race has been historically associated with different patterns of use, and this difference between the plans was addressed by relating the range of variables examined not only to their overall distribution in the two plans, but more specifically to race as well.

Age and sex differences between the two plans were not as pronounced. Overall, the difference in median age was 4 years (BC-BS, 28 years, GHA, 24 years; see Table 4.1); the largest difference was among those from 5 to 19 years. Age differences between racial groups tended to be wider, especially in GHA. In both plans the black median age was lower than for the white groups (by 5 years in BC-BS and by 7 years in GHA), and the black groups included in particular more school-age children and adolescents (5 to 19 years). Among whites, there was a higher proportion of adults 45 years or older, and in GHA the difference by race in this group was twofold. The distribution of males and females in the two plans, on the other hand, was virtually identical. Slightly more than half the sample was female in each plan, although in both plans women noticeably exceeded men among young black adults (ages 20 to 44).

Socioeconomic Characteristics

Education and Occupation

Educational levels in the two plan populations were determined by asking the survey respondents about the number of years of elementary, high school, and college education completed by adults in the family, and the educational level of the most highly educated adult in the household was then ascribed to each household member. By this measure, the plan populations did not differ much in the proportions who had finished high school (about a third each; Table 4.2), although in BC-BS the percentage of those in families where four years of college was the highest educational level was somewhat higher than in GHA (21 percent as compared to 15 percent), whereas in GHA a quarter had attended a college or university for more than four years. However, the unequal racial distribution of the two plans obscures considerable variation within and across racial groups, particularly in regard to the relative preponderance of white households at high educational levels in GHA. In 71 percent of white GHA families, the most educated adult had attended college for four years or more, as compared to 48 percent in BC-BS. On the other hand, levels of education were quite similar for the black groups in the two plans, so that differences in education within the plans by racial grouping were considerable. In BC-BS, half as many black as white household heads or their spouses had had five years or more of college, while an almost fivefold difference was observed in GHA.

A comparable pattern held for household occupational level, which was determined as the occupation of the male or female contract holder (or the male household head if employed full-time). While in both plans more than half lived in families in the professional/managerial category (Table 4.2), the most striking difference was again with regard to racial groupings. Only about one-third of the blacks in either plan were in families headed by professionals or managers, compared to more than two-thirds of BC-BS whites and as much as 85 percent of those in GHA. Conversely, more than twice as many blacks in BC-BS and four times as many in GHA were in blue collar occupations than among the respective white groups, although the relative proportion of blue collar families was higher in BC-BS than in GHA, regardless of race.

Income and Family Size

Similarly, while 20 percent in each plan were in families in the highest income category ($25,000 or more), this group was largely composed of whites (40 percent in GHA and 24 percent in BC-BS, as compared to roughly a tenth in the two black groups; Table 4.3). Differences in median family incomes by race were likewise substantial, and almost twofold in GHA. Again, this income differential by race in each plan was not reflected in the overall plan distributions, where differences in the percent living in families at different income brackets existed almost exclusively at the lowest income level (less than $10,000 per year), which was reported almost twice as often in GHA than in BC-BS (21 percent and 12 percent, respectively). On the other hand, there were no differences by either plan or race in the mean number of persons per household. A relative preponderance of families with more than six persons was observed in GHA (see Table 4.3). Roughly a quarter of blacks in each plan lived in large families, and 18 percent of the white group in GHA, while this was observed for only 11 percent in BC-BS. Also, there was little difference between plans in mean family size at various income levels (Table 4.4). In both plans, family size tended to increase with income, although this was less noticeable for families in the two black groups than for white families, where the range was more than twofold across income categories. Differences in family size between the race groups, therefore, existed mainly at the lower end of the income scale.

Parent Work Status

Almost all of the men in the survey population were employed full-time. Among the adult women in the study, who were either contract holders or wives of contract holders, 61 percent in BC-BS and 71 percent in GHA (but more than three-quarters among blacks and about half of whites in both plans) were employed full-time as well (Table 4.5). The presence of children seems to have had little effect on the work status of women in GHA where, even when three or more children were reported, 58 percent of female parents worked full time, as compared to 35 percent in BC-BS. This difference is largely due to the fact that white women with children were far less likely to be employed than black women in both plans; among those with three or more children, less than 20 percent worked full-time, as compared to roughly two-thirds of black women. The greater proportion of mothers in GHA who were employed full-time is reflected in the finding, also shown in Table 4.5, that 58 percent of children under age 16 in GHA lived in families where the only adult or both parents were employed full-time, as compared to 38 percent in BC-BS. Again, in both plans the vast majority of these children were black: two-thirds as against a quarter of white children. In view of the black/white ratios in both plans, therefore, parent availability in case of illness was presumably less in GHA.

Attitudes to Care

These general comparisons of the demographic composition of the two plans and of some of their members' social and economic characteristics were complemented by an assessment of their attitudes to the seeking of curative or preventive care. While in part associated with these characteristics (Rosenstock, 1969; Kasl and Cobb, 1966), such attitudes can also reflect previous experience with the availability of or access to services; health habits prevalent in different family and cultural settings; and psychological factors such as levels of dependency and self-reliance (see for example Mechanic, 1969, 1962; Hetherington and Hopkins, 1969). Another attitudinal factor of interest in the present context is satisfaction with previous care. While this factor has been shown to be a relatively weak predictor of use (Aday and Eichhorn, 1972), and the lack of survey instruments of sufficient sensitivity and reliability has been noted (Ware, 1978; Lebow, 1974), the presence in this study of two populations cared for in different organizational settings might provide some, admittedly indirect, evidence of different patterns of care.

Tendency to Use Physician Services
and Physical Examinations

In order to determine whether members of the two plans varied in their propensity to seek health care at roughly comparable levels of illness, contract holders were shown a list of 13 common symptoms and asked whether, in the presence of any of these, they would do nothing, wait to see if it disappears, try a remedy at hand, or contact a physician. Scores were then constructed based on the number of symptoms for which the respondent felt that a physician contact would be required; these were grouped as follows:

Affirmative Replies	Score
0–6	Low
7–9	Medium
10–13	High

The summed scores based on the replies of contract holders were attributed to each family member as an individual tendency score. Only about one-fourth in both plans scored low on this measure (Table 4.6), with BC-BS members most likely to have a medium score and GHA members to have a high score. The plan difference was small within race groups, although statistically significant among whites. In both plans, however, black members were considerably more likely than whites to have high scores. The higher overall tendency to use physician services in GHA was thus largely attributable to the black component in that plan.

Reported attitudes toward preventive care followed a similar pattern. The overwhelming majority of persons in both plans were in families who supported a routine physical examination once a year, even when "a person is feeling all right." The notable exception were whites in BC-BS, of whom 19 percent thought it "not worth the trouble" in the absence of a complaint. Attitudes to and previous use of preventive services were only roughly consistent, however. When asked whether family members had had a routine physical examination in the last two years, two-thirds of those in BC-BS and four-fifths in GHA reported such an examination overall; in BC-BS, close to 20 percent had never had one. In fact, only the white group in GHA recalled a recent physical examination in the absence of illness at a level commensurate with their reported attitude toward this type of use.

Satisfaction with Care

Satisfaction with medical care during the year before the start of the survey was measured by asking contract holders, in the first interview, whether or not they were completely satisfied with each of the following 13 items:

- Quality of the medical care received
- The time it took to get an appointment
- Waiting time in the physician's office or a clinic
- The length of time the physician spent with the patient
- Availability of medical care at night and on weekends
- Ease and convenience of getting to a physician from one's place of residence
- Expenditures for the medical care received, not counting the payroll deduction for insurance premiums
- The amount of information provided about the patient's complaint
- Courtesy and consideration shown by physicians
- Explanation of home treatment of illness
- Courtesy and consideration shown by nurses
- The follow-up care received after an initial treatment or operation
- The personal interest showed by physicians

Responses were then attributed to all members of the household.

Overall, BC-BS members expressed higher levels of satisfaction for 9 of 12 items where differences were statistically significant (Table 4.7). These differences between plans ranged from a low of 5 percent for explanations of treatments to a twofold difference for appointment waiting times. GHA members, on the other hand, were more satisfied with office or clinic waiting times, the availability of care at night and on weekends, and the cost of care exclusive of premiums. Whites in both plans tended to be more satisfied than the black groups. Differences within race groups across plans tended to follow the pattern of overall plan comparisons, although fewer and smaller differences were noted between the two white groups. By these measures, the black group in BC-BS was least satisfied of all.

If satisfaction were in fact a sufficient predictor of use, comparatively low levels of use should be expected in the prepaid group practice plan, particularly in view of its relatively large population of blacks. On the other hand, while some of the differences between plans on specific items seem reasonable and expected (e.g., longer appointment waiting times in GHA, less satisfaction with the cost of care in BC-BS), it is difficult to determine whether the differences in satisfaction between the black and white groups in each plan reflect actual differences in experience with services or different expectations of the health care system.

Summary

In terms of characteristics generally shown as predisposing to the use of health care (age, sex, race, education, occupational status, income, family size, work status of adults, and attitudes to the use of services), the following findings were made with regard to the two plan populations:

— In 1972 the racial composition of the two plan groups was strikingly dissimilar, with twice as many whites enrolled in the fee-for-service plan than in the prepaid group plan.

— The median age in BC-BS was slightly higher than in GHA. A larger proportion of adults above 45 years was found among whites, particularly in the prepaid group practice plan; the black groups included more school-age children and adolescents. There was no difference in the percentage of males and females in each plan.

— Overall, household educational level was similar in both plans except at college and post-college levels; the major difference was that in GHA as much as half of the white group belonged to families including at least one person with more than four years of college or university, compared to a fourth of whites in BC-BS and a tenth of blacks in both plans.

— A similar picture was observed for occupational status. A third of all black plan members, two-thirds of whites in BC-BS and 85 percent of whites in GHA lived in families headed by men or women in professional and managerial occupations.

— Median family income was highest among GHA whites and lowest among GHA blacks, and there were more large families in GHA than in BC-BS.

— While roughly two-thirds of women in both plans worked full time, 58 percent of women with three or more children in GHA were so employed, as compared to 35 percent in BC-BS. In both plans, black working women were far more frequent in proportion to their numbers than was found among whites, and three times as many black as white children lived in families where all adults were working full time. The availability of parents in case of illness thus appeared lower in GHA.

— Finally, GHA enrollees reported a higher tendency to use physician services and more favorable attitudes toward annual physical examinations, but less satisfaction with services, than those in BC-BS. They were also more likely to have had a recent physical examination. The black group in BC-BS was most likely never to have had a physical examination.

As far as factors predisposing to the use of services are concerned, therefore, whites in GHA would rank highest. Overall, however, the predominance of blacks in that plan and their generally lower ranking on most of these indicators would make it difficult to predict differences in use between the two plans on the basis of these considerations alone.

ENABLING FACTORS AND
SELECTED MEASURES OF ACCESS

Among the range of factors that contribute to making health service resources available to the individual or that facilitate access to care, health insurance is a major influence. Although by definition, every person in the sample had fairly comprehensive insurance coverage, to the extent to which coverage varied between the plans in this study (see Chapter 1), use may have varied as well. The most obvious difference in this respect is the fact that no out-of-pocket payments were required for ambulatory physician care under GHA, and that such services as preventive care, eye care, and visits to certain other practitioners were covered as well. The more generous coverage of mental health care in BC-BS should have enabled its members to make more use of this type of service. Overall, however, the benefit packages in both plans minimized the deterrent effect of financial costs. Also, differences in the number and type of medical providers among whom the members of the two plans could choose should not have affected their access to care, despite the fact that GHA members were limited to a closed panel of physicians with fairly well defined patterns of referral, whereas BC-BS members could theoretically choose among all fee-for-service practitioners in the Washington metropolitan area.

Nonetheless, even when these aspects are disregarded, several factors remain that may be indicative of differences between the two plan populations and of the structure and organization of services available to them. Length of plan membership and, by implication, knowledge of how one's insurance plan works, what coverage is available, and how to use it effectively should increase the ability to use services when necessary or desired.

A regular and known source of care, particularly a personal physician who is aware of patient history and needs, should enhance both access to services and continuity of care, and differences between the plans in this respect may be postulated to have affected use of services. Finally, differences in travel time, which were probably longer in GHA because of the limited number of GHA facilities (see also Table 4.7), and differences in the appointment systems between prepaid group practice and fee-for-service practice may well have affected the seeking of care. The extent to which the study populations varied in these respects, in particular with regard to a personal physician and waiting times for appointments, is examined below.

Length of Plan Membership

Overall, at least half of the study population belonged to families with at least seven years of plan membership (Table 4.8). However, more than one-third of members in BC-BS, but only 14 percent in GHA, belonged to families whose enrollment dated back to before 1960, the year when the Federal Employees Health Benefits Plan came into effect. In BC-BS, this was observed for blacks and whites; in GHA, 32 percent of whites were in member families of similarly long standing, but only 5 percent of blacks had been in that plan for more than 14 years. At the other end of the scale, a much smaller proportion in BC-BS (less than 10 percent overall and only 4 percent of these blacks) were in families who had joined BC-BS in the three years prior to the survey, while this was true of 23 percent in GHA, with no difference between the race groups. In the survey year, therefore, the GHA membership was about evenly divided among relatively recent members (one to six years of membership) and those who were members of long standing (seven or more years), with a preponderance of recent members among the black group; in BC-BS, over 70 percent had been in the plan for at least seven years, and very few of the blacks in that plan belonged to families who had recently joined the service benefit plan.

On the other hand, Table 4.8 also indicates that members of long standing were more likely to be older, and that this was the case particularly in GHA, where 57 percent of those whose families had been plan members for 14 or more years were 45 years or older, as compared to 41 percent in BC-BS. This group, while numerically small (roughly 8 percent of the GHA sample), might therefore have had a relatively high likelihood of use because of its age. It should be noted, though, that a large proportion of children 0 to 4 years of age, who also are a group at high risk of use, belonged to families who were relatively recent members, particularly in BC-BS.

Knowledge of Plan Benefits

If health insurance benefits are to be used, plan members must know that they exist. This is particularly so for instances of coverage where the patient or plan member must initiate the process by which the benefit is realized. Thus, to the extent that the expected cost of services affects the decision to seek or continue care, to be ignorant of specific benefits is equivalent to not having coverage or, conversely, to incurring unforeseen expenses. In addition, in BC-BS it was up to the subscriber to initiate and secure reimbursement for physician visits or prescriptions or for basic services provided by nonparticipating physicians. Those in GHA had to apply for reimbursement for the cost of out-of-plan care in life-threatening emergencies, for care obtained while away from the Washington area, and for certain prescription costs. Beyond that, the GHA enrollee had to be aware that only care provided by or with the express approval of GHA was covered and that procuring other care was, in effect, to deny oneself the financial benefits of the plan.

To determine knowledge of plan benefits as a predictor of use, contract holders or family respondents were asked in the initial interview to identify from a list of health services those for which they had any coverage under their insurance plan. Generally speaking, subscribers were more knowledgeable of instances of full than of partial coverage or of those requiring initiative to obtain reimbursement (Table 4.9); the latter included supplemental benefits in BC-BS and, in GHA, both prescription medicines which totalled over a certain sum per year ($50) and care obtained outside the GHA service area. Thus, in BC-BS, less than one-third knew about coverage for any supplemental benefit, including physician visits and prescriptions (although these are frequently obtained medical services), but virtually everyone in both plans knew about coverage for hospital care, a relatively rare event. With some exceptions, the differences between plans and between race groups for specific knowledge of coverage were wide and not always in the direction of greater knowledge under GHA, although when correct answers were summed and grouped into scores (0–5, low; 6–8, medium; 9–13, high), GHA members were twice as likely as their BC-BS counterparts to rank high on these scores (Table 4.10). Studies comparing knowledge of benefits in comparable plans have reported similar findings (Moustafa, Hopkins, and Klein, 1971). Differences between the two race groups in each plan were pronounced, the black group in BC-BS ranking lowest by far.

In part, this difference in knowledge of plan benefits may have been related to length of plan membership and presumably experience with plan services. In GHA, this was indeed the case, although whites with four to six years of plan membership were an exception (Table 4.10). Among BC-BS members, the expected positive relationship with years in plan was observed only among the relatively few black members with high knowledge scores, but among whites, new members exhibited the highest knowledge of benefits. The relationship between length of plan membership and knowledge of plan benefits was thus not entirely linear. Whether this was due to the previously observed differences in age distributions between the plans, involving greater use and thus more frequent exposure to questions of coverage by newer members in BC-BS and older members in GHA, is difficult to determine.

A point of interest here is the extent to which members of the service benefit plan did in fact claim supplemental benefits. About one-third of BC-BS households were found eligible to submit a claim for benefits for the year prior to the survey, according to data reported by respondents in the initial interview, but only 42 percent of those eligible filed claims, with more than twice as many white as black households filing claims (51 percent and 22 percent, respectively). Of those eligible who did not seek reimbursement, 37 percent were not aware that they might have been eligible under BC-BS supplemental benefits provisions; 25 percent reported that it was not worth the trouble because their expenditures for covered services did not substantially exceed the deductible; and another 16 percent said the claims were too complicated to complete.

Regular Sources of Care

A wide range of health services was available on a regular basis to those enrolled in the prepaid group practice plan; the health services used by members of the service benefit plan may be assumed to present a less homogeneous pattern. On the other hand, the availability of services at GHA offices did not necessarily imply an entirely uniform provision of such services. In particular, at least at the time of the study, not every member was treated on a continuing basis by a personal physician; for example, those using the walk-in clinic may have been seen by different staff physicians on different occasions. Family respondents were, therefore, also questioned as to the usual source of care of family members. Four major groups were distinguished among respondent answers:

- Those consulting a personal physician whenever medical care was desired
- Those consulting other physicians or a specifically mentioned medical group practice
- Those using the services of a hospital outpatient department or emergency room
- Those reporting no regular source of care

For GHA members consulting particular physicians, a further question, whether this physician was on the staff of GHA, was asked. Since very few (5 percent) regularly consulted physicians outside GHA, this subgroup will not be considered separately here (see, however, Chapter 6).

There was the expected marked difference between plans in the reporting of personal and other physicians as a regular source of care (Table 4.11). Although in both BC-BS and GHA, the majority thought it important to have a personal physician (nine-tenths in BC-BS and almost three-quarters in GHA), 82 percent in BC-BS consulted personal physicians (68 percent of blacks, 89 percent of whites), and only 6 percent overall consulted other physicians or medical groups, while in GHA a personal physician was the source of care for only two-fifths of members overall. Among whites, this was reported for 56 percent, and a large minority (39 percent) used an available GHA physician; among blacks only 36 percent had a personal physician while 52 percent were seen by available GHA medical staff. Thus, while the importance of the personal physician as regular source of care specifically in prepaid group practice plans has been noted by many (e.g., Fink, 1969; Weinerman, 1964, 1962), the data in this study support previous findings that creating and maintaining this source has been found difficult (Greenberg and Rodburg, 1971; Weinerman, 1962). Roughly one-tenth overall, but twice as many blacks in BC-BS as in GHA (21 and 11 percent, respectively), reported the hospital outpatient department or an emergency room as a regular source of care. It should be noted that since use of such facilities would be authorized by GHA only in emergencies, their reporting even by 8 percent of all GHA beneficiaries as a regular source of care is difficult to explain (see, however, Chapter 6 in this respect as well).

Access to Care

During the survey period GHA provided to its members in its main facility the services of an urgent visit clinic that required no appointments, as well as treatment at other GHA facilities. For BC-BS, no information was available on the number of providers who accepted patients without appointment, but it may be assumed that appointment patterns for those with a personal physician were typical of fee-for-service practice. In fact, more than twice as many visits by GHA members than by those in BC-BS were walk-in visits (39 percent compared to 18 percent; Table 4.12). Within each plan, slightly more visits made by the black groups were by appointment than those among whites. Also, for patient initiated appointments, which exclude visits where the appointment was suggested by the physician in a previous visit, substantial differences in appointment waiting times were observed (Table 4.13). Whereas almost half of the appointments in BC-BS were for visits within 24 hours, in GHA this was observed for only about one-fourth; for waits of 14 or more days, the difference between plans was threefold (GHA, 42 percent; BC-BS, 13 percent).

However, because of the general availability of services without appointment in GHA, a more accurate description of the accessibility of care is gained if all visits initiated by patients are combined, regardless of appointment status, and waits are measured by how long it took from the patient's decision to seek care to the actual time of the visit. In fact, prompt care was equally available in both plans. Close to two-thirds of walk-in visits as well as patient-initiated appointments in both plans occurred within 24 hours of the decision to seek care (Table 4.14), although twofold differences between the plans remain for intermediate waits of 2 to 7 days (BC-BS, 25 percent; GHA, 12 percent) and for waits of 14 or more days (BC-BS, 10 percent; GHA, 20 percent). More specifically, three-fourths of patient-initiated visits for diagnostic reasons in both plans occurred within 24 hours of the decision to seek care, and a similar proportion was observed for treatment visits; here a higher percentage occurred within 24 hours in GHA than in BC-BS (81 percent as compared to 75 percent; Table 4.15). Clearly, care could be and was obtained promptly in both plans when diagnosis or treatment was sought, particularly by the black group in GHA, for whom 24-hour waits for such visits were quite clearly the mode (79 percent of diagnostic visits and 85 percent of treatment visits). On the other hand, where waits of more than two weeks after the decision to seek care were incurred, they were found three times as often in GHA than in BC-BS for both diagnosis and treatment (3 percent in BC-BS; roughly 10 percent in GHA), but again, substantially lower percentages of long treatment waits were incurred by blacks in both plans.

Also, and as expected, differences in scheduling practices between GHA and fee-for-service providers were evident for checkups and routine physical examinations. In both plans fewer of these visits occurred within 24 hours than did diagnostic and treatment visits, but in GHA they were a smaller proportion of all visits in these categories than in BC-BS. For check-ups, 49 percent of BC-BS visits occurred within 24 hours, compared to 37 percent in GHA; for routine physical examinations, the corresponding fig-ures were 14 percent in BC-BS and 8 percent in GHA. Conversely, only 12 percent of checkups in BC-BS occurred 14 or more days after the decision to seek medical care, compared to 31 percent in GHA; for routine physical examinations, the difference was twofold and in the same direction (see Table 4.15). Finally, almost all visits in both plans for shots and immuniza-tions occurred within 24 hours of the decision to seek care. While this pattern of differences also prevailed within race groups across the plans, some interesting comparisons between race groups can be made. In GHA, for instance, almost twice the percentage of visits by blacks for checkups and physical examinations occurred within 24 hours as for the white group, with correspondingly lower percentages observed for visits made two weeks or longer after the decision to seek care. For BC-BS, a similar difference was noted for visits made for routine physical examinations.

At least for visits for treatment or diagnosis, therefore, the time required to obtain care was substantially the same in both plans. Scheduling practices for less urgent visits differed substantially between the plans, however, with visits for checkups and routine physical examinations involv-ing far longer waits in GHA than in BC-BS. It was also noted that treatment and diagnostic visits by the black group in GHA occurred more often within 24 hours of the decision to seek medical care than was observed for the white group in that plan. Contrary to expectations, this difference was not the result of a greater proportion of walk-in visits; black respondents, as a matter of fact, reported fewer walk-in visits than whites in both plans.

The distribution of all visits by office waiting times showed only small differences between the plans, with 5 percent more visits by BC-BS mem-bers having a waiting time of less than 15 minutes than in GHA (Table 4.16), and waiting times for about four-fifths of all visits less than 30 minutes. Here, however, waiting times for visits made by blacks tended to be longer than for those made by whites, particularly in BC-BS. Thus, waits of less than 15 minutes were reported for 40 percent of visits made by blacks in BC-BS compared with 61 percent of visits made by whites; in GHA, the difference was 48 percent versus 59 percent.

Summary

Several characteristics of the study population were examined as potential enabling factors with regard to their use of services. It was assumed that length of plan membership would be reflected in knowledge of plan benefits, and that these two factors in conjunction should enable plan members and their families to make efficient use of needed services for which coverage exists. It was found that while a larger proportion of BC-BS enrollees had been members of their plan for more than six years than was observed for GHA (73 percent versus 52 percent), twice as many GHA as BC-BS enrollees scored high on a knowledge of plan benefits scale. Furthermore, in BC-BS, a higher level of knowledge of plan benefits was found among more recent members than among those of long standing; the reverse was observed for GHA. The relationship between length of membership and knowledge of plan coverage was thus different for the two plans. It should also be noted that in BC-BS, almost three times as many whites as blacks were among recent members (one to three years at the time of the study), while the percentage of members of long standing was the same. In GHA, on the other hand, very few black members (5 percent) had joined the prepaid group plan before it became a federal benefit option (1960), compared to a third for whites. In view of these findings, and leaving aside other factors associated with use of services such as levels of illness, use should be greater among more recent members in BC-BS, and among members of long standing in GHA.

Strictly speaking, the third enabling factor, the regular availability of a source of care, should predict greater use under GHA, since membership in a prepaid group plan ensures both regular access to and availability of services. On the other hand, only half as many in GHA as those in BC-BS reported seeing a personal physician when seeking care. It remains to be examined whether the assurance of a regular source of care, regardless of whether care is continuously provided by the same physician or by several staff physicians, is a better predictor of use than the patient-physician relationship that generally exists in a fee-for-service system.

Finally, while a substantial percentage of all patient-initiated visits occurred within 24 hours in both plans, at least for nonurgent services the appointment system in GHA appeared to be more of a barrier to prompt medical care than was observed in the service benefit plan. This finding is reflected in the high degree of dissatisfaction with the GHA appointment system.

LEVELS OF ILLNESS

Information on health status and on specific instances of illness was obtained for each family member in the household survey. In the initial interview, questions were asked about each family member's general state of health and about any existing health problems lasting for more than three months; the latter are referred to, in subsequent analyses, as chronic health problems. Also, at each monthly interview, respondents were asked to enumerate and describe any occurrence of ill health or injury resulting in days of bed rest, restricted activity, or pain and worry. Thus, the data described in the following provide both an indicator of the individual's overall state of health at the beginning of the survey year, and a continuous record of illness events throughout the year.

It is noted that this information reflects perceptions of ill health and possibly of need for care rather than clinically verified morbidity. Also, it may reflect different thresholds of perception, i.e., the point at which the individual or someone in the family defined an event as worthy of being reported as illness or injury; for example, a backache mentioned as a health problem of long duration. It is known that attitudes toward health and illness as well as previous contacts with providers of care can affect perceptions of illness and the propensity toward illness behavior, such as restricting activity or staying in bed (Kasl and Cobb, 1966; see also Mott and Barclay, 1973; Shapiro, 1967). Differences in this respect between the two plan populations and between specific subgroups may, therefore, suggest possible differences in use.

Perceived Health Status. The general state of health of each family member as reported at the time of the first interview is shown by four categories in Table 4.17. Overall, about 70 percent were reported in very good health, and less than 10 percent in the fair to poor categories. The only exception to this was the black subgroup in GHA, where only 64 percent were reported as being in very good health. Among those reported not in very good health, adults 45 years or older were the largest single category among males and females in both plans, with slightly higher percentages among males in GHA; among those 20 to 44 years, females predominated in GHA. Older children and adolescents (5 to 19 years) were reported in less than good health more than twice as often among blacks than among whites in the prepaid group practice plan.

Chronic Illness. To determine the frequency of chronic health problems among the two study populations at the time of the first interview, respondents were handed the following list of health problems or illnesses of long duration and asked if a family member had any of these or another health problem which had continued for more than three months prior to interview:

Emphysema or chronic bronchitis

Repeated attacks of sinus trouble

Hemorrhoids or piles

Hay fever or other allergy

Tumor, cyst, or similar growth

Chronic gallbladder or liver trouble

Stomach ulcer or other chronic stomach trouble

Kidney stones or chronic kidney trouble

Thyroid trouble or goiter

Emotional, nervous, or mental trouble

Chronic skin trouble

Repeated trouble with back or spine

High blood pressure or hypertension

Any heart trouble, hardening of arteries, or arteriosclerosis

Diabetes

Repeated middle ear infections

Serious trouble with one or both eyes

Arthritis, bursitis, or rheumatism

Other

The proportion of those who mentioned a particular chronic health problem ranged from 0.3 percent for gallbladder problems in both plans to 7.8 percent in BC-BS and 10.5 percent in GHA for hay fever and asthma. For those problems where statistically significant differences existed between the plans, a higher burden of illness was observed in GHA (regardless of race); only sinus problems were more common in BC-BS. Statistically significant differences between the race groups appeared more often in GHA and indicated a heavier burden of chronic illness among whites in both plans, with the exception of hypertension. An aggregate of these distributions into three indicators of the presence of chronic problems (none, one, or two or more) confirmed the excess of chronic illness among the white subgroups in both plans, as well as among blacks in GHA as compared to those in BC-BS (Table 4.18). In both plans the percentage of those with at least one chronic problem was largest for those 45 years or older and higher in GHA for both males and females in this age group, regardless of race.

Of those reporting chronic ill health (34 percent in BC-BS and 39 percent in GHA), roughly three-fifths were under a physician's care for their problem. The range was from 55 percent for whites in BC-BS to 69 percent for whites in GHA (Table 4.19), and while the black group in BC-BS was least likely to report at least one chronic problem (29 percent as compared to 36 percent for GHA blacks) they were as likely to receive treatment when a problem existed (65 percent). GHA whites were both more likely to report a problem and to be treated for it than whites in BC-

BS or blacks in GHA. Females in both plans were somewhat more likely to be treated for a chronic problem than males.

Bed Days and Restricted Activity Days. A further measure of ill health, and possibly of need for care, consisted of days of bed rest or restricted activity summed over the survey year. By these measures of social dysfunction (Tables 4.20–4.21), which could be attributable either to a chronic problem or an acute condition, levels of ill health appear to have been slightly higher among the BC-BS population. Differences were most pronounced for the youngest age groups (0 to 19 years of age), where rates in BC-BS were substantially above those in GHA for both sexes, and by statistically significant margins in four out of eight comparisons. For the oldest male group, the pattern was reversed for both bed and restricted activity days. Differences were also noticeable between the two race groups, particularly in BC-BS, where the black group was substantially less likely to report bed days and restricted activity days than the white group in most age–sex categories, and by statistically significant margins in half of the comparisons. The pattern was similar in GHA.

Days of Pain and Worry. Days on which a health problem caused considerable pain or worry were reported for less than a third in each plan, with statistically significant plan differences observed only among the two black groups (Table 4.22). Although the previously observed differences by race persisted in most age–sex groups, in GHA young adults (20 to 44 years) of both sexes were an exception, with black rates equal to those of the white group in that plan.

Thus, the somewhat larger burden of chronic problems in GHA was only partly reflected in measures of social dysfunction and pain and worry. Differences by race were relatively large and, particularly in BC-BS, indicated less illness among the black groups. Despite the lower overall frequency of persons with bed days and restricted activity days in GHA, the presence in that plan of some groups with a relatively high likelihood of reporting one or several of these events reduced differences between plans. For example, among males 45 years or older, consistently higher rates of illness were observed in GHA for both race groups.

Also, statistically significant differences between the two plan populations in the mean volume of bed days, restricted activity days, and pain and worry days (Table 4.23) indicate higher measures in GHA than in BC-BS for the number of bed days among blacks and among older men of both races; in restricted activity days among all adult males; and in pain and worry days among adult black females. Means were higher in BC-BS only for bed days and restricted activity days reported for children. Thus, high levels of illness by these measures were concentrated among the young in BC-BS and among adults, particularly older men, in GHA.

SUMMARY AND CONCLUSIONS

This chapter has compared the members of a service benefit plan and prepaid group practice plan with respect to their characteristics in terms of predisposing and enabling factors, selected measures of access, and levels of illness. In part, this comparison was made to assess if differences in this respect between the two plan populations were of sufficient magnitude to explain the differences in hospital use that were observed in Phase I of the study (see Chapter 2); of equal importance to this study are its implications with regard to use of ambulatory services.

It is clear from the foregoing that there were few, if any, differences in the age and sex distribution of the two plan populations of sufficient magnitude to affect the use of services. A large difference was found in their racial composition, with relatively twice as many whites enrolled in the fee-for-service than in the prepaid group practice plan. Since this variable has been shown to be associated with different patterns of health services use in many studies of the United States population at the time (e.g., Aday and Eichhorn, 1972; National Center for Health Statistics, 1969a), the comparisons of member characteristics and levels of illness have focused not only on overall plan differences but also on differences within and across race groups. Of note here is the fact that there were somewhat larger proportions of white adults above 45 years, particularly in GHA, and a larger proportion of black school-age children.

While statistically significant differences between the plans were small with regard to most predisposing factors — household educational and occupational level, annual family income, family size, parent work status, and satisfaction with care — the imbalance in racial composition tended to obscure variations within and across plan groups. For example, over 50 percent of whites in GHA lived in households where the most highly educated adult had five or more years of college education, in contrast to 23 percent in BC-BS among whites and about 10 percent among blacks in both plans. Whites in GHA were least likely to be members of households where the occupational level of the head was classified in the category of craftsmen, foremen, operators, service workers and laborers, with the difference fourfold between race groups within that plan, but only twofold in BC-BS. Similarly, because of the higher percentage of blacks in both plans who were members of households in the lower income categories, the larger proportion of whites in GHA with family incomes of more than $25,000 per year (40 percent) was not reflected in overall plan distributions (see Table 4.3). Only with regard to family size did plan differences reflect the relatively large number of GHA families of six of more persons, though here, too, large black families were most frequent in both plans. The mean number of persons per household was similar among the four race and plan groups, however.

Plan differences were somewhat more pronounced with regard to attitudes, which were measured by the reported tendency to use physician services in the case of illness, attitudes towards and use of routine physical examinations, and satisfaction with care. In GHA a higher percentage were members of families where the contract holder reported a high tendency to use physician services; here, blacks in both plans reported a somewhat higher tendency to use such services than whites. GHA members reported more frequently a positive attitude toward physical examinations and were more likely to have had a physical examination within the past two years. Measures of satisfaction with a variety of aspects of care indicated strong differences by plan and also by race, generally indicating higher satisfaction by members of BC-BS and by the two white groups.

With regard to enabling factors, differences between the plans were clear and to some extent indicative of structural and organizational differences between the plans. Seventy-three percent of BC-BS members lived in households that had been enrolled in BC-BS for more than six years, in contrast to 52 percent for GHA. Here, the relatively low proportion of blacks who had joined BC-BS within one to three years of the survey (4 percent as compared to 11 percent of whites and roughly a quarter of GHA members) may suggest a preference for complete prepayment of services and full coverage for ambulatory care. Twice as many GHA as BC-BS contract holders scored high on a scale representing knowledge of plan benefits, and there was a difference between plans in the relationship between length of plan membership and knowledge of benefits. Here again, the fact that more blacks in BC-BS than in GHA were low on the knowledge scale is suggestive of differences within the black component in this study. In both plans, members were generally more aware of benefits that provided full coverage.

The data on regular sources of care clearly reflect the structural differences between the plans. Though most members in both plans, regardless of race, named a physician as their regular source of care, over 80 percent of BC-BS members identified a personal physician, in contrast to 43 percent in GHA. In the latter plan, 48 percent identified another physician as their regular source of care. Although in both plans whites reported a personal physician more frequently than the corresponding black groups, these findings must be seen in conjunction with appointment waiting times and of time to obtain care, where blacks in both plans obtained services more promptly than the respective white groups, indicating that there were few objective differences in access to care between the two race groups.

The final set of factors that might be explanatory of the differences in

Phase I and predictive of use of ambulatory services are levels of illness in the two study populations. In this phase of the study, only measures of perceived morbidity were employed because resources were not available to verify household reports by clinical and pathological indicators. Thus, the data in Tables 4.17 to 4.23 reflect questions that ascertained general health status, chronic complaints, and chronic problems under the care of a physician at the beginning of the survey year, days spent in bed or of restricted activity associated with illness or injury, and days of pain and worry about health problems over the couse of the survey.

As was found for the age–sex distributions of the two plan populations, overall patterns of illness did not indicate sufficiently large differences to warrant expectations of widely different levels of need for care. No major differences were found in perceived health status and, although some variation existed in the percent of members reporting specific chronic health problems in each plan, the overall distributions of the number of chronic health problems in the two populations were not dissimilar. However, BC-BS members were somewhat more likely than GHA members to have experienced bed and restricted activity days, particularly among children, and differences in groups defined by age and sex were indicative of a greater burden of chronic illness among older GHA males of both races and of social dysfunction among whites, particularly in BC-BS.

In general, then, among the many measures employed in this comparison of characteristics of members of BC-BS and GHA in 1972–73, few large differences were evident. The major exception to this general finding related to race, where a major difference in the composition of the two plans was found and where the pattern of differences between the races conforms to general findings of other studies (Aday and Eichhorn, 1972) for this period. Also, in both plans and both within and across race groups, some differences in the characteristics of certain subgroups suggested greater hospital and/or ambulatory use by BC-BS members, while others suggested greater use among GHA members. The collective impact of each of these on patterns of use within each plan is difficult to forecast because of the complex interrelationships of the predisposing, enabling, and illness factors suggested in these comparisons and observed in other studies. A further limitation is the fact that the study design could not include specific comparisons of the availability of resources and the direct effect of organizational and structural characteristics of the provider systems available to the members of each plan, permitting at best indirect assumptions as to the interaction of systems influences and consumer behavior. Hence, the evidence in this chapter does not offer an explanation for the major differences in hospital use observed; differences in ambulatory use between the two plans as well were expected to be relatively small.

Use of Health Care Resources

Table 4.1   Sociodemographic characteristics of two plan populations: Percentage distributions and medians by race, age, and sex

Characteristics	All BC–BS	All GHA	Black BC–BS	Black GHA	White BC–BS	White GHA
			Race			
Black	34	67	––	––	––	––
White	66	33	––	––	––	––
(n)	100 (1,368)	* 100 (1,323)				
			Age			
0 to 4 years	10	8	10	8	11	6
5 to 19 years	28	37	34	39	26	33
20 to 44 years	37	35	36	38	38	29
45 years or older	24	21	21	16	26	32
(n)	100 (1,367)[a]	* 100 (1,323)	100+ (461)	100++ (885)	100 (906)	* 100 (438)
Median	28	24	24	22	29	29
			Sex			
Male	48	49	47	48	49	49
Female	52	51	53	52	51	51
(n)	100 (1,368)	100 (1,323)	100 (462)	100 (885)	100 (906)	100 (438)
			Age and sex			
Males						
0 to 4 years	12	8	13	9	11	6
5 to 19 years	29	39	33	41	25	35
20 to 44 years	35	31	32	33	37	27
45 years or older	24	22	22	18	25	32
(n)	100 (658)	* 100 (644)	100 (216)	100++ (429)	100 (442)	* 100 (215)
Median	26	22	23	20	28	28
Females						
0 to 4 years	9	7	6	8	11	6
5 to 19 years	28	35	34	37	24	31
20 to 44 years	39	38	40	42	39	30
45 years or older	24	20	20	13	27	33
(n)	100 (709)	* 100 (678)	100+ (245)	100++ (456)	100 (464)	* 100 (222)
Median	28	25	26	23	30	31

[a]Age not ascertained in one case.

*P ≤ .05.

+P ≤ .05 for race groups, BC–BS.

++P ≤ .05 for race groups, GHA.

Table 4.2 Household education and occupation: Percentage distribution of two plan populations

	All		Black		White	
	BC–BS	GHA	BC–BS	GHA	BC–BS	GHA
	Years of education[a]					
Less than 12 years	6	8	11	12	3	1
4 years of high school	36	32	47	41	30	16
1 to 3 years of college	19	20	20	24	19	13
4 years of college	21	15	13	13	25	20
5 or more years of college or university	19	25	10	11	23	51
	100 *	100	100[+]	100[++]	100 *	100
	Occupation[b]					
Craftsmen, foremen, operators, service, and laborers	28	26	45	35	20	8
Clerical and sales	14	22	21	28	10	7
Professional, technical, manager, officials, and proprietors	58	52	34	36	70	85
	100 *	100	100[+] *	100[++]	100 *	100

[a]Of most highly educated household member.

[b]Of contract holder.

*$P \leqslant .05$.

[+]$P \leqslant 05$ for race groups, BC–BS.

[++]$P \leqslant .05$ for race groups, GHA.

Table 4.3   Annual family income and family size: Percentage distribution of two plan populations by family income and family size

	All		Black		White	
	BC–BS	GHA	BC–BS	GHA	BC–BS	GHA
Annual family income ($)						
Less than 10,000	12	21	25	29	6	4
10,000 to 14,999	22	18	29	22	18	9
15,000 to 24,999	45	42	33	39	51	47
25,000 or more	20	20	13	10	24	40
	100 *	100	100[+] *	100[++]	100 *	100
Median[a]	16,821	15,526	13,171	12,308	18,489	21,825
Number of persons in household						
1	11	12	10	13	12	12
2 to 3	36	29	37	25	36	37
4 to 5	37	34	27	35	42	33
6 or more	16	24	27	28	11	18
	100 *	100	100[+] *	100[++]	100	100
Mean	2.85	2.91	2.98	2.96	2.79	2.83

[a]Data on income were missing for 3 households in BC–BS and 6 households in GHA.
*P ≤ .05.   [+]P ≤ .05 for race groups, BC–BS.   [++]P ≤ .05 for race groups, GHA.

Table 4.4   Mean number of persons per household at four family income levels

Annual family income ($)	All		Black		White	
	BC–BS	GHA	BC–BS	GHA	BC–BS	GHA
Less than 10,000	1.9 (89)	2.1 (133)	2.3[+] (51)	2.2[++] (118)	1.4 * (38)	1.1 (15)
10,000 to 14,999	2.6 (116)	2.8 (83)	3.2[+] (41)	3.0[++] (65)	2.2 (75)	2.1 (18)
15,000 to 24,999	3.4 (184)	3.6 (152)	3.4 (45)	3.8[++] (89)	3.3 (139)	3.2 (63)
25,000 or more	3.2 (88)	3.2 (80)	3.5 (17)	3.5 (24)	3.1 (71)	3.1 (56)

*P ≤ .05.   [+]P ≤ .05 for race groups, BC–BS.   [++]P ≤ .05 for race groups, GHA.

Table 4.5 Work status: Percentage distribution of adult females, percent of females employed full-time by number of children, and percentage distribution of children less than 16 years of age by parent work status

	All		Black		White	
	BC–BS	GHA	BC–BS	GHA	BC–BS	GHA
Adult females						
Employed full time	61	71	76	82	54	51
Employed part time	9	6	5	5	11	9
Not employed	30	22	19	13	35	40
	100 *	100	100$^+$	100^{++}	100	100
(n)	(428)	(377)	(139)	(244)	(289)	(133)
Percent of females employed full time						
No children	87	81	85	89^{++}	88 *	70
	(183)	(145)	(54)	(85)	(129)	(60)
One to two children	44 *	70	74$^+$	84^{++}	31	44
	(173)	(141)	(56)	(91)	(117)	(50)
Three or more children	35 *	58	64$^+$	72^{++}	17	18
	(72)	(91)	(29)	(68)	(43)	(23)
Children less than 16 years[a]						
1 parent in household, employed full time	11	14	21	19	5	2
2 parents, employed full time	27	44	45	51	17	24
2 parents, one employed full time	62	42	34	30	78	74
	100 *	100	100$^+$	100^{++}	100	100
(n)	(432)	(446)	(160)	(329)	(272)	(117)

[a]Excludes 5 children for whom parent work status could not be determined.

*P ≤ .05. $^+$P ≤ .05 for race groups, BC–BS. $^{++}$P ≤ .05 for race groups, GHA.

Use of Health Care Resources

Table 4.6 Attitudes toward medical care: Percentage distribution of household members by three indicators

	All		Black		White	
	BC–BS	GHA	BC–BS	GHA	BC–BS	GHA
Tendency to use physician services						
Low	27	24	19	21	32	32
Medium	38	32	38	32	38	32
High	34	43	43	46	30	36
	100 *	100	100^+	100^{++}	100 *	100
Attitude to physical examination						
Positive	82	96	90	97	78	93
Negative	16	3	10	2	19	5
Don't know	2	1	0	1	2	2
	100 *	100	100^+ *	100^{++}	100 *	100
Prior physical examination						
Within 2 years	67	79	64	75	68	86
More than 2 years prior to survey year	16	10	13	11	17	8
Never	18	11	23	14	15	5
	100 *	100	100^+ *	100^{++}	100 *	100

*$P \leqslant .05$.

+$P \leqslant .05$ for race groups, BC–BS.

++$P \leqslant .05$ for race groups, GHA.

Table 4.7 Satisfaction with medical care: Percent of persons completely satisfied[a]

	All		Black		White	
Item of care	BC–BS	GHA	BC–BS	GHA	BC–BS	GHA
Quality of care	83 *	74	78[+] *	71[++]	86 *	80
Appointment waiting time	72 *	35	65[+] *	34	75 *	38
Waiting time in office	46 *	59	40[+] *	57[++]	49 *	63
Time spent with physician	85 *	76	84 *	71[++]	86	86
Availability of care	52 *	62	40[+] *	55[++]	57 *	75
Distance to medical facility	84 *	60	88 *	62	83 *	57
Cost of care, exclusive of premium	53 *	70	46[+] *	62[++]	56 *	85
Information from physician	78 *	69	80 *	63[++]	77 *	82
Courtesy of physician	93 *	86	93 *	85	93 *	88
Physician explanations of home treatment	91 *	86	89	83[++]	91	91
Courtesy of nurses	88	87	88	87	88	88
Follow-up care	86 *	79	84 *	76[++]	88	84
Physician's personal interest	82 *	70	76[+] *	67[++]	85 *	75

[a]At time of first household interview.

*P ≤ .05.

[+]P ≤ .05 for race groups, BC–BS.

[++]P ≤ .05 for race groups, GHA.

Use of Health Care Resources

Table 4.8 Length of plan membership and age: Percentage distribution of all plan members by length of family membership and percent 0 to 4 years of age and 45 years or older by length of family membership

Years of family plan membership	All		Black		White	
	BC–BS	GHA	BC–BS	GHA	BC–BS	GHA
All						
1 to 3	9	23	4	22	11	25
4 to 6	17	25	19	29	16	17
7 to 13	37	38	40	44	36	27
14 or more	36	14	36	5	37	32
	100 *	100	100[+] *	100[++]	100 *	100
Percent 0 to 4 years of age						
1 to 3	13	9	21	9	12	9
4 to 6	19	13	18	13	20	14
7 to 13	12 *	5	9	5	13 *	5
14 or more	4	2	5	7	4	0
Percent 45 years or older						
1 to 3	16 (119)	11 (307)	10[+] (19)	12 (198)	17 (100)	9 (109)
4 to 6	8 (235)	9 (324)	7 (89)	7[++] (252)	9 (146)	17 (72)
7 to 13	16 * (509)	21 (503)	14 (186)	18[++] (386)	18 * (323)	32 (117)
14 or more	41 * (496)	57 (181)	37 (167)	50 (44)	44 * (329)	59 (137)

*P ≤ .05.

[+]P ≤ .05 for race groups, BC–BS.

[++]P ≤ .05 for race groups, GHA.

Table 4.9 Knowledge of plan benefits: Percent of contract holders knowledgeable about coverage

	All		Black		White	
Service category	BC–BS	GHA	BC–BS	GHA	BC–BS	GHA
Inpatient hospital services in plan area	96 *	92	96 *	90[++]	97	97
Emergency care, everywhere in US	75 *	60	60[+] *	50[++]	82	79
Physician visits, ambulatory[a]	31 *	78	22[+] *	73[++]	35 *	90
Diagnostic tests, ambulatory	78 *	68	70[+] *	58[++]	82	88
Prescribed medicines[a]	31 *	40	14[+] *	37	40	46
Ambulatory psychiatric services (long-term)[a]	18 *	29	8[+] *	26	23 *	35
Nursing home care	26	27	27	24	26	32
Routine physical examination	53 *	92	49 *	89[++]	55 *	97
Eye examinations	7 *	83	7 *	81	7 *	87
Eye glasses or lenses	76 *	64	62[+]	57[++]	82	78
Routine dental services	88 *	68	80[+] *	61[++]	92 *	83
Physician visits, everywhere in US[a]	20	24	9[+] *	18[++]	24 *	36
Hospitalization, everywhere in US	73 *	43	63[+] *	36[++]	78 *	58
(n)	(480)	(453)	(155)	(298)	(325)	(155)

[a]Covered by supplemental benefits in BC–BS.

*P $\leqslant$ .05.

[+]P $\leqslant$ .05 for race groups, BC–BS.

[++]P $\leqslant$ .05 for race groups, GHA.

Table 4.10 Knowledge of plan benefits and length of family membership: Percentage distribution of all household members by contract holder's knowledge of plan benefits, and percent with high knowledge scores by years of membership

	All		Black		White	
	BC–BS	GHA	BC–BS	GHA	BC–BS	GHA
Knowledge score		*All*				
Low	23	18	43	23	13	7
Medium	55	40	50	49	58	21
High	21	43	7	28	29	72
	100 *	100	100[+] *	100[++]	100 *	100
Length of family plan membership	*Percent with high knowledge of plan benefits*					
1 to 3 years	34 (119)	30 (308)	–	13[++] (198)	40 * (100)	62 (110)
4 to 6 years	17 * (235)	28 (324)	4[+] * (89)	22[++] (252)	24 * (146)	47 (72)
7 years or more	21 * (1,006)	56 (684)	8[+] * (354)	40[++] (430)	28 * (652)	83 (254)

–Less than 1 percent of the total sample.

*P ⩽ .05.

[+]P ⩽ .05 for race groups, BC–BS.

[++]P ⩽ .05 for race groups, GHA.

Table 4.11 Regular sources of care: Percentage distribution of household
members by source of care and type of physician

Regular source of care[a]	All BC–BS	GHA	Black BC–BS	GHA	White BC–BS	GHA
None	2	1	4	1	2	2
Hospital clinic or emergency room	10	8	21	11	4	2
Personal physician	82	43	68	36	89	56
Other physician	6	48	7	52	5	39
	100 *	100	100[+] *	100[++]	100 *	100

[a]Includes out-of-plan physicians for members of GHA (approximately 5 percent of the GHA sample).

*P ⩽ .05.

[+]P ⩽ .05 for race groups, BC–BS.

[++]P ⩽ .05 for race groups, GHA.

Table 4.12 Appointment patterns: Percentage distribution of annual physician
visits by type of visit

Visit type	All BC–BS	GHA	Black BC–BS	GHA	White BC–BS	GHA
Appointment	82	61	85	63	82	59
Walk-in	18	39	15	37	18	41
Total	100 *	100	100[+] *	100[++]	100 *	100
(n)	(4,726)	(4,427)	(971)	(2,295)	(3,755)	(2,132)

*P ⩽ .05.

[+]P ⩽ .05 for race groups, BC–BS.

[++]P ⩽ .05 for race groups, GHA

Table 4.13 Appointment waiting times: Percentage distribution of patient-initiated physician appointments by days waited

Appointment waiting times	All		Black		White	
	BC–BS	GHA	BC–BS	GHA	BC–BS	GHA
1 day	48	26	45	27	48	26
2 to 7 days	36	26	41	27	35	25
8 to 14 days	3	6	3	6	3	5
More than 14 days	13	42	11	39	14	44
Total	100 *	100	100 *	100	100 *	100
(n)	(2,061)	(1,567)	(383)	(768)	(1,678)	(799)

*P ≤ .05.

Table 4.14 Time to obtain care: Percentage distribution of all patient-initiated physician visits by days from patient decision to seek care

Waiting times	ALL		Black		White	
	BC–BS	GHA	BC–BS	GHA	BC–BS	GHA
1 day or less	63	65	60	66	63	65
2 to 7 days	25	12	30	13	25	12
8 to 14 days	2	3	2	2	2	2
More than 14 days	10	20	8	19	10	21
Total	100 *	100	100 *	100	100 *	100
(n)	(2,901)	(3,291)	(529)	(1,620)	(2,372)	(1,671)

*P ≤ .05.

Table 4.15 Time to obtain care and reason for visit: Percent of patient-initiated physician visits occurring within 24 hours or more than 2 weeks after patient decision to seek care, by main reason for visit

Main reason for visit	All		Black		White	
	BC–BS	GHA	BC–BS	GHA	BC–BS	GHA
Percent occurring within 24 hours						
Diagnosis	75 (519)	75 (559)	76 (109)	79[++] (294)	75 (410)	71 (265)
Treatment	75 * (910)	81 (1,015)	79 * (177)	85[++] (607)	74 (733)	74 (408)
Check-up	49 * (424)	37 (322)	51 (87)	52[++] (153)	49 * (337)	24 (169)
Routine physical examination	14 * (392)	8 (458)	21[+] * (90)	10 (251)	12 * (302)	6 (207)
Lab work	57 (114)	63 (143)	—	57 (60)	57 (100)	68 (83)
Shots/Immunizations	94 * (384)	97 (613)	—	95[++] (148)	94 * (374)	98 (465)
Other	41 (158)	33 (181)	48 (42)	32 (107)	38 (116)	34 (74)
Percent occurring after more than two weeks						
Diagnosis	3 *	10	1	9	4 *	11
Treatment	3 *	8	1[+] *	6[++]	4 *	13
Check-up	12 *	31	10 *	22[++]	12 *	40
Routine physical examination	37 *	71	26[+] *	67[++]	40 *	76
Lab work	6 *	20	—	20	7 *	19
Shots/Immunizations	1	1	—	1	1	1
Other	18 *	32	14	27	19 *	38

—Less than 1 percent of total sample.

*P ≤ .05.

[+]P ≤ .05 for race groups, BC–BS.

[++]P ≤ .05 for race groups, GHA.

Use of Health Care Resources

Table 4.16 Office waiting times: Percentage distribution of all physician visits

Office waiting time	All		Black		White	
	BC–BS	GHA	BC–BS	GHA	BC–BS	GHA
15 minutes or less	57	52	40	48	61	59
16 to 30 minutes	24	28	31	30	22	26
31 to 60 minutes	12	12	16	13	11	10
More than 60 minutes	7	7	14	9	5	5
Total	100 * 100		100+ * 100++		100 * 100	
(n)	(4,633)	(4,324)	(943)	(2,243)	(3,690	(2,081

*P ≤ .05. +P ≤ .05 for race groups, BC–BS. ++P ≤ .05 for race groups, GHA.

Table 4.17 Overall state of health: Percentage distribution of plan members[a]
by categories of perceived health status and age-sex specific percent
of persons in less than very good health

	All		Black		White	
	BC–BS	GHA	BC–BS	GHA	BC–BS	GHA
Perceived health status						
Very good	72	66	71	64	72	70
Pretty good	23	27	24	29	23	24
Fair	4	6	4	6	4	5
Poor	1	1	0	1	1	1
	100	100	100	100	100	100
(n)	(1,364)	(1,312)	(462)	(879)	(902)	(433)
Percent in less than very good health						
Male						
0 to 4 years	23	24	29	24	19	—
5 to 19 years	19	25	24	31++	17	12
20 to 44 years	27	30	25	30	28	29
45 years or older	45	54	44	56	45	51
Female						
0 to 4 years	18	25	—	31	18	—
5 to 19 years	18	23	19	27++	17	12
20 to 44 years	29 * 39		32	42	27	32
45 years or older	45	49	44	48	46	50

[a]Contract holders and their covered dependents.

—Less than 1 percent of the total sample. *P ≤ .05. ++P ≤ .05 for race groups, GHA.

Table 4.18 Chronic health problems: Percentage distribution of plan members by number of problems and age-sex specific percent of persons with at least one chronic health problem

	All		Black		White	
	BC–BS	GHA	BC–BS	GHA	BC–BS	GHA
Chronic health problems						
None	65	61	71	64	62	55
One	23	25	22	24	24	26
Two or more	11	14	7	12	14	19
	100	100	100[+]	* 100[++]	100	* 100

Percent with at least one chronic health problem

	All		Black		White	
	BC–BS	GHA	BC–BS	GHA	BC–BS	GHA
Male						
0 to 4 years	10	15	14	10	8	—
5 to 19 years	21	26	19	26	22	27
20 to 44 years	42	40	28[+]	38	48	46
45 years or older	52	* 67	50	68	52	65
Female						
0 to 4 years	17	4	—	3	22	—
5 to 19 years	16	22	10	* 21	21	24
20 to 44 years	40	49	36	47	42	54
45 years or older	57	67	60	67	56	66

—Less than 1 percent of the total sample.

*P ≤ .05.

[+]P ≤ .05 for race groups, BC–BS.

[++]P ≤ .05 for race groups, GHA.

Table 4.19 Treated chronic health problems: Percent of plan members with chronic health problems under physician care for at least one problem

	All		Black		White	
	BC–BS	GHA	BC–BS	GHA	BC–BS	GHA
All	58	61	65	56[++]	55 *	69
	(476)	(521)	(133)	(322)	(343)	(199)
Male	55	55	64	53	52	59
	(226)	(251)	(61)	(155)	(165)	(96)
Female	61	67	67	60[++]	59 *	79
	(250)	(270)	(72)	(167)	(178)	(103)

*P ≤ .05. [++]P ≤ .05 for race groups, GHA.

Table 4.20 Social dysfunction: Percentage distribution of plan members by number of bed days and age-sex specific percent with any bed days

	All		Black		White	
	BC–BS	GHA	BC–BS	GHA	BC–BS	GHA
Bed days						
None	59	64	70	67	53	59
1 to 7 days	32	26	22	23	37	31
8 days or more	9	10	8	10	10	10
	100	* 100	100[+]	100[++]	100	100

Percent with any bed days

	All		Black		White	
	BC–BS	GHA	BC–BS	GHA	BC–BS	GHA
Male						
0 to 4 years	38	27	29	32	44	—
5 to 19 years	42	* 28	21[+]	22[++]	55	43
20 to 44 years	37	31	32	31	40	30
45 years or older	28	34	17	* 37	32	32
Female						
0 to 4 years	47	27	—	23	50	—
5 to 19 years	43	34	33[+]	30[++]	50	46
20 to 44 years	45	44	33[+]	44	52	46
45 years or older	46	49	38	44	49	53

—Less than 1 percent of the total sample.

*P ≤ .05.

[+]P ≤ .05 for race groups, BC–BS.

[++]P ≤ .05 for race groups, GHA.

Table 4.21 Social dysfunction: Percentage distribution of plan members by number of restricted activity days and age-sex specific percent with any restricted activity days

	All		Black		White	
	BC–BS	GHA	BC–BS	GHA	BC–BS	GHA
Restricted activity days						
None	58	65	71	71	52	53
1 to 7	26	22	20	19	30	27
8 or more	15	13	10	10	18	20
	100 *	100	100[+]	100[++]	100	100

Percent with any restricted activity days

	BC–BS	GHA	BC–BS	GHA	BC–BS	GHA
Male						
0 to 4 years	45	29	25[+]	24	56	—
5 to 19 years	47 *	28	29[+]	22[++]	58	43
20 to 44 years	35	34	24[+]	33	40	36
45 years or older	28 *	41	12[+] *	36	35	48
Female						
0 to 4 years	56 *	25	—	23	64	—
5 to 19 years	44 *	28	34[+]	22[++]	51	41
20 to 44 years	42	40	34	34[++]	46	58
45 years or older	46	47	40	36[++]	49	57

—Less than 1 percent of the total sample.

*P ≤ .05.

[+]P ≤ .05 for race groups, BC–BS.

[++]P ≤ .05 for race groups, GHA.

Table 4.22 Pain and worry: Percentage distribution of plan members by number of pain and worry days and age-sex specific percent with any pain and worry days

	All		Black		White	
	BC–BS	GHA	BC–BS	GHA	BC–BS	GHA
Pain and worry days						
None	71	71	82	76	65	62
1 to 7	16	14	12	13	18	16
8 or more	14	14	6	11	18	22
	100	100	100[+] * 100[++]		100	100

Percent with any pain and worry days

	All		Black		White	
	BC–BS	GHA	BC–BS	GHA	BC–BS	GHA
Male						
0 to 4 years	29	24	11[+]	21	40	–
5 to 19 years	25	28	14[+]	13[++]	32	31
20 to 44 years	29	26	15[+]	26	35	27
45 years or older	24	32	15	22[++]	28 * 44	
Female						
0 to 4 years	26	19	–	17	30	–
5 to 19 years	20	17	13	11[++]	25	30
20 to 44 years	38	40	25[+] * 40		45	38
45 years or older	39 * 52		33	43	41 * 60	

—Less than 1 percent of the total sample.

*P ≤ .05.

[+]P ≤ .05 for race groups, BC–BS.

[++]P ≤ .05 for race groups, GHA.

Table 4.23 Volume of illness days: Age-sex specific mean number of bed days, restricted activity days, and pain and worry days

	All		Black		White	
	BC–BS	GHA	BC–BS	GHA	BC–BS	GHA
Mean number of bed days						
Total	2.4	3.3	1.8$^+$ *	3.6	2.8	2.6
Male						
0 to 19 years	2.2 *	1.4	1.1$^+$	1.3	2.8 *	1.5
20 to 44 years	1.9	2.8	1.6	3.1	2.0	2.1
45 years or older	1.3 *	7.0	0.9	10.4	1.4	3.1
Female						
0 to 19 years	1.8	2.0	1.5	1.8	2.0	2.5
20 to 44 years	3.1	4.6	3.2	5.1	3.1	3.3
45 years or older	4.7	4.4	2.5	5.3	5.5	3.6
Mean number of restricted activity days						
Total	4.5	4.6	3.0$^+$	3.5^{++}	5.3	6.7
Male						
0 to 19 years	4.4 *	2.0	3.6	1.2^{++}	4.9	3.9
20 to 44 years	3.3	5.8	1.6$^+$ *	5.2	4.0	7.1
45 years or older	2.5 *	6.3	0.8$^+$ *	4.7	3.2 *	8.2
Female						
0 to 19 years	3.8 *	2.0	2.6$^+$	1.4^{++}	4.5	3.6
20 to 44 years	4.7	4.5	2.9$^+$	4.0	5.7	6.0
45 years or older	9.3	12.4	7.5	12.1	10.0	12.6
Mean number of pain and worry days						
Total	5.6	6.2	2.4$^+$ *	4.4^{++}	7.2	9.9
Male						
0 to 19 years	2.9	2.1	0.9$^+$	1.7	4.0	3.0
20 to 44 years	5.2	5.5	3.1	4.7	6.1	7.4
45 years or older	6.7	10.2	3.5	8.2	8.2	12.4
Female						
0 to 19 years	2.3	2.6	1.2$^+$	1.0^{++}	3.0	6.4
20 to 44 years	7.4	7.2	3.0$^+$ *	6.3	9.8	9.8
45 years or older	11.1	18.4	4.3$^+$ *	14.3	13.8	21.7

*P ≤ .05. $^+$P ≤ .05 for race groups, BC–BS. $^{++}$P ≤ .05 for race groups, GHA.

5

Use of Ambulatory Services

Sarina B. Hirshfeld and Samuel M. Meyers

In contrast to consistent findings of lower hospital use in prepaid group practice than under service benefit plans, comparisons of ambulatory care have been ambiguous. In a review of 12 large comparative studies, Diehr et al. (1976) reported that in at least half, rates of physician visits in prepaid group practice plans were similar or somewhat below those in fee-for-service plans; in the remaining studies, they were substantially lower in fee-for-service practice.

In the present study, patterns of ambulatory care were compared in order to address several questions raised by these other studies. Was there variation between the two types of plans in the extent to which plan members contacted physicians and other health professionals? Did rates of use of various types of health services differ between the two plans? Were differences in rates of use associated with differences between the plan populations in the distribution of predisposing and enabling and perceived illness factors? Is there, finally, any evidence of the effect of plan structure on the use of ambulatory care, including its substitution for inpatient care in the prepaid group practice plan?

To answer these questions, different points of emphasis were used in analyzing the data obtained in the 1972–1973 household survey. First, levels of use of ambulatory medical services by persons in both plans were compared, followed by an examination of the use of individual service components. Second, use was related to the set of predisposing, enabling, and illness variables outlined in Chapter 3. Third, the relative effect on use of these variables was analyzed by means of a multivariate technique, with particular attention to the effect of plan net of all other variables. Finally, the analytical perspective shifted from the user of services to the episode of illness, that is, the events connected with a defined health problem.

PATTERNS OF USE

Variables and Data Sources

In this comparison of the use of ambulatory services by members of a prepaid group practice and service benefit plan and their families, the unit of analysis was the individual covered by the plan. Use of health services, the dependent variable, was measured by contacts over a period of 12 months with the following providers or service components as established during the monthly household survey (see Chapter 3 for survey procedures):

Visits to a physician's office, clinic or laboratory (including those for preventive, diagnostic, or treatment reasons)

Purchase of prescribed medicines

Dentist visits

Telephone calls to a physician's office for advice (excluding appointments)

Home visits by a physician

Eye examinations (including those for vision problems)

Fitting of glasses or lenses

Emergency room visits

Purchase or rental of medical equipment

Visits to a mental health practitioner

Visits to other health practitioners

Ambulance trips

Three measures were employed to describe the frequency of use among the study population:

— *Likelihood of use*: the percentage of members in each plan making at least one contact with the respective service or provider over the course of the survey year

— *Total volume of use*: the mean number of such contacts per person in each plan

— *Volume of use per person using services*: the mean number of contacts by those with at least one instance of use of the respective service or provider

Measures of both likelihood and volume of contacts represent aggregated monthly totals over the survey year. Exceptions are purchases of prescribed medicines and of medical equipment, where counts were obtained of the total number of months in which such purchases (and, in the case of equipment, rentals) were made.

These measures reflect all use of ambulatory health services reported by survey respondents, including, in the case of GHA enrollees, services not obtained under the auspices of their plan. Physician visits were defined as office visits and visits to a clinic or laboratory, including hospital outpatient clinics, work clinics, and independent medical laboratories. Physician home visits were inquired into as well; 14 were reported by the entire sample population.

To permit classification into preventive, diagnostic, and treatment services, the main reason for each physician visit was elicited from the respondent in terms of the following:

1. To find out what was wrong
2. To have minor surgery
3. To obtain medical treatment
4. To have a checkup suggested by a physician (such as after a hospital stay, minor surgery, or taking prescribed medicines)
5. To have a checkup for a longstanding health problem or illness
6. To have x-rays, laboratory work, or other diagnostic tests that were ordered by a physician
7. To have a routine physical examination that the respondent thought necessary
8. To have a complete physical examination suggested by a physician
9. To talk about a personal or family problem
10. For a prenatal visit
11. For a well-baby checkup
12. To get shots or immunizations

Visits related to items 7 and 10–12 were considered as having been made for preventive reasons, and those related to items 1, 6, and 8 for diagnostic reasons; the remainder are classified as treatment visits.

Visits to a mental health practitioner included those described by the respondent as contacts with a psychiatrist, a psychologist, or any other mental health worker. Visits to other health practitioners included those made to a variety of practitioners, such as chiropractors, midwives, nurses, and podiatrists.

Use was further measured by three types of dependent variables. The first, ambulatory medical contacts, was intended to reflect an aggregate of ambulatory medical services used by the sample population over the course of the survey year. It comprises the following major categories:

— Visits to a physician's office, clinic, or laboratory for preventive, diagnostic, and treatment reasons

— Telephone calls to a physician's office (for medical advice only)

— Emergency room visits

— Eye examinations

— Visits to mental health practitioners

— Visits to other health practitioners

— Home visits by a physician

A second variable aggregating several types of contacts comprises entry visits; these were defined as initial or first visits for a specific health problem to a hospital clinic or emergency room, a physician's office, a laboratory, or other health practitioners. This measure permits an estimation of the relative frequency of first contacts with these services for specific health problems, as distinct from preventive or follow-up care. Preventive use of services was examined in terms of patient-initiated physical examinations in the absence of illness, of shots and immunizations, of prenatal services and infant care, and of eye examinations for common vision problems.

In view of the racial distribution of the BC-BS and GHA populations (the black-to-white ratio was 1:2 in BC-BS and 2:1 in GHA; see Table 4.1), data on overall rates of use are presented as race-specific rates in addition to total rates both unadjusted and adjusted for race, as prior studies have indicated persistent differences in ambulatory use between white and black populations (Newman, 1975; Kravits and Schneider, 1975; Andersen and Newman, 1973; Aday and Eichhorn, 1972; National Center for Health Statistics, 1969a).

Levels of Use

Selected Health Care Services. In both plans, use of the various service types varied as to the percentage of users and volume of use. As reflected in the race-adjusted rates, 67 percent of all respondents in BC-BS and 76 percent in GHA visited a physician's office or clinic; at least half bought prescribed medicines; and two-fifths saw a dentist. Roughly a quarter called a physician for advice at least once, and at least 15 percent had eye examinations; less than 10 percent bought or rented medical equipment, saw a mental health practitioner or other health personnel, or used an ambulance (Table 5.1). Both likelihood and volume of use were higher under the prepaid group practice plan for most types of services, in most cases by statistically significant margins. This was also observed for the differences between blacks and, respectively, whites in both plans (Tables 5.1-5.2). Greater use under BC-BS was found for emergency room visits, where both the percentage of users and the volume of use was at least twice that in GHA. Race-adjusted rates for those with at least one instance of use, however, showed less in the way of plan differences and no instances of statistical significance (Table 5.3).

The consistent margin of greater overall use by GHA members did not necessarily follow differences in insurance coverage. This is particularly noticeable with regard to use of mental health services, for which coverage by GHA was less complete than under BC-BS, but where there was more wide-spread use in terms of both likelihood and overall volume under the prepaid group practice plan. On the other hand, there was little difference between the plans in dentist use, for which there was no coverage under either plan, and in the likelihood of having purchased prescribed medicines during the survey year, where there was a difference in the deductible between BC-BS and GHA (see Chapter 1). The major differences between plans, therefore, were found to lie in the use of physician and related services and of eye care services. It should be pointed out that the latter comprise mainly common vision services; only 5 percent of all contacts in this category were for medical problems such as eye injuries.

Whites under both plans made considerably more use of most types of services than did blacks. Substantial and statistically significant differences in likelihood of use (Table 5.1) were observed for almost all types of use, particularly for preventive physician contacts, dentist visits, contacts with mental health and other practitioners, and telephone calls to the physician's office. These differences were even more pronounced in mean number of contacts by the entire study population, where they were well over twofold for some services (Table 5.2). They were less marked for volume of use among those who used services at least once (Table 5.3), but remained at statistically significant levels for total physician visits and visits for preventive reasons, calls for advice in GHA, purchases of prescribed medicines, and, in particular, mental health visits, where the difference by race in BC-BS was thirteenfold and sixfold in GHA. There was no statistically significant difference by race for those using any dental services, on the other hand.

As noted in Chapter 4, the different racial composition of the two plans tends to obscure differences in rates unadjusted for race. This is particularly well illustrated by the volume of physician visits (Table 5.2); here, the ratio of unadjusted total means was virtually identical (GHA/BC-BS = 1.01), while the race-adjusted ratio was 1.24, which more accurately reflects differences between plan in rates of use. The corresponding ratios for the two racial subgroups (blacks 1.33; whites 1.20) indicate a larger difference in use between the two black groups. Subsequent discussions of patterns of plan differences will refer in the main to rates adjusted for race.

In summary, despite wide differences in use by racial groupings, and with the exceptions noted (use of emergency rooms and dentists and the purchase of prescribed medicines), the difference between plans in overall use of services was in the direction of moderately greater use of ambulatory services under the prepaid group practice plan both in terms of race-adjusted and race-specific rates.

Components of Use. Plan differences were maintained when several components of ambulatory use were examined in greater detail. The first, a summary measure of ambulatory medical contacts, aggregates major types of physician use as well as eye care, mental health, and nonphysician services (Table 5.4). The plans clearly differed in likelihood, volume, and intensity of use per person with contact, both in terms of race-adjusted and race-specific rates, although the margin in favor of GHA decreased for the percent of persons using services and increased for both measures of volume; 81 percent of all GHA members and 75 percent in BC-BS had at least one such ambulatory contact in the survey year, while the mean number of contacts was 6.29 and 4.90, respectively.

Despite the lower frequency of health problem–related entry visits, a measure which excludes all follow-up and preventive use (Table 5.5), the difference between the two plans persisted and was particularly noticeable in the two black subgroups. For preventive use of services, as expected, there were more physical examinations in the absence of illness and vision examinations under the prepaid group practice plan (Table 5.6), although there was little difference in both likelihood and volume of prenatal contacts and well-baby visits, despite inequalities in coverage.

Correlates of Use

Given these findings of moderately higher rates of use of ambulatory services under the prepaid group practice plan, the following examines whether they persist when the known characteristics of the two study populations are taken into account (see Chapter 4). The questions here are the extent to which differences between the plans reveal the influence of factors known to be associated with use, and whether it is possible to discern the effect of the system of care on specific patterns of use.

Predisposing Factors

Sociodemographic Factors. As expected, use of ambulatory medical services in both plans was most frequent in the youngest and oldest age groupings (in this study, 0 to 4 years and 45 years and older; Table 5.7); females in both plans made more use of services than males. Gradients in use within each plan differed by age, however, and tended to be larger in BC-BS. On the other hand, the relationship of use to educational level, although evident in both plans, was closer in GHA than in BC-BS. It was particularly strong for volume of use, with a more than twofold range between members of families at the low end of the educational scale and those in which at least one adult reported five or more years of college (from 2.5 to 6.8 contacts). In BC-BS, this range was narrower, and there was no progression in the number of contacts from low to high educational levels. Although at the high end of the educational scale volume of use was higher under GHA than under BC-BS, at the low end of the scale it was substantially below that in BC-BS (2.5 as compared to 5.2 contacts). Overall, therefore, there was less evidence of consistently higher use under GHA when groups at similar levels of education were compared. Similarly, for rates of use by occupational level, the only statistically significant difference between plans was a greater volume of use by those in GHA professional and managerial families. In both plans, those in blue collar families were somewhat less likely to have contacted medical or related services than were those in clerical and sales and in professional and managerial occupations, and they also reported a lower volume of use.

An increase in likelihood of contacts with rising income was seen in both plans as well (from 72 to 82 percent in BC-BS and from 78 to 86 percent in GHA; see Table 5.7). The range in volume of contacts between the low and high income groups was relatively wide in GHA (from 4.5 to 6.8 contacts), while there was no progression in the number of contacts between low and high income groups in the service benefit plan. Thus, differences in volume of use by income level were more evident in GHA, despite the absence of financial barriers to use in that plan.

Finally, while the effect of family size on ambulatory medical contacts by children under 16 was in the direction of lower use by children in large households in both plans, it was particularly noticeable in GHA where the difference between children in small (two or three persons) and large families (six or more persons) was threefold in volume of use, and as much as 20 percent for likelihood of use as well. In this as in the previous comparisons of the influence of sociodemographic factors, therefore, the finding of higher levels of use under GHA was in some instances attenuated and in others reversed, particularly at the lower end of the scale. Nonetheless, most statistically significant plan differences remain in the direction of greater use under GHA.

Attitudinal Factors. As shown in Chapter 4, the distribution of attitude scores indicated consistent differences between the plans with regard to the tendency to use physician services, both in the case of illness and for physical examinations, and with regard to satisfaction with care. This raised the question whether, if users within each plan were grouped by these attitudes, actual measures of use would reflect this pattern. With regard to the tendency to use services, a direct association was evident in both plans (Table 5.8). There was a clear rise in likelihood of entry visits for a specific health problem from low to medium and high tendency scores, particularly in the service benefit plan where the range was 14 percentage points. Volume of use, on the other hand, was less clearly associated with these scores. Reported differences in attitudes to preventive care were likewise reflected in the likelihood of ambulatory medical contacts for those who approved of routine physical examinations and/or who had had such an examination recently, on one hand, and those who did not care for or never used this service, on the other hand. In both plans, an association between previous physical examinations and current use is likely, of course, as suggested by the relatively large differences in both plans in volume of contacts (see Table 5.8). Thus, overall plan differences were small and favored GHA only among those with high tendency scores and among those favoring and/or reporting physical examinations within two years of the survey. Finally, levels of satisfaction with care, which tended to be lower in the prepaid group practice plan, were not reflected in rates of use in either plan.

Enabling Factors

Factors Related to Plan Membership. In the present study, the type of plan took the place of health insurance coverage as an enabling factor. It was assumed that plan membership, in conjunction with knowledge of plan benefits, would be positively related to use of services. As discussed in Chapter 4, the distribution of the sample in this respect differed considerably, and Table 5.9 indeed indicates different relationships to use in the two plans. In BC-BS an inverse relation is observed, in that there was consistently greater use among those who joined the plan within three years of the 1972 household survey than among others. In GHA, the highest likelihood of use was among those whose families had been in the plan 14 years or longer. This difference in high use patterns may reflect the difference in characteristics of long-term and recent member families in the two plans. In GHA, 57 percent of those 45 years and older were members of long standing, as compared to 41 percent in BC-BS; the pattern was reversed for children from 0 to 4 years. Also, in GHA there was a strong association between high levels of knowledge of plan benefits and length of plan membership (see Table 4.10); in BC-BS, those with high knowledge scores were mainly found among recent member families. However, the distribution of levels of use related to knowledge of plan coverage was roughly similar in the plans, with a positive gradient between those with low and high knowledge scores of roughly 20 percentage points in BC-BS, and of 24 percent in GHA between those with low and medium scores.

Regular Source of Care. The association in this study between use and the reported availability and type of a regular source of care (see Table 5.9)

supports previous findings of the importance of the patient-physician relationship even in a prepaid group practice plan (Scitovsky, Benham, and
McCall, 1979). In fact, differences in the likelihood of ambulatory contacts
by those reporting a personal physician as compared to other physicians
were larger in GHA than in BC-BS (89 percent versus 74 percent as compared to a 7 percent difference in BC-BS), as was the difference in number
of contacts. On the other hand, inasmuch as a personal physician was the
regular source of care in BC-BS for four-fifths of members as compared to
less than half in GHA (see Table 4.11), it is hard to escape the conclusion
that despite the strong association between the presence of a personal physician and levels of use, the availability of a regular, free source of care
contributed to the overall margin in favor of GHA.

Selected Indicators of Illness

Whether this margin was due entirely to the absence of financial barriers in
GHA and unaffected by levels of illness is examined in the following. In the
initial interview, the family respondent was asked a series of questions as to
the general state of health of each family member. Most were reported as
being in very good health; very few (at most one in 14) were described as
being in fair or poor health. More specific questions into the presence of
chronic health problems indicated a slightly higher burden of chronic illness
in GHA (see Table 4.18), and a small excess in the likelihood of days of bed
rest and restricted activity in BC-BS (Tables 4.20 and 4.21).

However, the perception of general health at the beginning of the
survey year did not affect the difference in ambulatory medical contacts
between the two plans (Table 5.10). Both likelihood and volume of use were
higher under the prepaid group practice plan by statistically significant
margins, regardless of reported health status. Plan differences in likelihood
of use also persisted among those with one chronic health problem (78
percent in BC-BS, 88 percent in GHA), although it was similar and high for
those with treated chronic problems. This was found also for those with bed
and restricted activity days and days of pain and worry. The overall margin
in likelihood of use in favor of GHA cannot therefore be attributed to
different responses to illness. Also, volume of use was larger under the
prepaid group practice plan for both the well and the ill.

Differences by Racial Groups

This leaves the finding of differences in use between the racial groups in
both plans. They were large and consistent for most types of services and

for both the likelihood of having received care and the volume of services used (see Tables 5.1–5.6), confirming discrepancies in use of services reported in the literature (Aday and Eichhorn, 1972). While plan differences generally were in the direction of greater use under GHA regardless of race, differences in use by race were larger than by plan (Table 5.11). On the other hand, despite the differences in income, family size, and work status observed in Chapter 4, there were more similarities than differences between the two racial groups in this study in terms of barriers to care. Both black and white groups were covered by high option federal employee benefits and generally belonged to income groups above the poverty level. Also, differences in appointments, appointment waits, and time to obtain care do not appear to have limited either access to or availability of services for the black group in either plan (see Tables 4.12–4.15).

However, when race groups were adjusted for income, education, and family size, differences in likelihood and volume of ambulatory medical contacts were generally maintained. Differences also remained in the likelihood of entry visits (first visits for a specific health problem) when these were associated with the reported tendency to use physician services, the low tendency group in GHA being the exception. The reported availability of a personal physician did little to narrow the gap in use, particularly in BC-BS. Although in most of these comparisons, the margin of difference in favor of GHA was wider among blacks than among whites, this did not obliterate differences in use by race in the prepaid group practice plan. White members consistently reported higher levels of use, and mean numbers of visits by both black groups were a fraction of those reported by whites, with generally twofold differences regardless of plan.

In contrast to other studies (Kravits, 1975), the black groups in these plans did not report negative attitudes to medical care, and while overall rates of reported illness tended to be higher among the white groups, differences in volume of use were maintained even when levels of chronic problems and bed days were held constant (see Table 5.11). The differential in rates for illness-related entry visits (see Table 5.5) was likewise substantial. Of course, questions of different types of illness and levels of severity could not be answered in this phase of the study, since the only health problem information was from self-reported interview data. Also, while age–race differences in GHA indicated the possibility of a relatively large burden of chronic problems among the whites in that plan, the difference in age groups (see Table 4.1) was not sufficiently large to be a substantial explanatory factor in this respect. Thus, none of the findings in this study come even close to suggesting why rates of use should differ between racial groups when enabling and predisposing factors have been taken into account.

Summary

The examination of use of ambulatory services under a prepaid group practice and service benefit plan nonetheless permits several conclusions. There was consistent, if moderate, variation in the extent to which members of the two plans contacted physicians and other health professionals, as well as differences in the rates of use of various types of health services, with use generally higher under GHA. These differences were not clearly associated with the distribution of predisposing and enabling factors in the two plan populations, although they became substantially less pronounced when rates of use were adjusted for the influence of these factors. For a few subgroups, this adjustment resulted in both higher likelihood and volume of use in BC-BS, in particular for recent plan members and at the lower end of several socioeconomic indicators.

As to levels of illness, members of GHA reported more chronic health problems than were found in BC-BS; members of the service benefit plan were more likely to report bed and restricted activity days. However, while the margin of difference in likelihood of use by GHA members was reduced for groups at comparable levels of illness, the race-adjusted rates for volume of contacts persistently showed substantially more use in GHA than in BC-BS. In this connection, it should be noted that this larger volume of contacts in the prepaid group practice plan was apparently not entirely a result of provider decisions, since only about a quarter of visits to a physician's office in that plan were reported to have been suggested by the physician; the corresponding percentage in BC-BS was roughly two-fifths, a finding that would seem in line with more recent findings on fee-for-service practice (Rossiter, 1980).

Generally, there was only limited evidence of the influence of plan structure on the use of services, and the overall differential in rates of use was not large enough to suggest that ambulatory care in the prepaid group practice plan was a substantial substitute for inpatient care. The findings thus do not, by themselves, improve our understanding of the reasons for differences in hospital use shown in Chapter 2. What remains likewise unexplained is the large difference in ambulatory use between white and black members of both plans. It was shown that these were not due to differences in economic or attitudinal factors, as patterns of differential use were not eliminated when groups with similar characteristics were compared. The data suggested, however, a somewhat smaller margin of difference between blacks and whites in the prepaid group practice plan; the absence of copayment and deductibles apparently tends to encourage use among groups historically reported to have relatively low rates of ambulatory care use.

VARIANCE EXPLAINED IN USE
OF AMBULATORY SERVICES

Analytical Techniques
and Variables

The assumption that predisposing, enabling, and health status factors might have had a differential impact in the two plans, producing the observed variations in ambulatory use, was also tested by means of a relatively new multivariate technique (AUTOGRP). For purposes of this analysis, the two plan populations were combined and plan was used as one of a set of independent variables. It was expected that this approach would yield a more precise measure of the extent to which the volume of ambulatory use was a function primarily of plan membership or of other characteristics of the study populations.

An automated grouping (AUTOGRP; Mills et al., 1976; Theriault, Mills, and Elia, 1976) program was selected as the analytical tool, as it provided a flexible, interactive least squares technique that focuses on explanation rather than on statistical significance. The procedure suggests partitions of a data set into subgroups based on the values of an independent variable so as to reduce unexplained variance in the dependent variable (here, various types of ambulatory use). The mean number of instances of use, the standard deviation, and the number of cases are then calculated for each subgroup. This partitioning process is not automatic, however, and users can decide whether to accept or refuse each partition in favor of more meaningful ones; even when groups partitioned automatically are statistically well behaved, they may make little sense practically or theoretically. Also, AUTOGRP requires no restrictive assumptions, e.g., linearity, additivity, freedom from interaction, and absence of multicollinearity.

Results are summarized in the following to show both the extent to which each independent variable contributed to the reduction in the total variance of the dependent variable and the size of its contribution relative to the other variables examined.

The first step in the analysis required each independent variable to be tested to determine if the parent group, i.e., the entire sample, could be partitioned on that particular variable. Where partitions were suggested by the program, the variable indicating the highest reduction in variance was usually selected and the corresponding partitions accepted. The first step was repeated for each partition, again selecting the variable offering the largest variance reduction and accepting the partitions, until no further partitions were possible in accordance with analytical constraints. For reasons of economy, the reduction factor was set at 1 percent, i.e., partition of a group was suggested by the program only if the variance in the dependent variable in the parent group could be reduced by 1 percent or more. To achieve stable mean values, the minimum size of any partitioned group was set at 25 respondents (or approximately 1 percent of the total sample), and the number of partitions of any group was limited to three to minimize group proliferation. Finally, no attempt was made to partition any group, regardless of size, if the remaining sum of squares in that group was equal to or less than 1 percent of the total sum of squares. These constraints tended to reduce the explanatory power of the final set of variables by 1 or 2 percent, but their relative importance was not significantly affected. In addition to plan, the independent variables chosen (Table 5.12) were those proposed in Chapter 3 in accordance with the model of use by Andersen and Newman (1973). Separate analysis of each plan was not contemplated because one of the major objectives of this analysis was to assess the relative effect of plan as an independent variable in comparison with other variables. However, plan and race were combined into one variable with four categories (GHA black, GHA white, BC-BS black, BC-BS white) to account for the persistent differences in use between race groups within each plan. The effect of plan was not lost by this categorization because, if any of these categories had in fact appeared as a significant factor at an early stage of the analysis, the population would have been partitioned on this variable, resulting in separate analysis by each plan-race group or by a combination of these. The respective volumes of ambulatory medical contacts, entry visits, and diagnostic and treatment visits were used as dependent variables.

Findings

Ambulatory medical use among the members of the two plans was related more closely to perceived illness factors than to plan membership or race. Table 5.13 summarizes the contribution of each independent variable to the reduction in variance in ambulatory medical contacts. Of 19 independent variables originally entered in this analysis, 5 were eliminated by the variable selection process, indicating that marital status, occupation of the contract holder, time since the last physical examination, household educational level, and a reported personal physician each explained less than 1 percent of total variance in this type of contact. The overall variance explained by the remaining independent variables was 21 percent, comparable to that reported in other studies employing multivariate techniques (Kobashigawa and Berki, 1977; Wolinsky, 1976; Andersen, 1975, 1968; Hershey, Luft, and Gianaris, 1975; Newman, 1975; Wan and Soifer, 1974; Andersen and Newman, 1973). The number of disability days (bed and restricted activity days) contributed 9.2 percent to this, or almost half of the total variance explained, and the number of treated chronic problems accounted for 3.1 percent or 14.8 of total variance explained. Age and the plan-race variable each explained less than 2 percent of the total variance and represented less than 10 percent of the total variance explained. Significantly, all partitions were by race groups across plans, i.e. by the black and white subgroups, regardless of plan. The remaining ten variables each explained 1 percent or less of the total variance, though together they accounted for about a quarter of explained variance.

For treatment and diagnostic visits as the dependent variable, a slightly different sequence of the independent variables explained 38.4 percent of the variance in use (Table 5.14). While the number of disability days was the most powerful explanatory variable here as well (22.3 percent of the variance or about 58 percent of total variance explained), the number of pain and worry days ranked next (8.1 percent of variance and 21.1 percent of total variance explained), followed by the number of treated chronic problems (2.9 percent of variance and 7.6 percent of variance explained). Of the remaining independent variables, age was the only factor contributing more than 1 percent to the variance in use. Four variables did not partition any of the groups: family size, family income, number of hospitalizations in the year prior to the survey, and years of plan membership. Also, in 36 attempts at partition, grouping by plan and race contributed very little to the variance in treatment and diagnostic visits (0.2 percent).

For entry visits (Table 5.15), as few as 11 of the 19 independent variables were of any explanatory power. The variance explained overall was 33.1 percent, the number of disability days again accounting for over half of this total (18.1 percent). Here, age ranked as the second important predictor of this type of use, explaining 7.4 percent or 22.4 percent of total variance explained. Of the other variables, only the number of pain and worry days contributed more than 1 percent to variance (4.9 percent), so that for this type of use as well, three variables accounted for nine-tenths of explained variance. However, while plan by race again contributed only 0.5 percent of variance or 1.5 percent of the total variance explained, it was here used by the partitioning algorithm to form two groups from a parent group of 1,056 persons. A group of 153 GHA whites who were four or more years of age and who reported less than two disability and pain and worry days showed twice the mean number of contacts as a similar group composed of 912 GHA blacks and BC-BS blacks and whites (means, 1.0 and 0.5 contacts). This was the only instance where plan and not race exercised a differential effect. In the other two instances of partitioning involving this variable in the analysis of entry visits, however, the partitioning was again strictly by racial grouping, with twice the mean number of entry visits for the white group.

Summary

In this multivariate analysis of three different types of use, between 22 and 38 percent of the variance in the volume of contacts was explained by the set of independent variables. Two health status variables accounted for well over half the total variance explained in ambulatory medical contacts; nine-tenths of the total variance explained in diagnostic and treatment visits and in entry visits was attributable to a combination of indicators of need for care and age, with only marginal influence on this type of use by plan and race. Among the predisposing variables, only age was found to be of explanatory power for all types of use examined, and individual enabling variables did little to explain variance in use. The fact of plan membership, which was of particular interest in this analysis, was not found to contribute noticeably to an explanation of differences in ambulatory use. An analysis of the same set of variables by multiple regression showed substantially similar results (Meyers et al., 1977).

EPISODES OF ILLNESS

In the following, use is examined in a different context, that is, of discrete episodes of illness experienced by members of the two plans. More comprehensive than an episode of medical care, which is usually defined as a "block of one or more medical services received by an individual during a period of relatively continuous contact with one or more providers of service in relation to a particular medical problem" (Solon et al., 1967), the episode of illness used here as the unit of analysis also includes behavioral events associated with a reported health problem, such as disability days. An episode of illness is thus defined to reflect a range of illness behavior rather than isolated events of illness and use; it permits an analysis of such behavior within a specified framework, from the initial perception of illness to the end of the episode (see also Richardson, 1971).

Recent studies have focused on episodes of care defined from medical and provider records, occasionally supplemented by survey information (Kessler, 1978; Lohr and Brook, 1978; Kane et al., 1978, 1976; Lasdon and Sigman, 1977; Moscovice, 1977; Roos, Henteleff, and Roos, 1977; Roos, Roos, and Henteleff, 1977). The present analysis uses episodes of illness constructed entirely from responses given in the household interview to answer the following questions:

—To what extent is care seeking behavior different in episodes of illness experienced by members of the two plans?

— Does it differ between or within racial groups?

— Is there more use of services within episodes of illness by members of one plan than by members of the other?

— Finally, are there important differences between the plans in the overall incidence of episodes and in the number of episodes experienced by individual plan members?

Data Sources and Variables

Episodes of illness were constructed from household survey information on population characteristics, levels of illness, and use of services. They were based on the reported presence of a health problem associated with one or all of the following events: social dysfunction measured by disability days (days of bed rest and/or restricted activity), and use of services measured by any ambulatory medical contacts, and/or the purchase of prescription drugs, and/or hospital admissions. Thus, all instances of social dysfunction and use of services related to a specific perceived health problem were considered as constituting an episode of illness. Respondent perceptions of severity were not employed in the construction of these episodes, nor were the health problems clinically confirmed. No inferences as to clinical levels of illness in the two study populations can be made, therefore, from the following summations of episodes; rather they reflect illness perceptions and illness behavior.

Construction of Episodes

Information on episodes of illness was derived from the raw household survey data, and distinct episodes were created by aggregating events associated either directly or indirectly with a specific health problem. If the reported events were associated with a health problem of short duration, such as a cold or the flu, and had occurred within one or two consecutive survey months, they and all related events (provider contacts, disability days, drug purchases) were considered to be part of one episode of illness. For long-term health problems such as diabetes or high blood pressure, all associated events (regardless of their date of occurrence) were considered to be part of one continuous episode of illness, including intermittent purchases of prescription drugs for that health problem.

To define episodes within the twelve-month survey period, four categories were established:

— With a definite beginning and ending

— With a definite beginning but an indefinite ending

— With an indefinite beginning but a definite ending

— With both an indefinite beginning and ending

Within these categories, the length of specific episodes of illness could only be measured approximately, as actual dates of disability days or medical contacts were not obtained and only the month in which an event occurred was known from the household survey data. Thus, if an episode had a definite beginning and definite ending within the survey year, its span was the number of months between the beginning and ending of the episode. Episodes with a definite beginning but no definite ending in the survey year spanned the period from the month in which the first related event occurred through the last month of participation in the survey by the respondent. Episodes with an indefinite beginning but a definite ending spanned the months from the first survey month through the month when the episode ended. The span for episodes with both an indefinite beginning and ending equaled the number of months during which the respondent participated in the survey.

To provide a count of events related to each episode, the data for each episode were summarized as to number of days of disability and number of different types of use. A health problem name was assigned to each episode and coded as acute, chronic, or miscellaneous, using a scheme reported by Kravits and Schneider (1975). A total of 6,135 episodes were created by these methods. Eleven episodes were eliminated from analysis because of inconsistent data and 384 were excluded because final analysis was restricted to persons who had remained in the survey for the entire year, leaving a total of 5,740. The number of episodes analyzed, however, does not always equal 5,740; frequently smaller subgroups are examined, and where the entire sample is discussed, missing data are excluded from the computations.

The volume of episodes with medical contacts involving psychiatric and psychological health problems is probably understated, because the survey questions about visits to mental health practitioners did not specifically ask about the health problem leading to the visit. Since events not associated with a specific health problem were excluded from this analysis, visits to mental health practitioners are not reflected in the episodes described, although disability days and purchase of prescription drugs associated with psychological and psychiatric problems are included.

Findings

In the following, the data are again presented by plan and race, as well as race-adjusted rates, in view of the substantial difference in the percentage of episodes experienced by blacks and whites in the two plans. In GHA 52 percent of the episodes were experienced by blacks as against 48 percent for whites, while the population was 67 percent black and 33 percent white; in BC-BS the corresponding percentages were 22 percent and 78 percent, with a population distribution of 34 percent and 66 percent (see Chapter 4). The black to white episode ratio, therefore, was 0.28 in BC-BS and 1.08 in GHA.

Comparison of Episodes

Type and Length. About two-thirds of the episodes in both plans have both a definite beginning and ending and involved mainly acute problems (Table 5.16). About one-fifth had an indefinite beginning and ending, and most of these were associated with health problems defined as chronic by the coding scheme. The remaining two episode types include a combination of acute, chronic, and other health problems and accounted for roughly 15 percent of the total, with no difference between plan and race groups. Similarly, there were no differences in the mean length of episodes, which ranged from little more than a month for episodes with a definite beginning and ending, to three and a half months for those with a definite beginning but indefinite ending. It is clear from these data that most episodes were relatively short, but because these measures are based on counts of whole months per episode, they are of necessity crude.

Selected Sociodemographic Characteristics. Race-adjusted distributions by age indicate that more episodes in BC-BS were concentrated in the youngest age group (less than five years) than in GHA; this difference was reversed for those 45 years or older (Table 5.17). In BC-BS, the youngest age category in the white group experienced a somewhat higher proportion of episodes than the corresponding black group. In GHA, the major difference was between those 20 to 44 years and 45 years or older; episodes experienced by blacks accounted for two-fifths in the younger and for a fifth in the older of these groups, while almost the reverse was the case for whites. Within both race groups, plan differences by age were statistically significant as well. They were noticeable in the two older black age groups and across all white age groups. The distribution of episodes by age thus did not correspond to the age distribution of the study population (cf. Table 4.1). In BC-BS, there was a relative preponderance of episodes in both the youngest and oldest age groups; in GHA, this was found for the oldest age group only. Also, almost 60 percent of illness episodes involved females, while their proportion in the sample was 51 percent (see Table 4.1). No plan differences existed in race-adjusted rates, but in BC-BS, a higher percentage of episodes among blacks was experienced by females than among whites (63.7 percent of episodes compared to 56.4 percent).

Distributions by family income indicated plan differences in the percentage of episodes at the high end of the income scale (30.2 percent above $25,000 in GHA, 19.4 percent in BC-BS; see Table 5.17), and for those with incomes between $10,000 to $15,000 (26 percent in BC-BS, 10.5 percent in GHA). Episodes involving whites were least frequent in the two low income groups, particularly in GHA (less than 5 percent), and no more than a sixth of the episodes involving blacks was in the highest income group in either plan. The distribution of episodes by income, however, was substantially the same as the income distribution of the study population in BC-BS, while in GHA it shifted noticeably toward the higher income group (cf. Table 4.3).

Health Problems and Bed Days. The health problems underlying the respective episodes were grouped into acute problems (those presumed to run their course in less than three months), chronic problems (those assumed to last longer than three months), and other (miscellaneous problems including psychological complaints and those that could not be classified as either acute or chronic). There was no difference between the plans in the distribution of episodes in this respect, in that about 60 percent of all episodes were associated with an acute problem and roughly 30 percent with a chronic problem. Also, in both plans, over half of race-adjusted episodes included bed days, but it was noted that the black group in GHA had by far the lowest percentage of episodes without bed days, while no difference was observed among the other groups (36.1 percent versus roughly 45 percent for whites in GHA and both race groups in BC-BS).

Similarly, for the mean number of bed days in episodes involving either acute or chronic health problems, there was no difference between the plans in the race-adjusted means of days in bed per episode (about 3.5 days for episodes involving acute health problems, and a little more than seven days for episodes with chronic problems). However, episodes of the black group in GHA involved by far the highest number of bed days regardless of type of health problem; the overall mean (6.01 days) was almost twice that of the white group in GHA (3.03 days) and about a third more than observed in BC-BS (whites, 4.01 days; blacks, 4.54 days).

Use of Services Associated
with Episodes of Illness

An episode of illness for the purposes of this analysis was constituted by the presence of disability days (bed and/or restricted activity days) associated with a health problem, either in conjunction with or in the absence of use of services. Conversely, the use of services (medical contacts and/or the use of prescription drugs) for an acute or chronic health problem was considered as constituting part of an episode of illness, whether or not this was accompanied by disability days. The distribution of episodes by type of associated event differed only slightly between plans, with a greater likelihood in GHA of episodes involving medical contacts only (46.6 percent as compared to 42.3 percent in BC-BS; Table 5.18). The percentage of episodes involving disability days without any use of services was lowest for the black group in GHA (12 percent), highest for the white group in GHA (21 percent), and intermediate and similar for both groups in BC-BS (16.2 percent, blacks; 18.4 percent, whites). On the other hand, whites in GHA experienced the lowest proportion (22.9 percent) and blacks in that plan the highest proportion (30.8 percent) of episodes involving both disability days and medical contacts, whereas the respective percentages for BC-BS were again similar and intermediate. Of all episodes experienced by the black group in GHA, four-fifths involved a medical contact, as compared to 68.7 percent for the white group; in BC-BS, the percentages were 71.4 percent and 69.5, respectively.

Overall, therefore, the likelihood of medical contact within an episode of illness differed markedly from that observed when the unit of analysis was use by the individual plan member over the course of the survey (cf. Table 5.1). Differences between the plans adjusted for race were small and, although in general slightly higher percentages of episodes with medical contacts were observed under GHA than under BC-BS, the differences were rarely statistically significant. Also, when examined in the context of specific episodes of illness, the likelihood of use was not greater for the two white groups. Instead, it appears that the black group in GHA was far more likely to make a medical contact in the course of an episode of illness than its white counterpart. This was not observed for the service benefit plan, where the differences between the two racial groups were smaller and patterns less pronounced. However, here too the large differences in use by racial grouping observed earlier were not evident when specific episodes of illness were compared.

Also, there was little difference in the volume of contacts per episode (Table 5.19), which seems to have been largely influenced by the type of associated health problem; episodes with chronic health problems, with and without disability days, involved at least twice the number of medical contacts than did episodes with acute problems. There were no statistically significant differences in either plan by race groups, nor within race groups across plans, possibly indicating that the volume of contacts in an episode of illness is largely determined by provider decisions and does not reflect differences in patient behavior.

These findings do not support the assumption of a greater likelihood of use of services within an illness episode in GHA because of its comprehensive coverage for ambulatory medical care. Nor does the volume of use within an episode suggest greater emphasis on ambulatory services by the providers of care in the prepaid group practice plan. The following findings, which relate to those persons (2,230 in all) who were in the survey for the entire year, therefore focus on the likelihood of experiencing an episode of illness in the course of twelve months and on the number of episodes experienced. The race-adjusted rates show that this likelihood was almost equal and high in both plans (77.4 percent, BC-BS; 80.4 percent, GHA; Table 5.20), but there were clear differences between the race groups. Blacks in both plans were much less likely than whites to experience an episode of illness. The black group in BC-BS ranked lowest of all in this respect (66.3 percent, as compared to 73.9 percent of blacks in GHA and more than 85 percent for both white groups). In terms of overall volume of episodes, the mean in GHA was 2.61; in BC-BS, it was 2.32, and in both plans, whites experienced almost twice as many episodes as blacks. Whites in GHA had by far the highest mean number of episodes (3.32 as compared to 3.03 in BC-BS), notwithstanding their relatively low use of services within an illness episode. This pattern was also observed for the number of episodes among those with at least one episode of illness.

When episodes were compared by associated types of events, race-adjusted and race-specific means in GHA were higher than in BC-BS for persons with episodes with medical contacts and for a subset of persons who had episodes involving medical contacts but no disability days (Table 5.21). For episodes with disability days, there were no differences between plans, but whites had more than twice as many episodes including only disability days than blacks (0.72 and 0.23, GHA; 0.57 and 0.26, BC-BS), and GHA whites ranked ahead of BC-BS whites by roughly 20 percent. These differences decreased when both disability days and medical contacts were episode components, but the mean for blacks was again substantially below that for whites, with the black group in BC-BS lowest on this indicator of illness and use (0.44 as compared to 0.58 in GHA, and 0.85 and 0.80 for the two white groups).

Thus, if the number of illness episodes experienced by a population over the course of a year can be considered a general measure of its health status, these findings would indicate that GHA members experienced more episodes of illness than BC-BS members and thus, as a group, were more likely to seek care. A further finding is that both black groups experienced fewer episodes of illness than whites by these measures, but that within such episodes, the black group in GHA had a higher propensity to seek medical contact than the white group in GHA and both race groups in BC-BS.

SUMMARY AND CONCLUSIONS

This chapter has compared patterns of use of ambulatory services under a service benefit and a prepaid group practice plan to address some of the questions raised in Chapter 1. Specifically, the following aspects were examined:

— Was there any difference in the extent to which plan members contacted physicians and other health professionals?

— Were there differences in rates of use of various types of health services?

— Were these differences due to a differential effect of predisposing, enabling, and illness factors?

— Did the behavior of plan members as to the use of medical services differ during episodes of illness?

The independent variables chosen for these analyses were selected from those identified by Andersen and Newman (1973) as related to the use of health services.

Differences in use between BC-BS and GHA were fairly consistently observed across the range of services examined; it tended to be higher under GHA in terms both of likelihood and volume of contacts. In race-adjusted comparisons, 76 percent of GHA members had at least one visit to a physician office, clinic or laboratory, in contrast to 67 percent of BC-BS members (Table 5.1). The race-adjusted mean number of such contacts was 4.22 in GHA and 3.40 in BC-BS (Table 5.2), and for those members with any use of this type it was 5.41 and 4.88, respectively (Table 5.3). Similar differences were found between the two plans with respect to most other types of ambulatory use. For example, the overall volume of contacts was significantly higher under GHA for treatment and preventive visits, telephone calls to the physician's office, fitting of glasses or contact lenses, and visits to mental health practitioners. Only for emergency room visits did BC-BS members experience a significantly higher mean rate of use than GHA members. Equally consistent but much larger differences were apparent between the two racial groups within each plan. Use by whites was almost invariably higher in both plans, generally by substantial and statistically significant margins. The differential in use between plans was maintained for both race groups, however.

When a summary measure of ambulatory contacts was compared, which included visits to a physician's office, clinic or laboratory, telephone calls to a physician's office, emergency room visits, eye examinations, visits to mental health practitioners, and visits to other practitioners, use by GHA members was again higher than in BC-BS by statistically significant margins. Eighty-one percent of the GHA members had at least one such contact in the course of 12 months, in contrast to 75 percent of the BC-BS members; the mean volume of these contacts was 6.29 (GHA) and 4.90 (BC-BS), respectively, and the mean volume of ambulatory contacts per person with contacts was 7.52 and 6.27, respectively (Table 5.4).

Similar patterns of higher use in GHA were observed in a comparison of entry visits and use of preventive services. The race-adjusted mean of first contacts for a specific health problem (entry visits) was 1.09 for BC-BS members and 1.32 for GHA members (Table 5.5). GHA members were also more likely to have had at least one physical examination in the absence of illness, shots or immunizations, and vision examinations (Table 5.6).

Given these differences, the association of rates of use with predisposing and enabling factors was generally in the expected direction, although the margin in favor of GHA became in some instances less pronounced or even reversed. This was noticeable in particular for recent plan members and at the lower end of several socioeconomic indicators.

When rates of ambulatory contacts were adjusted for selected indicators of ill health, the overall margin of difference in favor of GHA was maintained regardless of level of illness, and the volume of contacts in particular indicated substantially more use in GHA than in BC-BS for members with two or more chronic health problems, with one or more days of bed rest or restricted activity days, and with days of pain and worry. Thus, the differences in levels of chronic illness and social dysfunction observed in Chapter 4 were not clearly associated with levels of use when the individual plan member was the unit of analysis. That the larger volume of contacts in the prepaid group practice plan was not entirely a result of provider decisions is indicated by the fact that only about a quarter of visits to a physician's office in that plan were reported to have been suggested by the physician; the corresponding percentage in BC-BS was roughly two-fifths. Also, the differences in ambulatory use observed in this study were not large enough to suggest that ambulatory care in the prepaid group practice plan was a substantial substitute for inpatient care.

Multivariate analysis of different types of ambulatory use indicated that while roughly one-third of the variance in volume of use was explained by the set of predisposing, enabling, and illness variables, they did not have a differential effect in the two plans. Although the contribution of specific independent variables differed with type of use, illness measured by disability days was, as in many analyses of this type, the most powerful explanatory variable of use of ambulatory services, followed by other indicators of acute or chronic ill health. Among the predisposing variables, only age had any explanatory value for the types of use examined. Enabling variables were of little explanatory power as well. Moreover, and in contrast to the generally consistent finding in the univariate analysis of use, plan and race contributed little to the variance explained. Finally, an analysis of episodes of illness showed that the types of episodes, their length, and the kind of associated health problem (acute or chronic) were substantially the same for both plans. Few overall differences were found between the plans in the percentage of illness episodes with medical contact and in the volume of medical contacts within an episode of illness; however, the behavior of the black group in GHA was remarkably different from that of the other three groups, in that they were substantially more likely to seek care within an episode of illness, and substantially less likely to experience episodes involving disability days only. On the other hand, more episodes of illness were observed in GHA than in BC-BS, for whites as compared to blacks, and for the black group in GHA as compared to that in BC-BS. The greater use of ambulatory services in GHA, and by whites in either plan, may thus reflect differences in the illness experience of the groups studied and in the number of episodes involving medical contacts.

Table 5.1 Use of selected categories of health services: Unadjusted, race adjusted, and race specific percent of members[a] of BC-BS and GHA with at least one contact within twelve months

Type of contact	Unadjusted		Race adjusted		Black		White	
	BC-BS	GHA	BC-BS	GHA	BC-BS	GHA	BC-BS	GHA
				Percent				
Visits to physician office, clinic, laboratory including	71	74 *	67 *	76	55+ *	69++	80	84
Preventive reasons	35 *	39	32 *	42	21+ *	32++	42 *	52
Diagnostic reasons	43	42	40 *	45	31+	35++	50	55
Treatment reasons	49	49	45 *	51	35+ *	44++	56	58
Purchase of prescribed medicines	60	57	57	60	46+ *	52++	67	67
Dentist visits	48 *	36	42 *	43	24+	21++	61	64
Telephone calls to physician office	25	25	22 *	28	10+ *	18++	33	38
Eye examinations	17	19	16 *	22	14+	13++	19 *	30
Fitting of glasses or contact lenses	14	14	13 *	16	11+	10++	15 *	21
Emergency room visits	16 *	7	16 *	7	17 *	8	15 *	6
Purchase or rental of medical equipment	5	4	5	4	3+	3	7	5
Visits to mental health practitioners	2	3	2 *	4	1	2++	2 *	7
Visits to other health practitioners	5	4	4	5	2+	2++	6	7
Ambulance use	1	1	1	1	1	2	1	1
(n)	(1,368)	(1,323)	(1,368)	(1,323)	(462)	(885)	(906)	(438)

[a]Contract holders and their covered dependents.

*P ≤ .05.

+P ≤ .05 for race groups, BC-BS.

++P ≤ .05 for race groups, GHA.

Table 5.2 Volume of use of selected categories of services: Unadjusted, race adjusted, and race specific mean number of contacts by plan members within twelve months

Type of contact	Unadjusted		Race adjusted		Black		White	
	BC–BS	GHA	BC–BS	GHA	BC–BS	GHA	BC–BS	GHA
				Mean				
Visits to physician office, clinic, laboratory including	3.77	3.80	3.40 *	4.22	2.22+ *	2.96++	4.57 *	5.48
Preventive reasons	1.11	1.15	0.95 *	1.36	0.46+ *	0.74++	1.44	1.98
Diagnostic reasons	1.12	1.04	1.02	1.14	0.74+	0.84++	1.31	1.45
Treatment reasons	1.47	1.50	1.36 *	1.61	1.00+ *	1.28++	1.71	1.93
Months in which prescribed medicines purchased	2.13 *	1.80	1.96	1.94	1.46+	1.50++	2.47	2.38
Dentist visits	1.69 *	1.29	1.49	1.60	0.87+	0.69++	2.11	2.50
Telephone calls to physician office	0.64	0.62	0.54 *	0.76	0.22+ *	0.34++	0.86	1.18
Eye examinations	0.21	0.24	0.20 *	0.28	0.17+	0.15++	0.24 *	0.41
Fitting of glasses or contact lenses	0.18	0.19	0.16 *	0.22	0.13+	0.14++	0.20 *	0.30
Emergency room visits	0.22 *	0.11	0.23 *	0.10	0.25 *	0.13++	0.21 *	0.07
Months in which medical equipment was purchased or rented	0.07	0.05	0.06	0.06	0.03+	0.05	0.09	0.06
Visits to mental health practitioners	0.32	0.44	0.24 *	0.64	0.02+	0.05++	0.47 *	1.23
Visits to other health practitioners	0.34	0.24	0.28	0.28	0.11+	0.15	0.46	0.42
Ambulance use	0.02	0.02	0.02	0.02	0.02	0.03	0.02 *	0.01
(n)	(1,368)	(1,323)	(1,368)	(1,323)	(462)	(885)	(906)	(438)

*P ≤ .05.

+P ≤ .05 for race groups, BC–BS.

++P ≤ .05 for race groups, GHA.

Table 5.3   Volume of use per person using selected categories of services: Unadjusted, race adjusted, and race specific mean number of contacts within twelve months

Type of contact	Unadjusted		Race adjusted		Black		White	
	BC-BS	GHA	BC-BS	GHA	BC-BS	GHA	BC-BS	GHA
				Mean				
Visits to physician office, clinic, laboratory including	5.29	5.13	4.88	5.41	4.02[+]	4.29[++]	5.75	6.53
Preventive reasons	3.18	2.97	2.81	3.05	2.19[+]	2.30[++]	3.43	3.80
Diagnostic reasons	2.56	2.50	2.51	2.52	2.40	2.37	2.62	2.66
Treatment reasons	3.03	3.06	2.97	3.10	2.85	2.89	3.09	3.31
Months in which pre- scribed medicines purchased	3.56 *	3.16	3.42	3.22	3.14[+]	2.90[++]	3.71	3.55
Dentist visits	3.49	3.64	3.54	3.58	3.62	3.25	3.47	3.90
Telephone calls to physician office	2.53	2.51	2.40	2.50	2.24	1.91[++]	2.57	3.08
Eye examinations	1.25	1.27	1.22	1.26	1.18	1.18	1.27	1.35
Fitting of glasses or contact lenses	1.27	1.40	1.24	1.40	1.18	1.37	1.30	1.42
Emergency room visits	1.42	1.53	1.43	1.44	1.48	1.64	1.38	1.23
Months in which medical equipment was purchased or rented	1.36	1.46	1.32	1.44	1.25	1.64	1.38	1.24
Visits to mental health practitioners	18.83	13.14	13.32	10.42	1.83[+]	2.93[++]	24.82	17.90
Visits to other health practitioners	7.23	6.12	6.36	6.08	5.10	5.86	7.62	6.31
Ambulance use	1.21	1.74	1.29	1.57	1.50	1.81	1.80	1.33

*P ≤ .05.   [+]P ≤ .05 for race groups, BC-BS.   [++]P ≤ .05 for race groups, GHA.

Table 5.4 Ambulatory medical contacts: Unadjusted, race adjusted, and race specific percent of plan members with at least one contact in twelve months, total volume of contacts, and volume of contacts for persons with at least one contact

	Unadjusted		Race adjusted		Black		White	
	BC–BS	GHA	BC–BS	GHA	BC–BS	GHA	BC–BS	GHA
Persons with at least one contact (percent)	79	79	75 *	81	65[+] *	74[++]	86	89
Volume of contacts (mean)	5.52	5.44	4.90 *	6.29	3.00[+] **	3.78[++]	6.81 *	8.81
Volume of contacts per person with contact (mean)	7.00	6.91	6.27 *	7.52	4.63[+]	5.13[++]	7.91 *	9.90

*P ⩽ .05.
[+]P ⩽ .05 for race groups, BC–BS.
[++]P ⩽ .05 for race groups, GHA.

Table 5.5 Entry visits: Unadjusted, race adjusted, and race specific percent of plan members with first contacts for a specific health problem and volume of entry visits

	Unadjusted		Race adjusted		Black		White	
	BC–BS	GHA	BC–BS	GHA	BC–BS	GHA	BC–BS	GHA
Persons with at least one entry visit (percent)	55	55	52 *	57	43 *	51	61	64
Volume of entry visits (mean)	1.18	1.24	1.09 *	1.32	0.82[+] *	1.10[++]	1.36	1.53

*P ⩽ .05.
[+]P ⩽ .05 for race groups, BC–BS.
[++]P ⩽ .05 for race groups, GHA.

Table 5.6 Use of preventive services: Unadjusted, race adjusted, and race specific percent of plan members using at least one preventive service and mean number of contacts for preventive services within twelve months

	Unadjusted		Race adjusted		Black		White	
	BC–BS	GHA	BC–BS	GHA	BC–BS	GHA	BC–BS	GHA
Percent with at least one service								
Physical examination in the absence of illness	24 *	30	22 *	33	15+ *	25++	29 *	40
Shots or immunizations	8	9	7 *	11	3+	5++	10 *	17
Prenatal contacts (Females 15 to 45 years)	7	5	6	5	6	4	7	6
Well-baby visits	73	66	69	70	57+	60	81	79
Vision examinations	16	18	15 *	20	14+	12++	17 *	29
Mean number of contacts								
Physical examination in the absence of illness	0.34	0.38	0.30 *	0.41	0.19+ *	0.31++	0.41 *	0.51
Shots or immunizations	0.51	0.57	0.41 *	0.73	0.08+ *	0.25++	0.73	1.21
Prenatal contacts (Females 15 to 45 years)	0.39	0.35	0.37	0.39	0.33	0.28	0.42	0.52
Well-baby visits	3.22	3.09	2.99	3.58	2.14	2.33	3.76	4.71
Vision examinations	0.20	0.22	0.20 *	0.28	0.16+	0.14++	0.24 *	0.41

*P ≤ .05.

+P ≤ .05 for race groups, BC–BS.

++P ≤ .05 for race groups, GHA.

Table 5.7   Ambulatory medical contacts and correlates of use: Race adjusted percent of plan members making contact and mean number of contacts by selected predisposing factors

	Percent making contact			Mean number of contacts		
	BC–BS		GHA	BC–BS		GHA
Age						
0–4 years	89		84	7.2		5.8
5–19 years	72		75	3.8		4.8
20–44 years	76	*	84	4.6	*	6.7
45 years and over	78	*	85	5.9	*	8.0
Sex						
Male	70	*	78	4.2	*	5.6
Female	80		84	5.6	*	7.0
Household educational level						
Less than 12 years	69		68	5.2	*	2.5
4 years of high school	72		74	4.8		5.6
1–3 years of college	77		82	3.8	*	5.4
4 years of college	76	*	85	5.6		6.9
5 or more years of college or university	84		90	5.1	*	6.8
Household occupational level						
Craftsmen, foremen, operators, service, and laborers	70		72	4.3		4.2
Clerical and sales	78		80	6.3		7.8
Professional, technical, manager, officials, and proprietors	80		82	5.0	*	6.4
Annual family income						
Less than $10,000	72		78	5.3		4.5
$10,000–14,999	76		77	5.7		6.6
$15,000–24,999	76	*	82	4.8	*	6.0
$25,000 or more	82		86	4.6	*	6.8
Family size[a]						
2–3 persons	83		86	5.8		7.9
4–5 persons	78		83	4.5		6.0
6 or more persons	70		69	4.4		2.6

[a]Contacts by children less than 16 years of age.   *P ⩽ .05.

Table 5.8   Use of services and correlates of use: Race adjusted percent of plan members making contact and mean number of contacts by selected attitudinal factors

	Percent making contact			Mean number of contacts		
	BC–BS		GHA	BC–BS		GHA
Tendency to use physician services[a]						
Low	41	*	51	0.8		1.0
Medium	56		60	1.2		1.4
High	55	*	62	1.2	*	1.5
Attitude toward physical examinations[b]						
Positive	76	*	82	5.2	*	6.5
Negative	69		70	3.4		3.5
Prior physical examination[b]						
Within 2 years	80	*	85	5.4	*	6.6
More than 2 years	68		71	4.0		4.8
Never	67		62	3.6		4.5
Satisfaction with medical care[b]						
Low	74	*	81	5.1		6.3
Moderate	74	*	81	4.3	*	6.4
High	78		82	5.4		6.2

[a]Entry visits.

[b]Ambulatory medical contacts.

*P ⩽ .05.

Table 5.9 Ambulatory medical contacts and correlates of use: Race adjusted percent of plan members making contact and mean number of contacts by selected enabling factors

	Percent making contact		Mean number of contacts	
	BC–BS	GHA	BC–BS	GHA
Length of plan membership				
1–3 years	90 *	79	7.2	5.8
4–6 years	74	78	3.8 *	6.0
7–13 years	76 *	82	5.1	6.6
14 or more years	74 *	88	4.8 *	7.1
Knowledge of plan benefits				
Low	67	60	4.6	3.4
Medium	78 *	84	4.7	4.7
High	88	82	6.3	7.0
Regular source of care[a]				
None	60	—	3.9	—
Hospital clinic or emergency room	62 *	80	5.6	4.2
Personal physician	79 *	89	5.2 *	7.4
Other physician	72	74	4.0	5.0

[a]Includes out-of-plan physicians in GHA; see Table 4.11.

—Less than one percent of total sample.

*P ≤ .05.

Table 5.10   Ambulatory medical contacts and illness: Race adjusted percent of plan members making contact and mean number of contacts for selected measures of ill health

Levels of illness	Percent making contact			Mean number of contacts		
	BC–BS		GHA	BC–BS		GHA
Perceived health status						
Very good	73	*	79	4.2	*	5.1
All others	81	*	87	6.4	*	8.8
Chronic health problems						
None	72		76	3.8		4.2
One	78	*	88	6.2		7.2
Two or more	94		96	8.9	*	12.0
Treated chronic problems						
None	72	*	78	3.8	*	4.6
One or more	90		92	8.9	*	10.8
Bed days						
None	67	*	74	3.7	*	4.9
One or more	92		95	6.8	*	8.7
Restricted activity days						
None	66	*	74	3.9		4.7
One or more	92		94	6.6	*	8.7
Days of pain and worry						
None	69	*	75	3.9	*	4.7
One or more	96		98	7.4	*	9.5

*P $\leq$ .05.

Table 5.11 Ambulatory medical contacts and race: Race specific percent of plan members making contact and mean number of contacts by selected correlates of use

	Percent making contact						Mean number of contacts					
	Black			White			Black			White		
Correlates of use	BC-BS		GHA	BC-BS		GHA	BC-BS		GHA	BC-BS		GHA
Total	65[+]	*	74[++]	86	*	89	3.0[+]	*	3.8[++]	6.8	*	8.8
Annual family income												
Less than $15,000	60[+]	*	71	88	*	81	3.0[+]		3.9[++]	7.9		7.8
$15,000 or more	71[+]		76[++]	85		90	3.0[+]		3.6[++]	6.5		9.0
Education												
Less than 12 years	65[+]	*	69	73		–	3.3[+]		3.7	7.1		–
4 years of high school	60[+]	*	69	84		79	3.0[+]		3.7[++]	6.7		7.4
1–3 years of college	68[+]		75[++]	86		89	2.5[+]		3.3[++]	5.2		7.5
4 years of college	67[+]		80	86		90	3.9[+]		4.8[++]	7.4		9.0
5 or more years of college or university	77[+]		88	90		92	2.6[+]	*	4.1[++]	7.6		9.6
Family size[a]												
2–3 persons	71[+]		77	90		–	4.4[+]		4.4	7.3		–
4–5 persons	63[+]		75[++]	92		90	2.0[+]		3.5[++]	7.0		8.5
6 or more persons	52[+]		64	88		74	2.0[+]		1.7[++]	6.9		3.6

Table 5.11 (Continued)

Correlates of use	Percent making contact						Mean number of contacts					
	Black			White			Black			White		
	BC-BS		GHA	BC-BS		GHA	BC-BS		GHA	BC-BS		GHA
Tendency to use physician services[b]												
Low	31+	*	50	51		52	0.6+	*	1.0	1.1	*	1.1
Medium	47+		53++	66		66	0.9+		1.2	1.5		1.5
High	45+		51++	65		72	0.9+		1.1++	1.5	*	1.9
Personal physician												
Yes	71+	*	84++	87	*	94	3.5+	*	4.6++	6.8	*	10.3
No	51+	*	68++	78		82	2.0+	*	3.3++	6.8		6.9
Bed days												
None	54+	*	64++	80		84	2.1+	*	2.7++	5.3	*	7.1
One or more	91		94	94		97	5.1+		6.1++	8.5	*	11.3
Chronic health problems												
None	60+	*	68++	84	*	83	2.3+	*	2.7++	5.2	*	5.8
One	70+	*	80++	87		95	4.1+	*	4.9++	8.4	*	9.6
Two or more	94		93	95		98	6.4+		7.5++	11.4	*	16.5

[a]Contacts by children less than 16 years of age. [b]Entry visits.

*P ≤ .05. +P ≤ .05 for race groups, BC–BS. ++P ≤ .05 for race groups, GHA.

—Less than one percent of the total sample.

Table 5.12   Multivariate analysis of use of ambulatory services: Independent
variables and coding categories

Predisposing factors	
Marital status	Never married; married; divorced, separated or widowed; less than 16 years of age
Occupation of contract holder	Professional and managerial; clerical and sales; other
Work status of contract holder's spouse	No spouse; spouse works full or part time; spouse not employed
Plan by race	GHA black; GHA white; BC–BS black; BC–BS white
Time since last physical examination	Never; more than two years ago; within last two years; less than one year
Age	Continuous from less than 1 to 73 years
Family size	Continuous from 1 to 12 family members
Family income	Nine continuous income groups
Household educational level[a]	Seven continuous educational attainment categories (from low to high)
Hospitalizations in year prior to survey	None; one or more
Tendency to use physician services for symptoms of ill health	Continuous from 0 to 13[b]
Religion	Protestant; Catholic; Jewish; no preference; other
Enabling factors	
Years in plan since 1960	Continuous from 1 to 13+ years
Personal physician	Yes; no
Knowledge of plan benefits	Continuous from 1 to 13[c]
Perceived illness	
Overall health status (reported health status[d] and number of reported chronic health problems)	0 = reported health status very good and no chronic health problems; 1 = reported health status not very good or at least one chronic health problem; 2 = health status not very good and at least one chronic health problem
Disability days[e]	Continuous from 0 to 365 days
Pain and worry days	Continuous from 0 to 365 days
Number of reported treated chronic problems	Continuous from 0 to 7

[a]Of most highly educated adult in household.

[b]Summary score based on responses for thirteen symptom categories.

[c]Summary score based on correct responses to thirteen benefit items.

[d]At beginning of survey year.   [e]Bed and restricted activity days.

Table 5.13   Proportion of variance explained in ambulatory medical contacts

Independent variable	Variance explained (%)	Percent of total variance explained
Number of disability days	9.2	43.7
Number of treated chronic problems	3.1	14.8
Plan by race[a]	1.6	7.6
Age	1.5	7.1
Health status	1.0	4.8
Religion	1.0	4.8
Number of pain and worry days	0.7	3.3
Family size	0.6	2.9
Plan knowledge	0.5	2.4
Years in plan	0.5	2.4
Household educational level	0.4	1.9
Hospitalization in year prior to survey	0.4	1.9
Work status of spouse of contract holder	0.3	1.4
Tendency to use physician services	0.2	1.0
Total variance explained	21.0	100.0

[a]All partitions were by race across plans.

Table 5.14   Proportion of variance explained in treatment and diagnostic visits

Independent variable	Variance explained (%)	Percent of total variance explained
Number of disability days	22.3	58.1
Number of pain and worry days	8.1	21.1
Number of treated chronic problems	2.9	7.6
Age	2.0	5.2
Tendency to use physician services	0.7	1.8
Having a personal physician	0.4	1.0
Work status of spouse of contract holder	0.4	1.0
Plan knowledge	0.3	0.8
Household educational level	0.3	0.8
Plan by race[a]	0.2	0.5
Religion	0.2	0.5
Health status	0.2	0.5
Occupation of contract holder	0.2	0.5
Sex	0.2	0.5
Time since last physical examination	0.0	0.0
Total variance explained	38.4	100.0

[a]All partitions were by race across plans.

Table 5.15   Proportion of variance explained in entry visits

Independent variable	Variance explained (%)	Percent of total variance explained
Number of disability days	18.1	54.7
Age	7.4	22.4
Number of pain and worry days	4.9	14.8
Tendency to use physician services	0.7	2.1
Plan by race[a]	0.5	1.5
Plan knowledge	0.5	1.5
Family size	0.3	0.9
Income	0.2	0.6
Religion	0.2	0.6
Years in plan	0.2	0.6
Work status of spouse of contract holder	0.1	0.3
Total variance explained	33.1	100.0

[a]See table 5.13–14. However, one partition here was GHA (white) vs. all others.

Table 5.16   Episodes of illness in BC-BS and GHA: Percentage distribution of episodes by type and length of episode

	All		Black		White	
Episode type	BC–BS	GHA	BC–BS	GHA	BC–BS	GHA
	Percent					
Definite beginning and ending	66.8	67.3	63.3	68.2	67.8	66.3
Definite beginning, indefinite ending	6.9	6.9	7.1	7.3	6.8	6.4
Indefinite beginning, definite ending	7.9	6.1	9.8	6.0	7.4	6.3
Indefinite beginning and ending	18.4	19.7	19.8	18.5	18.0	21.0
	100.0	100.0	100.0	100.0	100.0	100.0
	Mean number of months					
Definite beginning and ending	1.2	1.2	1.2	1.1	1.2	1.2
Definite beginning, indefinite ending	3.6	3.6	2.9	3.8	3.8	3.4
Indefinite beginning, definite ending	3.4	3.1	3.5	3.2	3.4	2.9
Indefinite beginning and ending	12.0	12.0	12.0	12.0	12.0	12.0
(n)	(3,089)	(2,651)	(686)	(1,386)	(2,403)	(1,265)

Table 5.17 Episodes of illness and selected predisposing factors: Percentage distribution of episodes by age, sex, and family income of members[a] of BC–BS and GHA experiencing episode

Predisposing factors	Unadjusted BC–BS	Unadjusted GHA	Race Adjusted BC–BS	Race Adjusted GHA	Black BC–BS	Black GHA	White BC–BS	White GHA
Age								
0 to 4 years	13.4	8.5	12.9	7.7	10.3	10.8	14.3	6.0
5 to 19 years	26.1	27.5	26.2	28.2	26.8	25.5	25.9	29.7
20 to 44 years	33.8	34.7	34.4	31.9	37.5	43.2	32.7	25.5
45 years and over	26.7	29.3	26.5	32.2	25.4	20.5	27.1	38.8
	100.0 *	100.0	100.0 *	100.0	100.0+ *	100.0++	100.0 *	100.0
Sex								
Male	42.0	43.1	41.0	43.1	36.3	44.4	43.6	42.3
Female	58.0	56.9	59.0	56.9	63.7	55.6	56.4	57.7
	100.0	100.0	100.0	100.0	100.0+	100.0	100.0	100.0
Family income								
Less than $10,000	10.7	17.7	11.6	13.7	21.4	29.3	6.1	4.9
$10,000 to $14,999	22.7	13.3	26.0	10.5	31.2	21.4	23.0	4.3
$15,000 to $24,999	45.2	43.3	43.0	45.6	32.7	36.8	48.8	50.5
$25,000 or more	21.4	25.7	19.4	30.2	14.7	12.5	22.1	40.3
	100.0 *	100.0	100.0 *	100.0	100.0+ *	100.0++	100.0 *	100.0

[a]Contract holders and their covered dependents.

*P ⩽ .05. +P ⩽ .05 for race groups, BC–BS. ++P ⩽ .05 for race groups, GHA.

Table 5.18 Events associated with episode of illness: Percentage distribution of episodes by selected indicators of social dysfunction and use of services

Events associated with episode	Unadjusted		Race Adjusted		Black		White	
	BC-BS	GHA	BC-BS	GHA	BC-BS	GHA	BC-BS	GHA
Medical contact only	42.0 *	47.0	42.3 *	46.6	44.0	48.1	41.4 *	45.8
Prescription drugs only	10.4 *	8.4	10.4	8.6	10.4 *	7.7	10.4	9.1
Disability days only	17.9	16.3	17.6	17.8	16.2 *	12.0++	18.4	21.0
Medical contact and/or disability days and/or prescription drugs	27.9	27.0	27.9	25.7	27.4	30.8++	28.1 *	22.9
Prescription drugs and disability days	1.8	1.3	1.8	1.3	2.0	1.4	1.7	1.2
	100.0	100.0	100.0	100.0	100.0	100.0	100.0	100.0

*P ≤ .05.   ++P ≤ .05 for race groups, GHA.

Table 5.19 Episodes of illness, social dysfunction, and volume of use of services: Mean number of medical contacts per episode by two measures of illness

Type of health problem	Unadjusted		Race Adjusted		Black		White	
	BC-BS	GHA	BC-BS	GHA	BC-BS	GHA	BC-BS	GHA
No disability days								
Acute problem	1.39	1.31	1.39	1.29	1.38	1.35	1.39	1.26
Chronic problem	2.76	3.00	2.70	3.12	2.32	2.51	2.90	3.43
Some disability days								
Acute problem	1.25	1.27	1.28	1.24	1.41	1.36	1.21	1.18
Chronic problem	5.43	4.79	5.18	4.95	4.40	4.41	5.80	5.38

Table 5.20 Persons with episodes of illness: Percent of plan members with at least one episode, volume of episodes, and number of episodes per person with at least one episode

	Unadjusted		Race Adjusted		Black		White	
	BC-BS	GHA	BC-BS	GHA	BC-BS	GHA	BC-BS	GHA
Persons with at least one episode (percent)	81.1	78.2	77.4	80.4	66.3+ *	73.9++	88.5	86.9
Volume of episodes (mean)	2.53	2.36	2.32 *	2.61	1.61+	1.89++	3.03	3.32
Number of episodes per person with episode (mean)	3.12	3.03	2.91 *	3.19	2.40+	2.56++	3.42 *	3.82

*P ⩽ .05.
+P ⩽ .05 for race groups, BC–BS.
++P ⩽ .05 for race groups, GHA.

Table 5.21 Episodes of illness, social dysfunction, and use of services: Mean number of episodes per person by type of events

	Unadjusted		Race Adjusted		Black		White	
Event associated with episode	BC-BS	GHA	BC-BS	GHA	BC-BS	GHA	BC-BS	GHA
Medical contact	1.75	1.75	1.61 *	1.89	1.15+ *	1.49++	2.07	2.28
Medical contact without disability days	1.04	1.10	0.97 *	1.19	0.71+ *	0.90++	1.23 *	1.48
Medical contact with disability days	0.71	0.66	0.65	0.69	0.44+ *	0.58++	0.85	0.80
Disability days only	0.47	0.39	0.41	0.47	0.26+	0.23++	0.57 *	0.72

*P ⩽ .05.
+P ⩽ .05 for race groups, BC–BS.
++P ⩽ .05 for race groups, GHA.

6

Use of Services Outside the Prepaid Group Practice Plan

Samuel M. Meyers

It was noted that use of health services reported by members of GHA included care obtained from providers and facilities outside the prepaid group practice plan. Out-of-plan ambulatory use may reflect dissatisfaction with the range of coverage or with quality and interpersonal skills of staff and convenience of service arrangements, as well as lack of knowledge about plan benefits and facilities. From the point of view of the prepaid group practice plan, which has undertaken to provide comprehensive care to its members, substantial levels of such use would tend to fragment care. From the point of view of the user, obtaining services outside the plan may add to the financial burden of health care.

Second, and of particular importance in view of the findings in Phase I, out-of-plan hospital use has been argued to account (at least in part) for lower hospital admission rates under prepaid group practice as compared to service benefit plans. GHA admission rates in this study and those published elsewhere were derived from plan records; out-of-plan hospitalizations would not appear in these records and this could have distorted admission rates. These aspects were addressed in Phase II by a range of questions inquiring into types of and reasons for use of services other than those provided by GHA or paid for on the patient's behalf.

Out-of-plan use is here defined as any instance of care or services provided to plan members by other than GHA medical or paramedical staff that was not authorized by GHA nor covered by plan benefits, regardless of whether or not it involved financial cost to the user (i.e., free-of-charge visits to work or neighborhood clinics as compared to emergency room visits or visits to other than plan physicians). Use of such services was measured in terms of hospital inpatient stays; visits to an emergency room of a hospital; visits to physician offices, clinics, or laboratories; visits to other health practitioners and to mental health practitioners; telephone calls for medical advice; home visits by physicians; and vision examinations. In short, it contains the major elements of ambulatory use examined in Chapter 5, and in addition all instances of hospital use not under GHA auspices.

The design of the study permits an examination of out-of-plan use from two perspectives. The first takes each instance of use as the unit of analysis, so as to determine the percentage of total use that occurred outside the plan and its overall volume. The second perspective is the individual user, so as to determine the percentage of all GHA members who made any out-of-plan use and some of their characteristics. Finally, reasons for use were determined.

LEVELS OF OUT-OF-PLAN SERVICES

Volume and Types of Contact

Figure 6.1 shows overall volume and types of out-of-plan use as a percentage of all contacts reported by GHA members in the respective service categories. The small proportion of out-of-plan hospitalizations (4 percent of all hospitalizations during the survey year) clearly speaks against any hypothesis that out-of-plan hospital use could have accounted for the lower hospitalization rates in GHA. Even when adjusted for this out-of-plan use,

Figure 6.1   Contacts with services and providers other than GHA as percent of all GHA contacts in each category

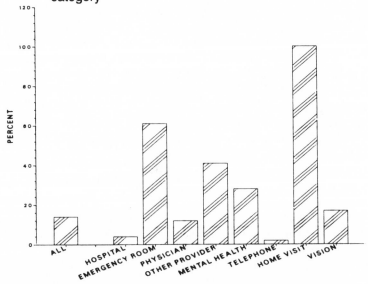

total GHA admissions were 72.1 per 1,000 population in 1972, or 58 percent of the BC-BS rate (121.2 per 1,000 population).

Overall, the proportion of out-of-plan use was not negligible (14 percent of all types of services examined) but remained within the range of findings from other studies, although direct comparisons are difficult because of the differences in methods used (Scitovsky, Benham, and McCall, 1981; Hetherington, Hopkins, and Roemer, 1975; Greenlick, 1972; Bashshur, Metzner, and Worden, 1967; Williams, Trussell, and Elinson, 1964; Weinerman, 1964; Freidson, 1961; Wolfman, 1961). Wide variation by type of use was noted in the present study, from 100 percent for home visits (three in all), to 2 percent for telephone contacts. In terms of percentages, emergency room visits and, as expected, contacts with mental health and nonphysician practitioners were relatively important aspects of out-of-plan use (see Chapter 1 for the GHA benefit structure); in terms of volume, a total of 519 contacts (Table 6.1) with other than plan physicians out of a total of 4,493 GHA physician contacts merits a closer look.

Figure 6.2 shows this numerically largest component of out-of-plan use by some of the characteristics of the study population. As a proportion of total physician visits, out-of-plan use was much more likely to occur among adults than among children and adolescents. The percentage was highest among those 45 years and older (19 percent) and almost nonexistent in the less than 5-year old group (only 1 percent of all visits). Among those with less than a high school education, 24 percent of physician contacts were out of plan, as compared to roughly a tenth in the other educational categories. For income as well, the highest percentage of out-of-plan physician visits was made by those living in households earning less than $15,000 (roughly a fifth of all physician visits for this group); the lowest out-of-plan use was in households with incomes between $15,000 and $24,999, where 5 percent of all physician contacts were out of plan, while 11 percent of such contacts were reported by those in households earning $25,000 or more. Also, since knowledge of the GHA benefit structure and the likelihood of use of services were shown to be related in Chapter 5, high knowledge of benefits should be inversely related with out-of-plan use of covered physician services. In fact, a threefold range in use in the expected direction was observed; of all physician visits made by members with low benefit knowledge, 20 percent were out of plan, as compared to 7 percent for persons with high plan knowledge and 16 percent for those with moderate knowledge of plan benefits.

In view of these findings, differences in patterns of use by race were not unexpected. While there was little difference in the overall percentage of out-of-plan use (51 percent of all out-of-plan contacts were made by black members, as compared to 49 percent for the white group; Figure 6.3), there were wide differences by type of contact. For out-of-plan visits to the

Figure 6.2   Out-of-plan physician contacts as a percent of all
GHA physician contacts, by selected patient
characteristics

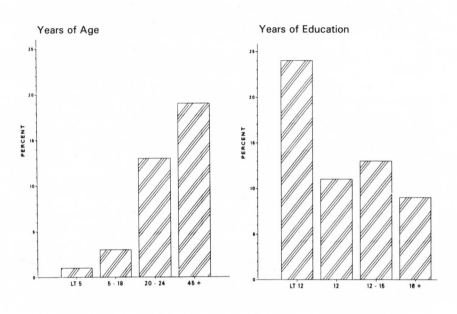

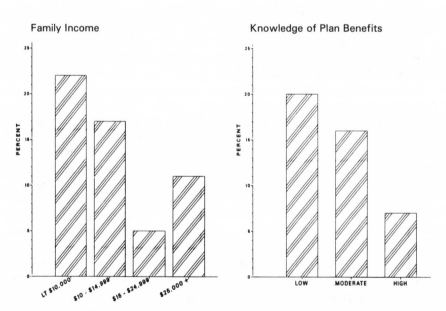

Figure 6.3   Percentage distributions of out-of-plan contact
categories by race

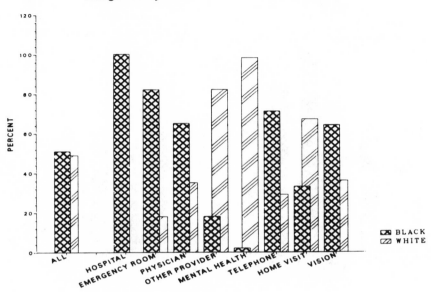

physician's office and vision examinations, for instance, contacts by blacks
predominated, while out-of-plan use of other health practitioners and mental health services was almost entirely attributable to whites.

Persons Using Out-of-Plan Services

Overall, about 20 percent of the GHA population made at least one out-of-plan contact of any of the types examined, for a total of 258 persons during the survey year. The overall racial distribution for persons making any out-of-plan use (63 percent black and 37 percent white) was not noticeably different from this distribution in the GHA population (67 percent and 33 percent, respectively). There was wide variation by type of out-of-plan use, however, with the black group accounting for 83 percent of persons making use of emergency rooms (and for all of the four out-of-plan hospital stays); relatively high percentages of whites reported out-of-plan visits to mental health practitioners (89 percent; Figure 6.4) and to other health practitioners (59 percent).

The characteristics of persons making use of any out-of-plan services or providers are shown in Table 6.2. There was no difference between the proportion of males and females who made any out-of-plan use and, as for contacts (see Figure 6.2), older people were more likely to make out-of-plan

Figure 6.4   Race specific percent of persons using services
             and providers outside GHA

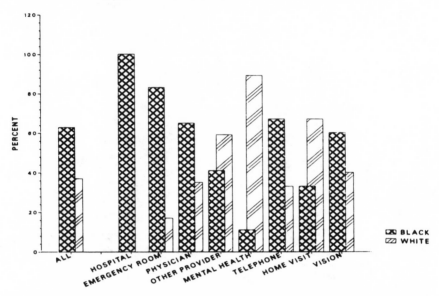

visits than those in younger age groups (30 percent of those 45 years or older reported at least one out-of-plan visit during the survey year, as compared to 12 percent of those in the 5 to 19 year group and 7 percent in the 0 to 4 year group). Education had relatively little effect in terms of the number of persons making out-of-plan use. The overall difference between the black and the white group was small, despite the differences in types of use observed. Income was of moderate importance, those in families earning less than $15,000 and more than $25,000 being more likely to make out-of-plan use than those in intermediate income households, but again, persons who knew less about the benefit structure of the plan seemed more likely to make out-of-plan contacts than those with a high knowledge score (range, 24 to 15 percent). Of those in the prepaid group practice plan less than three years, 26 percent reported out-of-plan use, compared to 18 percent of those who had been plan members for three or more years at the time of the survey, which may reflect the direct relationship of knowledge of GHA benefits to length of membership in that plan observed in Table 4.10. On the other hand, overall levels of satisfaction with medical care in the prepaid group practice plan as reported in the interview had little direct effect on the proportion of persons making any out-of-plan use. Of those highly satisfied with their medical care, 16 percent reported at least one instance of such use, while only a slightly higher proportion (21 percent) of those with low or moderate levels of satisfaction used providers and services outside GHA.

Figure 6.5   Race specific percentage distributions of reasons
for use of providers and services outside GHA

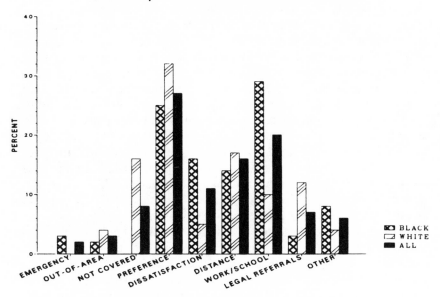

REASONS FOR OUT-OF-PLAN USE

Respondents were also asked for their reasons for out-of-plan use. Of interest here is whether such use was attributable to (1) circumstances ruling out GHA services (i.e., use for emergencies or by those outside the GHA service area at the time, or lack of coverage); (2) personal preferences sufficiently strong to overcome the financial disincentives involved (e.g., dissatisfaction with plan services, distance from plan facilities, or similar personal choices); or (3) factors extrinsic to the relationship between the plan and its members.

As to the first reason, a relatively small proportion of visits was attributed to emergencies (none by whites) and out-of-area visits, indicating that these were relatively insignificant (Figure 6.5). (For the present purpose, use reported for reasons of medical emergency was so classified, regardless of whether or not it was subsequently approved by GHA.) Services not covered by plan benefits accounted for a total of 8 percent of out-of-plan use; this reason was given by the white group only. Preference factors, on the other hand, appear a more substantial reason. A personal preference for a physician or other provider of services outside GHA accounted for 27 percent of all out-of-plan contacts, with a larger percentage of whites stating this as their reason (32 percent) than blacks (25 percent). An example of such use was out-of-plan visits to mental health practitioners (140 in all), 137 of which were made by whites, and 90 percent being associated with preference for providers outside of GHA. Dissatisfaction with the plan, whether with its physicians or staff, the appointment system, or other organizational aspects, appeared as a reason for 11 percent of out-of-plan use; it was stated three times as frequently by blacks than by whites (16 percent versus 5 percent; see also Table 4.7). If those contacts attributed to distance from GHA offices are included (16 percent, with little difference between racial groupings), over half of out-of-plan contacts in each race group can be attributed to the personal preference of the GHA members involved.

The additional reasons stated for out-of-plan contacts, i.e., that care was received at school or work and that respondents had been referred for services by a lawyer, relate at least partly to extrinsic factors. Care at school or work accounted for a fifth of total out-of-plan use, with a fairly large percentage of contacts reported by blacks (29 versus 10 percent for whites). This rather large proportion was probably associated with factors peculiar to this study population, which was comprised entirely of federal employees and their families. Federal agencies usually have occupational health units which offer a variety of health services to employees without charge, including periodic and other health examinations; immunizations for tetanus, polio, smallpox, and influenza; periodic disease detection programs for diabetes, cancer, defective hearing and vision, and other conditions; emergency treatment of illness and injury; and first aid or palliative treatment to enable the employee to complete the current work shift. Also, the District of Columbia Police and Fire Departments (whose members were federal employees and thus eligible for Federal Employees Health Benefits) required that medical care for their staff be obtained at the Police and Firemen's Clinic, with written approval required for exceptions. Those contacts described as suggested by a lawyer were probably an anomaly. Several respondents had been involved in automobile accidents and were being treated, on the advice of their lawyers, by specifically designated physicians, probably without cost to the patient. These persons, mainly whites, accounted for almost all of the visits in this category.

Overall, therefore, the largest single group of reasons for out-of-plan use can be attributed to the choice of GHA members to seek services or providers other than those offered by their plan. Although some overlap cannot be discounted, somewhat less than a third of contacts were apparently made for reasons extrinsic to the relationship between the plan and the members; in part these may have been for administrative reasons, and in part they were probably dictated by reasons of immediate convenience not involving financial outlays, such as the use of employee health clinics. Only a small proportion of contacts éxcluded choice entirely, i.e., were for medical emergencies.

SUMMARY AND CONCLUSIONS

Fourteen percent of all health care contacts by members of GHA were out of plan, and 20 percent of members made at least one out-of-plan contact during the survey year. These findings are entirely within the range reported in other studies (Scitovsky, Benham, and McCall, 1981; Hetherington, Hopkins, and Roemer, 1975; Greenlick, 1972; Bashshur, Metzner, and Worden, 1967; Williams, Trussell, and Elinson, 1964; Weinerman, 1964; Freidson, 1961; Wolfman, 1961). Only 4 percent of the hospitalizations reported for this period (100 in all) were not under GHA auspices, and it is apparent that this level of out-of-plan hospital use cannot have distorted the reported admission rates for GHA members. Therefore, any notion that such hospitalizations may have accounted for the substantial difference in hospital admission rates between GHA and BC-BS cannot be sustained.

Persons who made out-of-plan use tended to be in older age groups, to live in lower income families, and to be less knowledgeable about plan benefits. Differences by race were observed in types of and reasons for out-of-plan use, but overall, race-specific proportions of those reporting any out-of-plan use were not dissimilar. However, preference for other than GHA physicians was most often reported by whites, whereas dissatisfaction with GHA staff or services was a major reason for out-of-plan use stated by black GHA members. Whether a stated preference for other services and dissatisfaction with the services available are only different ways of justifying or explaining one's choice may be a moot question. The large proportion of out-of-plan use of mental health practitioners, on the other hand, which was reported almost entirely by the white component, indicates that different aspects of choice may have been involved for the two racial groups.

Whether out-of-plan use by GHA members, in terms of persons or volume, should be termed inappropriate is likewise a question of definition. If contacts made at work, for treatment not covered or obtained on the advice of lawyers, and for care outside the service area of GHA are discounted (about 45 percent of all out-of-plan contacts), less than a tenth of all contacts reported by GHA members were out-of-plan use of a type probably involving financial outlays beyond those normally incurred by members of a prepaid group practice plan with similar benefits. While it does appear that some of this use may be due to a lack of understanding on the part of recent GHA members of how to avail themselves of the services provided, the remainder may well represent an irreducible element of personal choice.

Table 6.1   Out-of-plan use in GHA: Number of plan members[a] making out-of-plan use and of out-of-plan contacts

Type of service	Number of persons			Number of contacts		
	All	Black	White	All	Black	White
Hospital	4	4	0	4	4	0
Emergency room	52	43	9	61	50	11
Physician visit	159	103	56	519	337	182
Nonphysician service	17	7	10	108	19	89
Mental health	9	1	8	140	3	137
Telephone consultation	12	8	3	14	11	4
Home visit	3	1	2	3	1	2
Vision examination	42	25	17	50	32	18
Total	258	163	95	899	457	442
Percent of all GHA persons	20	18	22			
Percent of all GHA contacts				14	15	13

[a]Contract holders and their covered dependents.

Table 6.2   Characteristics of GHA plan members making out-of-plan use

Characteristics	Percent using out-of-plan services
Sex	
Male	20
Female	19
Age (years)	
0 to 4	7
5 to 19	12
20 to 44	24
45 and over	30
Race	
Black	18
White	22
Family income	
Less than $15,000	24
$15,000 to $24,999	15
$25,000 or more	20
Educational level	
High school and some college	21
College	15
College and beyond	20
Plan knowledge	
Low	24
Moderate	19
High	15
Years in Plan	
3	26
3 or more	18
Satisfaction with care	
Low	21
Moderate	21
High	16

7

Health Care Expenditures: Annual Out-of-Pocket Expenses

Susan S. Jack and Samuel M. Meyers

The relative levels of out-of-pocket health care expenditures by the members of the two health plans were an important question in this study. The substantially lower hospital admission rates under GHA (see Chapter 2) would seem to warrant the expectation that GHA premium costs should have been lower than under BC-BS. On the other hand, any savings resulting from lower admission rates might well have been offset by the cost of the more comprehensive ambulatory benefits available to GHA members. Also, and aside from premiums, the cost of medical care includes direct out-of-pocket expenditures for services that are not or only partly covered by the benefit packages of the two plans. Here as well, expenditures should have been lower for GHA members because of first dollar coverage for most services, although the cost of out-of-plan use to GHA members would have to be considered. At the time the study was designed, little was known about such expenditures other than the premium expense, but information obtained in Phase II should help to clarify the relationship between out-of-pocket expenditures and type of health plan.

METHODS OF DATA COLLECTION AND ANALYSIS

In the following, the unit of analysis is the household or family covered by the respective contract. The sample comprised 480 contracts in BC-BS and 454 in GHA; single person contracts amounted to 29 percent in BC-BS and 35 percent in GHA. Health care expenditures for all covered persons in each household in the sample were obtained every month as part of the 12-month household survey (see Chapter 3 for survey procedures and response rates). Respondents were asked for any amounts expended during the month before the interview for the following range of services:

— Nursing home, rest home, or convalescent home

— Inpatient hospital stays

— Emergency room care

— Inpatient medical care billed by any physician

— Examinations for and costs of eyeglasses or contact lenses

— Visits to psychiatrists or other persons for emotional problems

— Visits to a physician's office, clinic, or laboratory

— Medical advice received from physicians over the telephone

— Home visits by physicians

— Services of other practitioners such as visiting nurses or physical therapists

— Ambulance services

— Prescription drugs or refills

— Medical items bought or rented, such as wheelchairs, crutches, hearing aids

— Other items or services

For every household, each type of service expense was summed for every month during which the household was in the survey, providing annual estimates of gross total service expenses. In addition, respondents were asked each month if they had received any monies or refunds as a result of claims filed with BC-BS, GHA, or other insurance carriers for expenditures incurred for any medical service. Reported refunds were then summed and subtracted from the gross total to obtain the total annual service expense. These expenditures for services are not directly related to specific instances of use but reflect totals actually spent by each contract holder for services, prescribed medicines, or equipment obtained during the survey year or for bills outstanding from the period prior to the survey year. Records of any bills unpaid at the end of the year were not obtained. Finally, premium deductions from salaries for 1973 (exclusive of employer contributions) were added to the service expense, yielding net annual household expenditures.

The expenditures of families not in the sample throughout the survey year were weighted according to their time in the survey to provide an estimate of total annual expenditures for the entire sample. Also, to enable meaningful plan comparisons, the data were standardized for race and contract type.

EXPENDITURES AND PATTERNS
OF DISBURSEMENTS

In interpreting the findings that follow, two sets of facts should be considered. First, the premiums of the two plans in 1973 were not strictly comparable. Aside from differences due to differences in benefits, the actuarial methods used in the calculation of the respective premiums were dissimilar. The GHA premium was based not only on the actual use by federal employees covered under GHA's high option federal contract, but also on the use of those covered by other GHA high option contracts; it primarily reflected the cost of obtaining medical care in the Washington, D.C. area in 1972. The BC-BS premium was based on the experience of all high option federal employees and dependents across the nation covered under the Government-Wide Service Benefit Plan and thus reflected the average cost of care in the United States at the time. If similar actuarial methods had been used in the two plans, the premiums might have been different from those observed. Second, the premiums represent only one year (1973) and no generalizations can be made about other years because of frequent changes in annual premiums at different rates. For example, the BC-BS premium increased by 19 percent from 1973 to 1974 (the year following the study) whereas the GHA premium remained the same (Table 7.1).

Total Expenditures

Total amounts expended under each plan for specific services, refunds, and premiums and their relative share of net expenditures are shown in Table 7.2. Apart from premiums, which amounted to 79 percent of GHA expenditures and 61 percent of those in BC-BS (means, $442.00 in GHA and $299.00 in BC-BS), the major difference between plans was in expenses for physician and other practitioner services ($98.71 for BC-BS and $15.14 for GHA). These accounted for 20 percent of expenditures in BC-BS and for 3 percent in GHA, a not unexpected difference in view of the benefit structure of the two plans. It should be noted that at least some of the expenses reported by GHA households in this category were attributable to out-of-plan use (see also Table 7.4 and Chapter 6). A statistically significant difference in service expenses between the two health plans was noted for only one other category, i.e., for vision examinations and eyeglasses or contact lenses ($29.93 for BC-BS and $20.75 for GHA), probably reflecting the coverage for vision examinations in GHA and the lack of such coverage in BC-BS.

The fifteenfold difference in refunds clearly reflects the plan benefit structures, in that BC-BS members could receive refunds for amounts paid for covered basic services when the provider did not participate in BC-BS, or for services covered as supplementary benefits after appropriate deductibles were met; GHA members received a partial refund only for prescription drug expenditures after the deductible had been met, and for out-of-pocket expenses for approved services received outside the GHA service area. In all, the mean out-of-pocket service expense after refunds was higher in BC-BS than in GHA ($190.39 as compared to $117.71). However, as GHA households spent almost a quarter as much as their premiums for services either not covered by the plan (e.g., glasses, podiatrists) or for covered services that were obtained from sources outside the prepaid group practice plan, GHA mean net expenditures including premiums were higher than those in BC-BS by a statistically significant margin (means, $559.71 and $489.39).

Expenditures by Contract Type

A comparison of expenses for different contract types showed differences not only between expenditures by single persons and families but also in the patterns between plans and the ranking for each category (Table 7.3). Regardless of contract status, physician and related expenses were the largest single service expense in BC-BS, followed by prescription drugs; in GHA the latter ranked first and physician expenses third for single-person contracts, and fourth for family contracts. Overall, the net expenditure per year of single BC-BS subscribers exceeded that of single GHA subscribers only slightly, while their out-of-pocket service expenses were almost three times those in GHA (mean, $109.41 and $40.92, respectively); for family contracts, the difference in annual net expenditure between BC-BS and GHA was about $100 (mean, $594.88 and $702.29, respectively), while BC-BS out-of-pocket service expenses were only 1.5 times those in GHA ($228.88 and $153.29).

An interesting difference between plans is the expense for mental health practitioners. It was high ($25) and ranked third for BC-BS single members, and low ($1) and sixth in rank for those in GHA; at $5 and $32, respectively, this type of expense ranked fifth for family contracts in BC-BS but second in GHA, for a sixfold difference in mean expense, reflecting both more restricted coverage for such services under the prepaid group practice plan and the relatively high use by its members (see also Chapter 5, Table 5.1).

GHA single members, then, apparently paid a premium and little else (about $3 a month). Out-of-pocket expenditures by single BC-BS members exceeded those of BC-BS families in two categories, notably for mental health practitioners, and their mean net expenditures were as much as 44 percent of BC-BS families. In GHA, this fraction was 36 percent, with families having mean expenses of $153 above the premium.

TOTAL EXPENDITURES AND
OUT-OF-PLAN USE IN GHA

As pointed out in Chapter 6, 20 percent of GHA enrollees made at least one out-of-plan medical contact during the survey year. While no financial outlay was required in about a fifth of these contacts, out-of-plan use in general entails additional outlays and thus was expected to increase total GHA service expense and decrease plan differences in net expenditure. Total service expense and annual net expenditure of GHA households both with and without out-of-plan use were, therefore, compared with expenses of BC-BS households. For this purpose, GHA households were divided into families where no member reported any out-of-plan use, and those where at least one reported any instance of out-of-plan use. (Considered at the family or household level, about 43 percent of all GHA households reported at least some out-of-plan use.) Overall, the mean total service expense for GHA households without any out-of-plan use was about $45.00 less than for those with some out-of-plan use (Table 7.4), but while a comparison of net annual expenditures of the former group with BC-BS expenses reduced the margin of difference, it did not eliminate it (GHA, $538.89; BC-BS, $489.39), although it was no longer statistically significant.

A similar reduction in annual net expenditure by contract type was noted for those who used only services covered by GHA, although it was less for family contracts, where the difference between plans remained statistically significant (Table 7.5). For single contracts, on the other hand, where no overall difference between plans in annual net expenditure was observed in Table 7.3, a statistically significant difference existed for those with and without out-of-plan use, while the margin between GHA members without such use and those in BC-BS increased ($237.29 compared to $262.41 for BC-BS).

SUMMARY AND CONCLUSIONS

Annual net out-of-pocket expenditures (including premiums) of GHA families were 14 percent higher in 1973 compared with those in BC-BS, though, as noted, the actuarial methods for calculating the premiums were dissimilar. Little difference was noted between the plans for single contracts; for family contracts, GHA expenditures were 18 percent higher. Out-of-pocket expenditures for services were substantially lower for GHA families. That this difference between the plans was not as large as expected was due mainly to expenses connected with out-of-plan use and for services not covered by the GHA. But even when out-of-plan expenditures were eliminated, the net expenditures of GHA households in general remained somewhat higher than in BC-BS, due largely to the substantially higher GHA premium. The reasons for this higher GHA premium in 1973 are not immediately apparent and could not be investigated in this study. Premium rates are the result of complex actuarial and accounting procedures and include such factors as the use and cost of medical services, both past and expected, financial reserves, efficiency and effectiveness of operations, federal requirements, and marketing strategies. GHA was not alone among prepaid plans participating in the Federal Employees Health Benefits Program in having higher premiums than BC-BS. In 1973, of 26 comprehensive plans (the federal government's name for prepaid plans) 18 had higher premiums for family contracts than BC-BS, and 10 had higher premiums than BC-BS for single contracts (U.S. Civil Service Commission, 1974).

These findings are not in agreement with those of Luft (1978, 1981) that out-of-pocket expenditures for medical care are lower in prepaid plans than in the more conventional insurance plans. As Luft points out, his findings were based on a limited number of studies, none of which examined the experience of the Federal Employees Health Benefits Program. Also, the studies reviewed were conducted mainly in California, where the marketing and competitive environment may have been different from that in the Washington area. Finally, the group health plans involved in these studies were under the auspices of Kaiser-Permanente and are not necessarily representative of all prepaid group practice plans.

Table 7.1   BC–BS and GHA Premiums for 1973 and 1974[a]

| | | BC–BS | | | | | GHA | | | |
| | | Paid by employee | | Paid by employer | | | Paid by employee | | Paid by employer | |
Contract type	Total premium	Amount	%	Amount	%	Total premium	Amount	%	Amount	%
Single										
1973	$258.70	$153.66	59	$105.04	41	$318.76	$213.72	67	$105.04	33
1974	308.88	166.14	54	142.74	46	318.76	176.02	55	142.74	45
Family										
1973	631.28	366.86	58	264.42	42	813.02	548.60	67	264.42	33
1974	753.22	397.80	53	355.42	47	813.02	457.60	56	355.42	44

[a]The year following the Phase II study.

Source: Rate Sheet, U.S. Civil Service Commission, Bureau of Retirement, Insurance and Occupational Health, 1974.

Table 7.2   Out-of-pocket health care expenditures: Mean annual expenses for services and premiums by BC–BS and GHA households, adjusted for race and contract type

| | BC–BS | | | | GHA | | |
Expense category	Mean ($)	Rank	Percent of total		Mean ($)	Rank	Percent of total
Physicians and other health practitioners[a]	98.71	1	20	*	15.14	4	3
Prescribed medicines	51.63	2	10		44.69	1	8
Vision examinations, fitting of eyeglasses or contact lenses	29.93	3	6	*	20.75	3	4
Medical equipment	12.52	4	3		4.70	6	1
Mental health services	11.27	5	2		22.19	2	4
Other[b]	5.44	6	1		4.86	7	1
Emergency room services	2.71	7	1		1.82	8	—
Hospital services	2.53	8	1		5.11	5	1
Gross total service expenses	214.74		44	*	119.26		22
Less refund	24.35		5	*	1.55		—
Total service expense	190.39		39	*	117.71		22
Premium	299.00		61		442.00		79
Net expenditure	489.39		100	*	559.71		100

[a]Other practitioners include among others optometrists, podiatrists, nutritionists, and physical therapists.

[b]Nursing home, ambulance services, miscellaneous.

—Less than 1 percent.

*P ≤ .05.

Table 7.3 Annual out-of-pocket health care expenditures and contract type: Race adjusted mean expenses for services and premiums by single persons and families

Expense category	Single Contracts						Family Contracts					
	BC-BS			GHA			BC-BS			GHA		
	Mean Expense ($)	Rank	Percent	Mean Expense ($)	Rank	Percent	Mean Expense ($)	Rank	Percent	Mean Expense ($)	Rank	Percent
Physicians and other health practitioners[a]	51.15	1	19 *	6.85	3	3	121.07	1	20 *	19.02	4	3
Prescribed medicines	34.44	2	13 *	22.61	1	9	59.68	2	10	55.03	1	7
Vision examinations, fitting of eyeglasses or contact lenses	20.11	4	8 *	7.82	2	3	34.54	3	6	26.81	3	4
Medical equipment	2.48	6	1	2.92	4	1	17.22	4	3	5.54	7	1
Mental health services	24.94	3	9	1.07	6	—	4.86	5	1 *	32.09	2	5
Other[b]	8.14	5	3	1.30	5	—	4.18	6	1	6.25	6	1
Emergency room services	1.38	7	1	0.41	7	—	3.34	8	—	2.49	8	—
Hospital services	0.69	8	—	0.00	8	—	3.39	7	—	7.40	5	1
Gross total service expenses	144.33		54 *	42.98		17	248.28		41 *	154.63		22
Less refund	34.92		13 *	2.06		1	19.40		3 *	1.34		—
Total service expense	109.41		41 *	40.92		16	228.88		38 *	153.29		22
Premium	154.00		59	214.00		84	366.00		62	549.00		78
Net expenditure	262.41		100	254.92		100	594.88		100 *	702.29		100

[a]Other practitioners include among others optometrists, podiatrists, nutritionists, and physical therapists.

[b]Nursing home, ambulance services, miscellaneous.

—Less than 1 percent.

*P ≤ .05.

Table 7.4   Annual out-of-pocket health care expenditures and out-of-plan use: Mean total expenses for services and premiums, adjusted for race and contract type

Expense ($)	BC–BS		All	GHA No out-of-plan use	Some out-of-plan use
Total service expense	190.39	*	117.71	96.89**	143.38***
Premium	299.00		442.00	442.00	442.00
Net expenditure	489.39	*	559.71	538.89	585.37***

*P ≤ .05.

**P ≤ .05, BC–BS and GHA, no out-of-plan use.

***P ≤ .05, GHA, no out-of-plan and some out-of-plan use.

Table 7.5 Annual out-of-pocket health care expenditures, out-of-plan use, and contract type: Race adjusted mean total expenses for services and premiums, by contract type

	Single				Family			
		GHA				GHA		
Expense ($)	BC-BS	All	No out-of-plan use	Some out-of-plan use	BC-BS	All	No out-of-plan use	Some out-of-plan use
Total service expense	108.41 *	40.92	23.29	69.49***	228.88 *	153.29	131.38**	178.00
Premium	154.00	214.00	214.00	214.00	366.00	549.00	549.00	549.00
Net expenditure	262.41	254.92	237.29	283.49***	594.88 *	702.29	680.38**	727.00

*P ≤ .05.

**P ≤ .05, BC–BS and GHA, no out-of-plan use.

***P ≤ .05, GHA, no out-of-plan and some out-of-plan use.

8

Diagnostic-Specific Assessment of Care

Samuel M. Meyers and Donald C. Riedel

Phase I of this study has documented the differences in hospital admission rates between persons enrolled in either Group Health Association, Inc. (GHA) or in Blue Cross and Blue Shield (BC-BS), the government-wide service benefit plan. Phase II examined in detail the characteristics of the members enrolled in each plan, their patterns of ambulatory use, and whether these variables in concert would account for the differences in hospital admissions observed in Phase I. Phase III presents a more focused analysis of patterns of patient and physician behavior associated with a specific episode of illness resulting in hospitalization. The comparisons are between members of GHA and BC-BS who were hospitalized with similar diagnoses, and the analysis centers on the period prior to and during their hospitalization.

Numerous studies on hospital use had been reported in the literature when this study was conceived and carried out. For example, some investigators had studied hospital records to reveal changes in patient composition by age, sex, or diagnostic category and high and low users of hospital services at a certain point in time (Lerner, 1963, 1961, 1960; Sinai and Patton, 1949). Some made systematic comparisons of the use of hospitals among several areas with known bed and physician resources (Roemer, 1961a,b; Klarman, 1963). Many other studies compared use of hospitals by members of two types of medical practices — group practice with prepayment and fee-for-service in private practice (Hastings et al., 1973; Shipman, Lampman, and Miyamoto, 1962; United Steel Workers of America, 1960; Anderson and Sheatsley, 1959; Darsky, Sinai, and Axelrod, 1958; Densen, Balamuth, and Shapiro, 1958; Williams, Trussell, and Elinson, 1957). Control or experimental groups in service benefit plans were employed to test if providing comprehensive ambulatory care would reduce hospital use (Hill and Veney, 1970; Kelly, 1965). Hospital use has also been analyzed in the light of criteria developed by medical committees of various specialties and applied to the hospital records of persons actually hospitalized (Payne and Lyons, 1972; Riedel and Fitzpatrick, 1964; Fitzpatrick, Riedel, and Payne, 1962). Cartwright (1964) reviewed patterns of hospital use on the basis of patient and physician interviews, viewing the hospital as a community resource influenced by interrelated medical and social factors. Also, social surveys of hospital patients and of physicians involved in their admissions and discharges have been employed to depict hospitalization as a progression of interrelated events (Anderson and Sheatsley, 1967).

These studies confirmed that both hospitalization rates and length of hospital stays vary under the influence of a number of factors, but no single study explored the range of these factors to account for the variations found. Furthermore, while some studies pioneered in evaluating hospitalizations but restricted themselves to medical criteria and hospital records, others depended too heavily on judgments of patients and physicians.

Phase III of the present study was designed as an attempt to fuse many of these approaches. It compares the complex of care received by hospitalized members of GHA and BC-BS and examines hospitalization not as an isolated occurrence but as one of a progression of events in patient care over the entire period of an illness. Illness behavior was not viewed in a single dimension of time but in sequential time frames, and both the medical criteria approach and social survey methods were incorporated to seek out factors related to the various decisions made in an illness episode resulting in hospitalization. Finally, analysis on a diagnostic-specific basis and a relatively homogeneous sample including only federal employees and their families covered under high-option plans made it possible to examine in considerable detail, and in two types of practice settings, episodes of illness that were similar in relative medical care need but without variation in hospital benefits.

The study also sought to answer a number of specific questions. Did patterns of medical care under two health plans differ for patients hospitalized with the same diagnosis? Were differences found mainly in the prehospital stage or in the hospital? What were the factors that accounted for these differences? Did they lie in the personal characteristics and the illness behavior of the BC-BS and GHA sample? In the characteristics and type of medical practice of the physicians attending the two groups of patients? In the types of hospitals in which the patients were hospitalized? Or were differences due to a combination of these variables, some having more importance than others? Finally, were there differences in the severity of illness at admission and, according to criteria generally accepted by the medical community, in appropriateness of admission and hospital care by providers in the two plans?

PROCEDURES AND METHODS

Selection of Diagnostic Categories

With this multitude of considerations, a small number of diagnostic categories were selected. Specific criteria for selection included differences in admission rates for each category between the two plans as established in Phase I; availability of acceptable evaluation criteria and standardized medical record abstract forms; a likelihood of differences in patterns of ambulatory care, as evident from earlier studies and Phase II, between prepaid group practice and service benefit plans; and the involvement of a range of medical specialties in the care and treatment of patients. The following 13 diagnostic categories were selected initially (see Table 8.1):

— Appendicitis

— Cystic disease of the breast

— Nonmetastatic malignant neoplasms of the breast

— Diabetes mellitus

— Diseases of the gallbladder and biliary duct

— Arteriosclerotic and hypertensive heart disease

— Acute myocardial infarction

— Pneumonia

— Hyperplasia of tonsils and adenoids

— Uterine fibroids

— Disorders of menstruation

— Urinary tract infections

— Benign prostatic hypertrophy and prostatitis

Several pairs of related diagnostic categories were selected because the presenting symptoms are often the same in each diagnosis within each pair, and the correct diagnosis can be made only after final definition by the physician after extensive testing and/or during hospitalization. In both cystic disease and malignant neoplasms of the breast, the presenting symptom is a lesion or lump in the breast. In uterine fibroids and disorders of menstruation, unusual menstrual bleeding is most often the presenting symptom, while in men with benign prostatic hypertrophy and prostatitis, a urinary tract infection may be the presenting symptom. Thus, the pattern of care in each pair may be similar at first, but differs subsequently. For the prehospital period, it was intended to treat each pair as one category to obtain a more realistic assessment of patient behavior and admission patterns prior to diagnosis.

For patients discharged in each of the 13 categories specified above, complete sets of data were collected. However, three categories were subsequently eliminated from analysis: disorders of menstruation, urinary tract infections, and hypertrophy of the prostate and prostatitis. The last two were excluded because the small number of cases in GHA made meaningful comparisons impossible; disorders of menstruation were excluded because of the unavailability of an acceptable set of criteria for assessing appropriateness of care, and because the known, extensive use of an "in and out" surgical facility by GHA physicians for patients in this category, coupled with lack of knowledge concerning the use of similar facilities by BC-BS physicians, complicated the interpretation of any differences noted.

Survey Methods

Data Sources

The data for Phase III were obtained from five sources. Interviews with patients discharged from a hospital during the study period in one of the selected diagnostic categories were conducted in person with the patient, or with a proxy if the patient was a minor, too ill, or deceased. The sampling frame was the population of members of the two health plans and their dependents discharged from hospital during the survey period (August 1973–July 1974); it thus differs from that in both Phases I and II.

Hospital records for the discharged patients were abstracted on forms developed at the Yale-New Haven Hospital (1974). The abstracts included demographic data, admission and final discharge diagnoses, reasons for current admission, admission history, physical examination and consultation findings, surgical and diagnostic procedures performed, summary of hospital course, discharge information, and disposition on discharge.

Personal interviews were conducted with physicians identified by respondents as having first suggested hospitalization and/or arranged for hospital admission, and/or being mainly responsible for in-hospital care. Depending upon the diagnostic category, more than one physician may have been identified by the respondent as being involved in the care provided. These interviews obtained information both on patients treated or referred and on physician characteristics. Published sources were used to obtain characteristics of those physicians who could not be interviewed (American Medical Association, 1974). The characteristics of the hospitals to which the patients were admitted were likewise obtained from published sources (American Hospital Association, 1974; American Medical Association, 1969, 1967).

Sampling

Approximately 200 cases per diagnostic category were required for each plan to obtain a sufficiently large sample for analytical purposes; this number was based on assumptions concerning the probable size of differences between plans and the levels of statistical significance to be used in evaluating these differences. For paired diagnoses, 200 cases were considered sufficient for each pair, with the number selected for each diagnosis within a pair to be based on its proportion in the total number of cases for both categories combined. Because of anticipated losses due to ineligibility, inability to locate prospective respondents, or patient refusal to grant an interview, the sample target was set at 230 cases per diagnostic category. Because of the large number of discharges in each of the selected categories, sampling of patients was required for BC-BS; for GHA, all cases discharged from hospital with the selected diagnoses were included in the study, as information provided by GHA during the design stage indicated that the total number of discharges available for analysis in each diagnostic category would be considerably less than 230. While the number of GHA cases could have been increased by extending the data collection period, this approach was ruled out for a number of technical and practical reasons. As a result, the relatively small number of GHA patients available for analysis in some of the diagnostic categories tends to restrict the conclusions that can be drawn.

Patients were interviewed approximately six weeks after hospital discharge to minimize recall problems, to allow time for sufficient recovery for an interview, and to provide for reporting on posthospital care. The sample period was from August 1973 through July 1974. All GHA cases discharged during this period were included on a continuous basis. A systematic sampling procedure was developed for continuous sampling of BC-BS cases, with a different sampling fraction for each diagnosis because of expected differences in the number of discharges in each diagnostic category. All claims for payment submitted to the local BC-BS plan by local hospitals were examined on a weekly basis. Claims for which the first recorded discharge diagnosis fell into one of the selected diagnostic categories were included in the sample, provided that the contract holder or subscriber lived within the study area (the D.C. metropolitan area) and was an active employee of the federal government or the District of Columbia at the time the claim was submitted. As GHA used the same fiscal intermediary, it was possible to have GHA hospital claims screened by the same staff, ensuring that GHA patients in the appropriate diagnostic categories would be selected on the basis of the same criteria and methods.

After selection of the claims for each week, they were further screened for eligibility, and ineligible claims, e.g., by patients who had retired or who had questionable diagnoses, were eliminated. Remaining claims were numbered sequentially throughout the sampling period, with a unique sequence of numbers for each diagnostic category. BC-BS claims were sampled according to the sampling fraction. Sampling was monitored closely because of the crudeness of original estimates of discharges within each of the selected diagnostic categories, and periodic adjustments were made in the sampling fractions to take into account revised projections of total discharges and to ensure that the targeted samples would be obtained.

Survey Instruments

The overall development of the survey instruments was based on earlier work by Anderson and Sheatsley (1967).

Patient Questionnaire. Information was obtained on sociodemographic characteristics of the patients; the early history of the condition related to the episode of illness; contacts with various physicians during the episode, among them the first physician seen, the physician who first suggested hospitalization, and the attending physician during the inpatient period; delays in hospitalization, if any; patient perception of the severity of illness during the episode and the presence or absence of social dysfunction; outpatient treatment; satisfaction with care received in the hospital; worries about cost of hospital care; and posthospital care.

Since the focus of this phase of the study was a specific episode of illness eventually leading to hospitalization, it was essential to establish an exact starting date for each episode. Precise determination of this date was complicated in some cases by the particular circumstances of the illness that led to hospitalization and by some conditions of long standing. For emergency admissions, i.e., for those instances where patients were admitted to the hospital on the day they first saw a physician, the starting date of the episode was considered equal to the admission date. For patients with conditions of long standing such as diabetes or arteriosclerotic heart disease, the starting date was established by asking the patient when ". . . this most recent trouble started that brought you to the hospital this time" or, if there was no recent trouble, "When did you decide to do something about the condition this time?" For conditions of relatively recent onset, the starting date was the date when the patient first saw a physician about the condition, and for patients who had been hospitalized previously for the same condition, the episode excluded that hospitalization.

Hospital Record Abstracts. A different medical record abstract form was developed for each diagnostic category so as to capture all relevant data concerning events related to admission to the hospital. The following data categories were recorded:

- Patient identification
- Length of stay
- Previous admissions and discharge diagnoses
- Reasons for admission
- Admission history
- Consultations and physical examinations
- Surgical procedures
- Diagnostic tests
- Discharge information
- Disposition on discharge

Each form was designed to allow application of pre-established criteria for evaluation of appropriateness of admission, services received, and length of stay, including provision for definition of any concomitant or complicating disorders. The abstractors were nurses familiar with the record systems and idiosyncracies of notation employed in the hospitals where the sampled patients were interned; they were trained for the abstracting task by a nurse-supervisor with many years of experience in developing record abstracts and the application of evaluation criteria.

Physician Questionnaires. Two physician questionnaires were administered, one focusing on practice and professional characteristics, the other on the care provided to each patient. The first questionnaire elicited information on staff appointments in hospitals, primary practice arrangements, hours devoted to various types of patient care and other professional activities, referral practices, continuing education, practice staffing patterns, length of time in practice, completed residencies, and board certification status.

The second questionnaire centered on the medical care provided to the patient and was composed of four sections. The first inquired into the period prior to hospitalization, with questions designed to obtain information on patient history, preliminary diagnoses, medicine and treatments prescribed, and recommendations for hospitalization. The second section inquired into reasons for hospitalization, including the rationale for recommending admission, assessment of the urgency and necessity of hospitalization, whether the illness could have been treated on an outpatient basis, and reasons for delays in hospitalization, if any. The third section dealt with hospital inpatient care and included questions about medical procedures ordered, physician satisfaction with staff performance in carrying out procedures, discharge planning, and nonmedical reasons, if any, for longer than expected lengths of stay. Finally, a number of questions on posthospital care were asked.

Data Collection

Field Procedures. Cases included in the household survey sample were forwarded to the field staff. If the discharge date was less than six weeks from the sample date, the case was held until six weeks had elapsed before it was assigned to a trained professional interviewer, who either interviewed the person listed on the claim or the proxy. Respondents were asked to sign permission forms authorizing both abstracting of the hospital records for the episode of illness discussed in the interview, and the contacting of physicians identified by respondents as having provided care during the episode. After completion of the patient interviews, the corresponding hospital record was abstracted by a specially recruited and trained group of professional nurses. The case was then assigned for physician interview, wherever possible by the same interviewer who had conducted the patient interview. Physicians were offered an honorarium for completion of an interview.

Completion Rates. Table 8.2 shows the assignment and completion rates for interviews with patients and physicians and for the hospital abstracts. For the diagnostic categories analyzed, the overall patient interview completion rate was substantially the same for both plans (88.5 percent for BC-BS and 89.4 percent for GHA). These rates varied somewhat by diagnostic category, ranging from 97.5 percent for gallbladder patients to 83.3 percent for breast cancer and diabetes mellitus in GHA, and from 91.7 percent for hyperplasia of tonsils and adenoids to 85 percent for diabetes mellitus in BC-BS. Response rates for breast cancer, uterine fibroids, and heart disease tended to be relatively low in both plans. Of a total of 1,863 patient records assigned for abstracting, 95 percent overall were acceptable (80 percent of cases assigned for interviewing), with little difference noted between the plans. About 9 percent of patients who had completed an interview refused to give permission to abstract the hospital record; this refusal rate as well varied by diagnostic category. Overall, by the end of abstracting phase, both patient interview and hospital abstracts were available for about 75 percent of cases initially assigned for patient interviews; the largest noncompletion rates were observed for heart disease, breast cancer, and uterine fibroids.

Since provider information was sought from the physician or physicians who first suggested hospitalization, arranged for hospitalization, and/or provided care during hospitalization, a precise estimate of the completion rate for physician interviews was difficult. In nonsurgical cases, the same physician usually filled these three roles, but in surgical cases, more than one physician tended to be involved and was assigned for interview, particularly for cases of appendicitis and diseases of the gallbladder and biliary duct. This should be borne in mind with regard to both the numbers of physicians interviewed and the overall completion rate for matched physician/patient interviews (84.4 percent for BC-BS and 85.7 for GHA). The response rate for GHA physicians tended to be higher in most diagnostic categories because they had agreed to participate prior to the study, and all granted at least one interview, with a final completion rate of 89 percent. Prior agreement by BC-BS physicians could not be obtained, and their initial response rate was 89 percent or an 81 percent final completion rate.

Quality Checks. In both the patient and physician interview phases, 15 percent of each interviewer's cases were verified by the field supervisor. If the interviewer's work was not up to standard, additional training was given. Continued substandard work was ground for dismissal. In addition to supervisory monitoring, all interviews were edited by trained editors. Problems were routed back to the supervisors and then to the interviewers for correction. For the abstract phase, a random sample of each nurse abstractor's work was reabstracted independently by another nurse. Differences noted were discussed and resolved, and if necessary additional training was scheduled.

Data Reduction

Computer files were created for each diagnostic category. The final number of patients in each file is shown in Table 8.2. Each file contained the data derived from the interview with the patient as well as, if available, the hospital record abstract data, physician data on care provided, and the practice and professional characteristics of the physician or physicians involved in the episode of care. Missing data for physicians with several patients in the sample were obtained by using information available from interviews relating to one of their patients for the remaining patients. If the physician had not been interviewed at all, whether because of patient refusal to permit an interview or the physician's refusal to grant one, information available from published sources was added (American Medical Association, 1974).

DATA ANALYSIS

Because of the range of questions addressed in Chapters 9–13, the analysis is based on different subsets of the data, although the patient is the unit of analysis throughout. In Chapters 9 and 10, which describe the discharged patient sample and the providers of care, as well as aspects of prehospital care provided during the episode of illness, most data were derived from patient and physician interviews. In Chapters 11 to 13, which examine aspects of inpatient care, the basic data set comprises the subset of cases where both the practice and professional characteristics of the attending physician in the hospital and medical record abstract data were available. Thus, the number of patients available for analysis in these chapters is relatively small in some of the diagnostic categories; also, the numbers used in analysis may vary among tables because of the difference in completion rates mentioned above (see Table 8.2); all relevant available data were used in each analysis. Percentage distributions may not in all cases add to 100 because of rounding.

Methods of Analysis

The basic analytical technique used in Chapters 9–12 is a simple cross-tabulation of variables. In addition, partial correlations were used in Chapter 13 to assess the relationship between plan type and the dependent variable, which in that analysis was the number of unmet criteria of care, while controlling for the effects of other variables. While each of the diagnostic categories required separate analysis, the results are presented across all categories.

In interpreting the results, various tests of significance were used as required by the data, such as Student's t-test, z-test, chi square, Fisher's exact test of probabilities when the numbers in a fourfold table were small, and the Kolmogorov-Smirnov test. Differences between the plans were considered to be statistically significant at $P \leq .05$.

Even though the GHA study population comprised the entire population of persons discharged from hospital during the survey year in all of the selected diagnostic categories, they were assumed to be a sample of cases from a larger universe defined by time. Thus, the calculation of the standard error of the difference between means or percentages required an error term for both BC-BS and GHA, for in the absence of this assumption, there would have been no sampling error for the GHA population and the standard error of the difference between means or percentages would have contained the error term for the BC-BS sample only. This assumption rendered the test more conservative, i.e., differences between plans were judged statistically significant less often.

Limitations of the Data

Cannell and Fowler (1965, 1963) have demonstrated that under-reporting of information increases with the time between an event and the interview reporting it. The data may thus be affected by recall errors and omissions. While every effort was made to interview patients approximately six weeks after their discharge from the hospital, this was not always possible. Sometimes hospital claims were submitted to BC-BS months after the patient had been discharged from the hospital, or it was difficult to find the patient or to schedule an appointment for the interview. Moreover, it was recognized that while respondents probably gave reasonably accurate information about events close to the interview, they might have reported less accurately on those in the more distant past, e.g., those connected with the onset of the condition in cases of long standing. Because of these variations in time between discharge and patient interview, posthospital experiences were not comparable and thus are excluded from analysis.

Recall problems also existed for the physicians because they were not interviewed until the abstract had been completed; this could have been within one month following patient interview or as much as six months later, depending upon the availability of the hospital record to the abstractor. Physicians were encouraged, however, to consult their own records about the care provided to the particular patient.

Furthermore, as in any study concentrating on a subset of the population selected by nonrandom methods, questions must be raised concerning the generalizability of the findings. These questions extend beyond the study limitations outlined in Chapter 1. Together, the diagnostic categories represent a fraction of the estimated total hospitalized population in each plan for 1973–1974 (approximately 18 percent in BC-BS and 9 percent in GHA). The fraction would have been slightly larger if the three categories originally included in the study design had been retained, but the group would still represent only a minority of the patient population, whether counted by patients or diagnostic entities.

However, the inclusion of the various categories described earlier in this chapter was justified by the purpose of Phase III, which was to provide diagnostic-specific descriptions and evaluations of patterns of provider and patient behavior in the two plans. In conjunction with the data collected in Phases I and II, the data which follow add yet another dimension to our understanding of the process of care and impact of the two plans on the patients served. Their strength must be assessed in relation to these other findings and in terms of increasing our ability to comprehend the whole.

Table 8.1 Diagnostic categories used in Phase III analyses of hospital use

| Category | ICDA–8 codes included[a] | |
	Number	Description
Cystic disease of the breast[b]	610	Chronic cystic disease of breast
Cancer of the breast	174	Malignant neoplasm of breast
Uterine fibroids[b]	218	Uterine fibroma
Diseases of menstruation[b]	626	Disorders of menstruation
Diabetes mellitus[b]	250	Diabetes mellitus
	962.3	Adverse effects of insulin and antidiabetic agents
Myocardial infarction	410	Acute myocardial infarction
Arteriosclerotic and hypertensive heart disease	400	Malignant hypertension
	401	Essential benign hypertension
	402	Hypertensive heart disease
	411	Other acute and subacute forms of ischemic heart disease
	412	Chronic ischemic heart disease
	413	Angina pectoris
	414	Asymptomatic ischemic heart disease
Pneumonia[b]	480	Viral pneumonia
	481	Pneumococcal pneumonia
	482	Other bacterial pneumonia
	483	Pneumonia due to other specified organism
	484	Acute interstitial pneumonia
	485	Bronchopneumonia, unspecified
	486	Pneumonia, unspecified
Hypertrophy of tonsils and adenoids[b]	500	Hypertrophy of tonsils and adenoids
Appendicitis[b]	540	Acute appendicitis
	541	Appendicitis, unqualified
	542	Other appendicitis
Diseases of gall bladder and biliary ducts[b]	211.5	Benign neoplasm of liver and biliary passages
	574	Cholelithiasis
	575	Cholecystitis and cholangitis
	576	Other diseases of gall bladder and biliary ducts
Urinary tract infections	590	Infections of kidney
Hyperplasia of prostate and prostatitis[b]	600	Hyperplasia of prostate
	601	Prostatitis

[a]National Center for Health Statistics. 1967. *International Classification of Diseases, Adapted for Use in the United States.* Eighth Revision. DHEW Publication no. (PHS) 1693. Washington: Government Printing Office.

[b]Corresponds directly to a diagnostic category used in Phase I.

Table 8.2   Phase III patient interviews, medical record abstracts, and physician interviews: Completion rates for a sample of discharged patients in BC-BS and GHA

Diagnostic category	Patient interviews			Medical record abstracts[b] (%)	Matched physician/patient interviews	
	Assigned (n)	Com-pleted (%)	Used[a] (%)		Assigned (n)	Com-pleted (%)
Appendicitis						
BC–BS	(242)	90.0	87.9	80.0	(231)	85.3
GHA	(39)	92.3	89.7	76.9	(36)	100.0
Cystic breast disease						
BC–BS	(192)	87.5	85.4	78.6	(167)	85.4
GHA	(48)	93.8	93.8	83.3	(43)	100.0
Breast cancer						
BC–BS	(87)	87.0	69.0	69.0	(65)	84.6
GHA	(18)	83.3	72.2	55.6	(10)	100.0
Diabetes mellitus						
BC–BS	(246)	85.0	78.9	82.9	(188)	86.7
GHA	(18)	83.3	83.3	72.2	(16)	81.3
Diseases of gall bladder and biliary duct						
BC–BS	(272)	90.1	89.0	82.4	(283)	85.2
GHA	(40)	97.5	97.5	85.0	(44)	97.7
Arteriosclerotic and hyper-tensive heart disease and myocardial infarction						
BC–BS	(354)	88.0	81.0	72.0	(269)	91.4
GHA	(43)	88.4	81.4	74.4	(33)	87.9
Pneumonia						
BC–BS	(187)	90.9	90.4	82.9	(159)	81.8
GHA	(20)	85.0	65.0	55.0	(15)	93.3
Hyperplasia of tonsils and adenoids						
BC–BS	(121)	91.7	91.7	88.4	(118)	83.4
GHA	(78)	91.9	90.5	82.4	(71)	63.4
Uterine fibroids						
BC–BS	(217)	86.2	87.1[c]	74.4[c]	(159)	81.8
GHA	(84)	88.1	85.7	71.4	(60)	80.0
Diagnostic categories analyzed						
BC–BS	(1,918)	88.5	84.7	77.3	(1,629)	84.4
GHA	(388)	89.4	86.1	75.0	(328)	85.7
Diagnostic categories unanalyzed[d]						
BC–BS	(468)	87.0	81.4	71.8	(333)	79.3
GHA	(54)	83.3	79.6	61.1	(37)	89.2
All						
BC–BS	(2,386)	88.2	84.0	76.2	(1,973)	83.5
GHA	(438)	89.5	86.1	74.2	(365)	86.0

[a]Excludes patients with diagnoses found to be inappropriate after examination of the hospital record.

[b]Accepted for analysis.

[c]Some patients with disorders of menstruation found to have uterine fibroids.

[d]Disorders of menstruation; urinary tract infections; hyperplasia of the prostate and prostatitis.

9

Patient and Provider Characteristics

Thelma Myint

The findings in Phases I and II led to several assumptions regarding the characteristics of the patients studied, and of the providers of care and the structure of their practice in the third phase of the study:

- Some differences in the age and sex distribution of the patient samples would be expected in accordance with the composition of the populations at risk, but to a lesser extent than for other demographic and socioeconomic variables, as the analysis in this phase was specific to diagnostic categories.
- The physicians providing care to the GHA population should have constituted a more homogeneous group than the physicians caring for BC-BS patients, particularly with regard to age, qualification, and related professional aspects. An exception to this were surgical specialists, who were not part of GHA staff at the time.
- Organizational arrangements in GHA would have restricted its physicians to hospitalizing patients in a relatively small number of institutions; in contrast, BC-BS physicians could be expected to have had admitting privileges in a greater number of hospitals.
- Referral patterns would vary between the plans, as direct access to specialists in GHA was limited to pediatricians, gynecologists, and internists. On the other hand, referrals to modal specialists should have been higher in GHA.
- Because prepaid group practices are known to encourage and foster continuing educational activities and formal and informal peer review, in addition to providing a set number of working hours per week, GHA physicians should have been more likely than their BC-BS counterparts to participate in grand and teaching rounds, scientific meetings, and formal medical educational courses, as well as in both formal and informal patient care review and evaluation procedures.

— GHA patients should have been more likely than BC-BS patients to have been cared for in larger hospitals with a university teaching affiliation, since at the time of the survey, GHA tended to admit its patients to major teaching hospitals, while BC-BS patients could be admitted to any hospital of the physician's and patient's choice.

VARIABLES AND DATA SOURCES

Data on age, sex, and race of the discharged patients under both plans who are the unit of analysis throughout this and the following chapters were obtained from patient interviews conducted from August 1973 to July 1974 (see Chapter 8 for survey methods). The providers of care as identified by survey respondents were categorized by three physician roles, i.e., the physician who first suggested hospitalization, the physician who arranged for hospitalizing the patient, and the attending physician who had primary responsibility for the patient in hospital. The following characteristics were established for each physician:

— Specialty status (board eligibility or board certification)

— Participation in continuing education activities in the past year (attendance at grand and teaching rounds, scientific meetings, and enrollment in formal medical education courses)

— Peer review and evaluation (general patient review and evaluation, and review of patient care by use of statistical methods such as the Medical Audit Program (MAP) and the Professional Activities Study (PAS) of the Commission on Professional and Hospital Activities)

Also, the number of hospitals at which the physician had admitting privileges was determined. Rough estimates of referral patterns were established by asking the physicians what percentage of their patients, in an average work week, were referred to them by other physicians and what percentage were referred by them. Finally, the amount of time spent per week in direct patient care and formal medical teaching, and years of practice were determined. Hospital characteristics included the size of the institution and the type of its teaching affiliation, as obtained from the Guide Issue of the *Journal of the American Hospital Association* (1974). In this chapter, this refers to the teaching status of the institution, regardless of whether its specialties included training for the specific diagnostic category under study or not. A somewhat different definition is used in Chapter 13.

PATIENT CHARACTERISTICS

Sex. In both plans, and as expected, relatively more males were discharged with diagnoses of arteriosclerotic and hypertensive heart disease and myocardial infarction than females; for the latter diagnosis, this was especially observed in BC-BS (88 percent versus 57 percent in GHA; Table 9.1). The female proportion was predictably higher in both plans for diseases of the gallbladder and biliary duct and, to a lesser degree, hyperplasia of tonsils and adenoids. In addition to myocardial infarction, plan differences were observed for diabetes mellitus, a diagnosis for which the BC-BS sample had almost perfect dichotomy by sex whereas almost three-fourths of the GHA cases were male, and for appendicitis (almost two-thirds of the BC-BS cases but less than half of GHA cases were male).

Race. The racial composition of the study population (two-thirds white in BC-BS and one-third in GHA; see also Table 4.1) was fairly closely approximated by the distribution of patients hospitalized for breast mass, arteriosclerotic and hypertensive heart disease, and hyperplasia of the tonsils and adenoids. In both plans, the relative proportion of blacks was higher in the diagnostic categories of uterine fibroids and diabetes mellitus; the reverse held for patients hospitalized with myocardial infarction and appendicitis. Plan differences were noted for patients with diagnoses of pneumonia and gallbladder disease; a slightly higher relative proportion of blacks in the former category and of whites in the latter category were hospitalized in BC-BS. In GHA, patient distribution by race approximated the membership ratios more closely for these diagnostic categories (see Table 9.1).

Age. Differences between the plans in patient age were restricted to appendicitis, breast mass, and diabetes mellitus. Patients in GHA tended to be somewhat younger than those hospitalized under BC-BS while the reverse held for patients with arteriosclerotic and hypertensive heart disease, pneumonia, and hyperplasia of the tonsils and adenoids. Overall, therefore, it would appear that GHA admitted younger patients except for heart disease and respiratory system and throat conditions (see Table 9.1).

PHYSICIAN CHARACTERISTICS

The assumption that differences in the organizational structure of the two health plans would be reflected in the characteristics of providers of care to the discharged patient sample was confirmed, although these differences were not always as anticipated. GHA physicians, for example, were not a more homogeneous group than their counterparts in BC-BS. There were fairly wide ranges across diagnostic categories for most physician character-istics, with the possible exception of residency training, participation in grand and teaching rounds, and patient care review and evaluation. Simi-larly, the expectation that a prepaid practice group like GHA would attract more highly qualified physicians was not supported throughout. Overall, the following differences and similarities were noted.

Residency Training and Board Certification. While almost all physi-cians in both plans had completed a residency program, the range across diagnostic categories was narrower in the prepaid group practice plan (79–99 percent for BC-BS, 91–100 percent for GHA). For board certifica-tion, these ranges were somewhat wider in both plans (49–91 percent for BC-BS and 41–100 percent for GHA) and the preponderance of specialists varied among plans in the diagnostic categories examined. GHA patients were more likely to have been cared for by board certified specialists for hyperplasia of tonsils and adenoids, diabetes mellitus, and pneumonia, whereas this was observed for BC-BS patients in the three surgical catego-ries of breast mass, uterine fibroids, and diseases of the gallbladder and biliary duct. No differences were noted for the two heart disease categories or appendicitis.

Years in Practice. The assumption that GHA patients would be more likely to have been cared for by physicians with less years in practice was borne out only in four of the six surgical categories (appendicitis, breast mass, diseases of the gallbladder and biliary duct, and uterine fibroids). There was no difference between plans in this respect for patients with arteriosclerotic and hypertensive heart disease and diabetes mellitus, and GHA physicians who cared for pneumonia patients were more, rather than less likely to have been more than ten years in practice.

Allocation of Time. On the other hand, there was evidence that BC-BS physicians in general averaged more hours per week in direct patient care (range, 50–58 hours) than physicians in GHA (range, 25–51 hours). The largest differences (on the order of 20 hours per week) were observed in the surgical categories and may be due to the inclusion of surgeons who were not on GHA staff; when only the nonsurgical and gynecological categories were examined the difference narrowed considerably, and a range of 45–51 patient care hours per week in GHA was observed. To some extent, the differences in the surgical categories may have been due to the greater teaching load of the GHA physicians treating patients in these categories; they averaged over ten teaching hours per week as compared to roughly eight hours for the BC-BS physicians in these diagnostic groups. In the internal medical categories, however, patients under BC-BS were more likely than those under GHA to be cared for by physicians with greater medical teaching responsibilities.

Admitting Privileges. As noted, at the time of the study GHA admitting privileges were restricted to a few hospitals; this is reflected in the finding that BC-BS physicians admitted their patients to a much wider range of hospitals. The difference between plans in the percentage of patients with physicians having admitting privileges at three or more hospitals was generally at least twofold (range, 51–86 percent for BC-BS as compared to 0–44 percent for GHA).

Referral Patterns. Inspection of referral patterns revealed an expected direction. In categories where patients are more often treated surgically, there was a tendency in both plans for the attending physician to be the receiver of referrals, rather than initiator, followed closely by the proportions for "hospitalizing" physicians (often one and the same) and "suggesting" physicians. In categories involving mixes of treatment modes, and in those where patients are usually treated medically, there was a greater probability of having a nonspecialist (and hence nonreceiver of referrals) acting as hospitalizing physician and attending physician. Differences between plans were expected, as the referral network involving specialty care for surgically treated patients and complex medical conditions was more rigid in GHA than in BC-BS, where most physicians worked in solo or other than group practice. Referrals initiated and received by the GHA physicians of patients with uterine fibroids, diabetes mellitus, and the two heart disease categories were indeed lower than in BC-BS, while referrals to practitioners in GHA were at higher levels than in BC-BS for all four major surgical categories (appendicitis, breast mass, gallbladder disease, and hyperplasia of tonsils and adenoids). The GHA physicians treating pneumonia patients were the exception. They received no referrals, but initiated them at a higher level than BC-BS physicians.

Professional and Continuing Educational Activities. Finally, the expectation that GHA patients would be more likely than BC-BS patients to have been cared for by physicians who participated in grand and teaching rounds, attended scientific meetings, and undertook formal review and evaluation of patient care was largely met. The exception here was formal continuing education courses and systematic statistical review of patient care employing such methods as PAS or MAP, where only those GHA physicians caring for patients in the internal medicine categories were more actively involved than BC-BS physicians; for all surgical categories, the reverse was true.

HOSPITAL CHARACTERISTICS

The comparison of provider characteristics between the service benefit and group practice plans also included the hospitals at which the patients under the two health plans were treated. The characteristics chosen were the bed size of the institution and the presence and level of teaching affiliation.

Bed Size. For all diagnoses except hyperplasia of tonsils and adenoids, GHA patients were far more likely than patients admitted under BC-BS to have been cared for in hospitals with more than 500 beds (Table 9.2). GHA proportions ranged from a high of 100 percent for uterine fibroid cases to 60 percent for diabetes mellitus, while for BC-BS patients these proportions varied from a low of 22 percent for hyperplasia of tonsils and adenoids to a high of 36 percent for diseases of the gallbladder and biliary duct. Roughly half of BC-BS patients across all diagnostic categories were cared for in medium sized (250–500 bed) hospitals. None of the GHA patients admitted for scheduled surgical interventions (breast mass, gallbladder, tonsillectomy and adenoidectomy, and uterine fibroids) nor any of GHA's myocardial infarction patients were cared for in hospitals with less than 250 beds, although in the three other medical categories (diabetes, arteriosclerotic and hypertensive heart disease, and pneumonia) and the surgical category of appendicitis, there were some GHA admissions to smaller hospitals, probably due to the need for emergency care; they ranged from a low of roughly 10 percent for appendicitis and heart patients to a high of roughly 25 percent for diabetes mellitus and pneumonia. In contrast, the proportion of BC-BS patients admitted to these smaller hospitals ranged from a low of 11 percent of the gallbladder cases to a high of 26 percent of the uterine fibroid cases. All tonsils and adenoid cases in GHA were cared for in medium sized (250–500 beds) hospitals, while the BC-BS cases were admitted across the whole range of facilities examined, with the majority of cases (49 percent) in medium sized hospitals, almost 30 percent in smaller institutions of less than 250 beds, and 22 percent in hospitals with more than 500 beds.

Teaching Affiliation. GHA patients in most diagnostic categories were also much more likely than BC-BS patients to have been cared for in a university teaching hospital or one with a major university affiliation. In the surgical categories, again except for hyperplasia of tonsils and adenoids, all GHA cases were cared for in this type of hospital, compared to only about a quarter of BC-BS patients in the same diagnostic categories (see Table 9.2). Conversely, of the BC-BS surgical patients, 9 percent of the uterine fibroid cases and roughly a fifth in the other four surgical categories (appendicitis, breast mass, gallbladder disease, and hyperplasia of tonsils and adenoids) were cared for in hospitals without any teaching programs.

In the four medical categories (arteriosclerotic and hypertensive heart disease, myocardial infarction, pneumonia, and diabetes), the proportions of GHA patients admitted to a university teaching or university affiliated hospital were generally lower than for the surgical groups, ranging from a high of 86 percent of patients with diabetes mellitus to a low of 57 percent of those with myocardial infarction. BC-BS patients in these categories, on the other hand, were most likely to have been cared for in hospitals with limited teaching facilities; the proportions cared for in either university or university affiliated teaching institutions exhibited a narrow range across the medical categories, from a low of about a fourth for diabetes and the two heart category patients to 29 percent for the pneumonia cases, with 15–20 percent cared for in hospitals that did not have any teaching programs. The only exception to this pattern was again in the pediatric category (hyperplasia of tonsils and adenoids), where less than half of GHA patients were admitted to a university teaching hospital and the remainder to a hospital with limited teaching affiliation.

As expected, the hospitals providing care to the patients of both health plans differed clearly in the two characteristics examined. With few exceptions, GHA patients were more likely than BC-BS cases to have been hospitalized in large institutions, either teaching hospitals or with university teaching affiliation. Conversely, the greater freedom of hospital selection for BC-BS physicians and patients is reflected in the wider range of hospital types to which their plan members were admitted. Dependent probably on bed availability and convenience to the patient and/or physician, BC-BS patients were as likely to have been cared for in small as in large hospitals, and in those with or without teaching facilities.

Thus, of the assumptions regarding patient and provider characteristics in Phase III of this study, only those relating to the type and size of hospital to which patients were admitted were fully met. The findings relating to patients and physicians were more ambiguous, although length of involvement in medical practice and, in particular, referral patterns were obviously related to the structures of fee-for-service and prepaid group practice.

Table 9.1 Sociodemographic characteristics of members of BC-BS and GHA[a] discharged from hospital in selected diagnostic categories: Percentage distributions by sex and race and mean years of age by sex and race

Diagnostic Category

	Appendicitis		Breast mass[b]		Diabetes mellitus		Gall bladder and biliary duct disease		Arteriosclerotic and hypertensive heart disease		Myocardial infarction		Pneumonia		Hyperplasia of tonsils and adenoids		Uterine fibroids	
	BC-BS	GHA	BC-BS	GHA	BC-BS	GHA	BC-BS	GHA	BC-BS	GHA	BC-BS	GHA	BC-BS	GHA	BC-BS	GHA	BC-BS	GHA
Percent by sex and race																		
Male	63	49	1	0	50	73	25	25	61	57	88	57	53	62	44	42	—	—
White	81	44	70	33	48	7	79	38	60	40	86	50	56	31	69	28	50	15
Mean years of age (n)																		
All	24* (210)	22 (35)	40 (233)	37 (58)	39 (193)	34 (15)	42 (241)	42 (39)	50* (190)	55 (21)	53 (94)	54 (14)	21* (169)	31 (13)	13 (111)	15 (67)	42 (188)	42 (72)
Male	23 (133)	19 (17)	55 (2)	—	41 (97)	34 (11)	48 (66)	50 (10)	50* (117)	57 (12)	52 (83)	55 (8)	20 (91)	27 (8)	10 (49)	11 (28)	—	—
Female	24 (77)	25 (18)	40 (231)	37 (58)	38 (96)	33 (4)	40 (175)	39 (29)	50 (73)	52 (9)	56 (11)	54 (6)	23 (78)	38 (5)	15 (62)	17 (39)	42 (188)	42 (72)
Black	22 (41)	21 (19)	36 (71)	34 (39)	42 (101)	33 (14)	38 (50)	39 (24)	47 (76)	52 (13)	54 (13)	53 (7)	21 (74)	29 (9)	14 (34)	16 (48)	40 (93)	42 (61)
White	24 (169)	23 (16)	41 (162)	42 (19)	37 (92)	50 (1)	43 (191)	46 (15)	52 (114)	59 (8)	52 (81)	55 (7)	22 (95)	36 (4)	12 (77)	12 (19)	45 (95)	46 (11)
Black male	23 (28)	19 (10)	—	—	45* (45)	33 (10)	44 (10)	42 (3)	47 (42)	56 (7)	54 (10)	53 (5)	20 (37)	25 (6)	10 (16)	12 (19)	—	—
White male	24 (105)	20 (7)	55 (2)	—	37* (52)	50 (1)	48 (56)	53 (1)	52* (75)	59 (5)	52 (73)	56 (3)	21* (54)	34 (2)	10 (33)	9 (9)	—	—
Black female	20 (13)	24 (9)	36 (71)	34 (39)	39 (56)	33 (4)	37 (40)	39 (21)	48 (34)	48 (6)	53 (3)	53 (2)	21 (37)	38 (3)	17 (18)	18 (29)	40 (93)	42 (61)
White female	25 (64)	25 (9)	41 (160)	42 (19)	37 (40)	—	41 (135)	40 (8)	52* (39)	58 (3)	57 (8)	54 (4)	24 (41)	37 (2)	14 (44)	15 (10)	45 (95)	46 (11)

[a] Contract holders and their covered dependents.

[b] Cystic breast disease and breast cancer.   — Not applicable.   *P ≤ .05.

Table 9.2 Characteristics of hospitals providing care to patients under two plans: Percentage distributions of BC–BS and GHA patients by hospital teaching status and bed size

	Appendicitis		Breast mass		Diabetes mellitus		Gall bladder and biliary duct disease		Arteriosclerotic and hypertensive heart disease		Myocardial infarction		Pneumonia		Hyperplasia of tonsils and adenoids		Uterine fibroids	
	BC-BS	GHA	BC-BS	GHA	BC-BS	GHA	BC-BS	GHA	BC-BS	GHA	BC-BS	GHA	BC-BS	GHA	BC-BS	GHA	BC-BS	GHA
Bed size																		
Less than 250 beds	19	9	14	0	20	27	11	0	18	10	13	0	21	23	29	0	26	0
250 to 500 beds	54	0	56	2	50	13	53	3	55	19	58	36	47	8	49	100	45	0
More than 500 beds	28	91	30	98	30	60	36	97	27	71	29	64	31	69	22	0	29	100
Total	100 *	100	100 *	100	100 *	100	100 *	100	100 *	100	100 *	100	100 *	100	100 *	100	100 *	100
Teaching status																		
University or university affiliated	25	100	23	100	25	86	24	100	25	76	26	57	29	77	20	42	19	100
Other teaching programs	55	0	55	0	60	14	57	0	59	19	52	43	55	23	57	58	72	0
No teaching program	20	0	21	0	15	0	19	0	16	5	22	0	15	0	23	0	9	0
Total	100 *	100	100 *	100	100 *	100	100 *	100	100 *	100	100 *	100	100 *	100	100 *	100	100 *	100

*P ⩽ .05.

10

Patterns of Prehospital Care and Length of Stay

Thelma Myint

This chapter examines the events preceding hospital admission of the discharged patient sample in BC-BS and GHA, with particular regard to entry into the care system, delays in use or provision of services, and sources of care for the episode which resulted in hospitalization. The patients' perception of the severity of their condition at the time of the first physician visit in this episode and their degree of social functioning were examined as well. The questions addressed here are whether any differences in this respect reflect the behavior of the patients in the two health plans; obstacles to seeking care arising from benefit coverage or the organizational structure of the two plans; or levels of perceived severity and urgency that might have occasioned different patterns of care or variations in the length of the episode before hospitalization.

One of the assumptions underlying this examination was that differences in coverage and provider arrangements between the service benefit and the prepaid group practice plan might indeed have contributed to imbalances in hospital use (see also Aday and Eichhorn, 1972). Under BC-BS, inpatient services were covered more fully than ambulatory care. Although high-option subscribers (of which the present sample was comprised) could seek reimbursement for a portion of physician and other ambulatory care expenses under a supplemental benefits mechanism, such a benefit structure has been argued to provide a financial incentive for both physicians and patients to obtain care on an inpatient basis (for full discussions of these arguments and associated evidence, see Donabedian, 1969, 1965; Luft, 1980a,b, 1978). In contrast, GHA offered relatively comprehensive health care coverage for a range of specified services, regardless of whether these were provided on an ambulatory basis or in hospital, and could exercise some control over hospitalization rates; for instance, by requiring agreement between primary care physicians and specialists on surgical procedures for its members. Also, at the time of this study, the prepaid group practice physicians had both individual and organizational incentives to reduce hospitalizations; they received an annual bonus which was inversely proportional to plan hospitalization rates and in general should have been concerned with holding plan expenditures to a level where premiums could remain competitive.

It might be argued, therefore, that the prospect of out-of-pocket expenses could have induced BC-BS subscribers to wait a while before contacting a physician, while the GHA patient, in the absence of a cost deterrent, should have been more prompt in seeking care, always given similar levels of illness severity. On the other hand, factors other than direct cost may have influenced the use of services, such as appointment patterns, office waiting times, and the availability of a regular physician as a source of care. Although in the present study the GHA appointment system does not seem to have inhibited prompt use of ambulatory services in the case of illness (see Chapter 4, Table 4.15), the GHA appointment and physician assignment procedure may nonetheless have produced some queuing effects.

With regard to the availability of hospital beds in the two plans, it must be remembered that while BC-BS patients were cared for by physicians who had appointments at several hospitals in the study area, GHA admissions were limited almost entirely to a few large hospitals at the time of the study. Further, while BC-BS patients could seek care from or be referred to any surgeon or hospital based specialist, GHA had no general surgeons on its full-time staff at the time of the study, and surgery for its members was performed by surgeons retained by the plan and on call at specified hospitals. Thus, for hospital care in general and for scheduled surgery in particular, these constraints could have resulted in longer delays in admission for GHA patients. The sequence of events after the patients entered the system of care might, therefore, provide some explanation of differences between the two plans with regard to the hospitalization of patients with comparable diagnoses, particularly in those diagnostic categories that involve scheduled surgical interventions and medical conditions of long standing.

In summary, the following factors were assumed to be potential determinants of patterns of prehospital care under the two health plans:

— As far as initial entry into the health care system at the start of an episode of illness is concerned, the cost deterrent factor under BC-BS might be offset by the appointment system and other procedural deterrents in GHA; thus, no substantial plan difference in delays in contacting a physician was anticipated. For life-threatening or severe symptoms, not only should there have been no delay, but under both plans entry would probably have been via the emergency unit of a hospital.

—Since patients in both plans could thus be expected to seek care equally promptly once definite symptoms were recognized, and patients in one plan were not expected to be sicker than those in the other *at the time they first contacted a physician*, differences in delays between the first physician contact and admission might have been due to differences in approaches to hospitalization between the physicians under the two plans, or to factors such as availability of hospital beds. This does not, however, assume equal incidence of morbidity in the two populations.

—Considering the predominance of a personal physician-patient relationship in the fee-for-service system and the relative ease of making appointments, BC-BS patients should have been more likely than those under GHA to have made their first contact at the start of the episode with their personal physician, whereas GHA patients would have been more likely to have bypassed the appointment system and entered the care system through the walk-in or urgent clinic. It follows that BC-BS patients would have been more likely to have made appointments to see their first physician in this episode of illness than GHA patients, and to have had a choice in selecting a particular physician.

—For those GHA patients who did make an appointment to see their first physician, longer waiting periods were expected.

—A variety of GHA organizational constraints, compared to what might be an economic advantage of inhospital care for both patient and physician in BC-BS, could have led GHA physicians to be less prompt than fee-for-service physicians to suggest admission in cases not requiring emergency care.

—Once hospital admission had been suggested to a patient (again with the exception of emergency cases), BC-BS patients, especially those admitted for scheduled surgery, would be likely to experience less delay than GHA patients in being admitted to hospital because of their direct access to specialists and surgeons, and also because of stricter GHA control over hospital admissions.

—It is known from Phase I of this study that overall hospital admission rates under GHA were lower than under BC-BS, while lengths of hospital stay were roughly comparable overall. At least for non-urgent conditions, therefore, GHA providers may first have attempted to handle problems on an ambulatory basis, and GHA patients may have received more extensive care prior to admission in terms of visits, x-rays, tests, and medication than corresponding BC-BS patients.

VARIABLES AND DATA SOURCES

The information used to describe the sequence of care events from the first signs of the episode of illness up to eventual hospital admission was obtained in personal interviews with patients or proxies (see Chapter 8). Lengths of stay were obtained from the hospital record abstracts.

The patient interviews first determined the nature of the illness as perceived by the patient, the date of its inception or of first symptoms, prior hospitalization for the same condition, and the degree of patient delay in seeking care, if any, at the start of the present episode leading to hospitalization. The time of inception of the condition was established by asking when the first signs of illness had appeared prior to this admission; this, in conjunction with the date of hospitalization, permitted calculation of the number of years the patient had been aware of the condition. For emergency admissions, in which patients were hospitalized within 24 hours of the first sign of illness or renewed symptoms, or in those instances where the patient was admitted to the hospital within 24 hours of the first physician contact, the date of admission was considered to be the starting date of the episode. For patients with conditions of longer standing, such as diabetes or arteriosclerotic heart disease, the starting date was established by asking the patient when ". . . this most recent trouble started that brought you to the hospital this time" or, if there was no recent trouble, "When did you decide to do something about the condition this time?" In some instances, this was the date when the patient first saw a physician about the condition after a prior hospitalization.

The question of whether access to services differed for the subscribers to the two health plans overall and for each of the selected diagnostic categories was examined by determining the extent to which those not admitted on an emergency basis had appointments with a physician prior to hospitalization. Also, for both scheduled and emergency admissions, respondents were asked whether their first physician contact was with their regular source of care, i.e., a physician previously consulted on a regular basis, or a referral from this physician. Patients were then classified as to whether they saw their regular physician or were referred by him, or whether they had no choice, i.e., were assigned to a physician on duty or in the emergency room.

In order to gain some insight into the relative severity of the condition as perceived by patients or proxies, and into patient functional status at the time of the first physician contact in this episode of care, patients were asked about their level of pain and discomfort just before they saw a physician and their perception of the seriousness of their condition. In addition, patients not admitted on an emergency basis were asked whether they had been able to keep up their usual activities, had had to limit normal function, or were sick in bed.

Comparisons of the time spans both before and after the patients' entry into the system of care up to the date of admission took into account appropriate differences for the various diagnostic categories.

Prehospital ambulatory care during the period from the first physician contact in this episode of illness up to the date of hospital admission is shown in terms of the number of outpatient physician visits and the percentages of patients who stated that they were taking medicines prescribed by a physician, were getting treatment from any doctor, had had any x-rays, or received any special tests for the health problem in question. Finally, lengths of hospital stay were examined in terms of mean lengths of stay and of preoperative stays for each diagnostic category.

PATIENT BEHAVIOR

History of Illness. There were few differences between the two health plans in the number of years respondents in each diagnostic category reported having suffered from the illness in question, in the percentage of those whose condition dated back less than one year, and in the percentage previously hospitalized for the same condition. Exceptions were observed for arteriosclerotic and hypertensive heart disease and uterine fibroids, where GHA patients were more likely than those in BC-BS to have had the condition for four or more years (Table 10.1), although GHA patients with uterine fibroids were almost three times less likely to have been hospitalized previously. In general, previous hospitalizations tended to be less frequently reported by GHA patients, with the possible exception of the diabetes mellitus group.

Patterns of Access. As all of the patients in Phase III of the study were in fact hospitalized in the course of their episode of illness, whether it was a condition of recent onset or a chronic complaint, a comparison of three patterns of entry into the system of care was considered of interest: the extent of emergency admissions (which excluded patients with breast mass, hyperplasia of tonsils and adenoids, and uterine fibroids, practically all of whom were admitted on a scheduled basis); levels of physician appointments and appointment waits for nonemergency cases; and the extent to which patients had a choice in seeing a particular physician.

Similar proportions of emergency admissions were reported in each plan, the only variation being among diagnostic categories. The proportion so admitted ranged from roughly 90 percent of patients in the myocardial infarction group, and 80 percent of appendicitis cases, to 15 percent for diseases of the gallbladder and biliary duct. Among patients admitted on a scheduled basis, statistically significant differences in the expected direction of fewer GHA physician appointments for the first visit in the episode were found only for breast mass, diabetes mellitus, and tonsil and adenoid patients. In all cases of appointments, however, average waits for GHA patients were at least twice as long as for BC-BS patients, and in one category (gallbladder and biliary duct disease), this difference was more than fourfold.

Finally, and also as expected, the first source of care at the start of this episode for BC-BS patients was more often than not their regular physician (or a physician to whom they were referred by their physician) in seven out of nine diagnostic categories; in GHA, the reverse was found. The proportion in BC-BS who had a choice of physician ranged from a high of 82 percent for breast mass patients to a low of 35 percent for myocardial infarction patients, while in GHA this range was from a high of 71 percent for uterine fibroid patients to zero for pneumonia. Differences between plans were large and statistically significant for appendicitis, breast mass, diseases of the gallbladder and biliary duct, and pneumonia. Even in the case of tonsil and adenoid patients, where there was less difference between plans in the proportion who first saw their regular physician, 45 percent of GHA patients were seen to have had no choice of physician. This pattern was substantially the same for both scheduled and emergency admission, although the margin of difference was less.

Perceived Severity and Functional Status. Reported levels of pain and seriousness of the patient's condition at the time of the first physician visit varied markedly by diagnosis but little between plans. Over 70 percent of patients admitted with appendicitis, myocardial infarction, pneumonia, and gallbladder and biliary duct complaints were in pain, followed by approximately 50 to 60 percent of patients with arteriosclerotic and hypertensive heart disease and hyperplasia of tonsils and adenoids, and 40 to 45 percent of uterine fibroid patients.

While there were some differences between the two plans in the direction of higher levels of perceived severity among GHA patients (mainly for appendicitis and arteriosclerotic and hypertensive heart disease and to some extent also for pneumonia and diabetes mellitus), none were statistically significant. Levels of functioning also varied more by diagnosis than among the plans, an excess of social dysfunction in GHA among patients with arteriosclerotic heart disease being the exception. Overall, therefore, patients in the diagnostic categories examined were at roughly comparable levels of perceived severity at the time of their first physician visit (see Chapter 12 for indicators of severity at the time of hospital admission).

PATTERNS OF CARE PRIOR TO
HOSPITAL ADMISSION

Time Sequences in
the Care System

Four time sequences were defined for each diagnostic group to establish how promptly patients under two health plans were hospitalized for similar conditions. Given that all members of the sample were eventually admitted, whether on a scheduled or an emergency basis, the time frames of interest are from the start of the present episode to the first physician contact; from the first physician contact to the date of hospital suggestion; from the date of hospital suggestion to admission; and, finally, the entire ambulatory care period from the date of the first physician contact until admission. With the possible exception of emergency admissions, the first of these (Table 10.2), may be considered as mainly determined by patient attitudes and by appointment patterns; the sequence of subsequent events (Tables 10.3 to 10.5) should reflect more specifically the pattern of services as determined by provider decisions (e.g., referrals, hospital suggestions) and the availability of hospital beds to members of the two health plans.

Appendicitis. There was no appreciable difference in the time lapses for BC-BS and GHA patients prior to their hospitalization for appendicitis. The progression of events from first recognition of signs to the first physician visit, until hospitalization was first suggested, and until admission, seems to have been both rapid and appropriate in view of the condition involved. Once a patient had contacted a physician under either plan, more than 90 percent were in hospital within a week, and over three-fourths in both plans were admitted within 24 hours of first seeking care.

Breast Mass (Cystic Breast Disease and Breast Cancer). In both plans, once patients had contacted a physician (in almost half of the cases within 24 hours after noticing signs or symptoms), hospitalization was recommended for two-fifths of the patients on the day of the visit and for an equal proportion after a lapse of at least one week. On the other hand, GHA patients were almost twice as likely to have waited more than 30 days from the date of hospital suggestion to admission (BC-BS 14 percent, GHA 26 percent). However, seen in the context of the period from first visit to admission, roughly half of all patients were admitted within a month.

Diabetes Mellitus. About one-half in BC-BS and two-thirds of GHA patients had seen a physician within 24 hours of the start of the episode. Admission was suggested to about two-thirds of patients in both plans within a similar period, and roughly 90 percent in both plans were admitted within two weeks after hospital suggestion. For only 7 percent of GHA patients hospitalized for diabetes mellitus did the time from their first physician contact to hospital admission exceed more than two weeks, compared to 25 percent for BC-BS cases.

Diseases of the Gallbladder and Biliary Duct. Roughly half of the patients in both plans contacted a physician within 24 hours from the start of the present episode; hospital admission was suggested to about 40 percent within a day, while similar proportions stated that the suggestion was made after more than two weeks. In contrast, the time from the date of hospital suggestion to admission was more likely to have been in excess of two weeks for GHA patients (74 percent as compared to 53 percent in BC-BS). Overall, for almost 60 percent of the patients in both plans, the period from first physician contact to admission was more than 30 days.

Arteriosclerotic and Hypertensive Heart Disease. About two-thirds of the patients in both plans saw a physician within 24 hours, and of these, more than 70 percent were referred to hospital and admitted within 24 hours, respectively. The period from first physician contact to hospital admission exceeded seven days for 28 percent in BC-BS and 19 percent in GHA.

Myocardial Infarction. In this category, emergency admissions constituted an even greater proportion of all cases (BC-BS 87 percent, GHA 93 percent), and the time lapse at any stage was rarely in excess of 24 hours.

Pneumonia. While roughly half of the patients in both plans had waited for as long as a week before their first physician visit, hospitalization was recommended to a majority (BC-BS 59 percent, GHA 77 percent) within 24 hours of the first visit. Also, once hospitalization had been suggested, more than four-fifths of patients in both plans were admitted within 24 hours. For this acutely ill patient group the period prior to admission tended to be short; it exceeded a week for only 17 percent of BC-BS and 8 percent of GHA patients.

Hyperplasia of Tonsils and Adenoids. Well over half of all patients in both plans had seen a physician within 24 hours from the start of the episode, and 59 percent in BC-BS and 43 percent in GHA were recommended for admission within 24 hours of the visit. Once hospitalization had been suggested, however, GHA patients were much more likely to have waited more than two months to admission (BC-BS 23 percent, GHA 39 percent). The entire prehospital period for this episode was thus more likely to have extended well beyond 60 days for GHA patients.

Uterine Fibroids. In this category as well, physicians in both plans recommended inpatient surgery for almost two-thirds of the patients within 24 hours of the first visit, and for only a fifth one month after the first contact. GHA patients were almost three times as likely to have waited for more than three months until admission (31 percent as compared to 12 percent in BC-BS), and the period from first physician contact to hospital admission was considerably longer for patients in the prepaid group practice plan, only 3 percent being admitted within 15 days of entry into the system, as compared to 21 percent of the BC-BS cases. Conversely, two-fifths of the GHA patients but only a fourth in BC-BS stated that it took more than three months to be admitted to a hospital after their first visit.

There were few important differences between the two health plans in patient delays in contacting a physician, at least in terms of percentage distributions for the individual diagnostic categories. The apparently greater differences between plans in the mean days from the start of the episode to the first physician visit (see Table 10.2) seem largely due to some extreme values; the difference between plans was statistically significant only in the uterine fibroid category. Overall, relatively small proportions of patients in each plan waited for more than a week to contact a physician. For the second time frame of interest, from the first physician contact to hospital suggestion, there were again no statistically significant plan differences for any of the nine diagnostic categories examined (see Table 10.3). In both plans, patients with emergency conditions were almost equally likely to have been recommended for hospitalization within 24 hours (appendicitis, 80–85 percent, myocardial infarction, approximately 90 percent, and arteriosclerotic and hypertensive heart disease, 70–75 percent). For the four scheduled surgical categories as well — breast mass, diseases of the gallbladder and biliary duct, hyperplasia of tonsils and adenoids, and uterine fibroids — it would be difficult to imply differences in physician attitudes concerning hospitalization. Only for patients hospitalized in the two categories primarily treated medically, diabetes mellitus and pneumonia, is there some suggestion of a difference between plans; in the case of diabetes, the mean delay for GHA patients was just 3 days while BC-BS patients averaged 16 days, and for pneumonia patients, the average was 2 days for GHA and 7 days for BC-BS. Whether the mean delays in GHA for these two categories indicate that the hospitalized patients were in need of admission at an earlier date in this episode of illness than those hospitalized by BC-BS cannot be determined here (but see Chapter 12). Thus, the assumption of generally greater delay in suggesting hospitalization for GHA patients was not supported. However, it must be remembered that the patients considered here were all eventually hospitalized; there is no comparable information on cases where hospitalization was suggested but postponed and who were sustained on an ambulatory basis.

On the other hand, there is some evidence that once hospitalization was suggested, there was less delay in admission under the service benefit plan for scheduled breast mass surgery, gallbladder and biliary duct complaints, tonsillectomies and adenoidectomies, and hysterectomies, where longer waits under the prepaid group practice plan for scheduled surgery were the mode (Table 10.4).

For the total prehospital period experienced by the patients in this episode of illness, differences between the two plans in hospitalization patterns were relatively small (Table 10.5) for appendicitis, heart disease, diabetes mellitus, and pneumonia and most scheduled surgery. However, in the case of hyperplasia of tonsils and adenoids and uterine fibroids, prehospital periods under GHA were longer by statistically significant margins. In the former category, 44 percent in BC-BS as compared to 66 percent in GHA were hospitalized more than 60 days after their first physician contact; in the case of uterine fibroids, a time lapse of more than 90 days was reported by only a fourth of BC-BS but by 41 percent of GHA patients. Inasmuch as these two diagnostic categories represented quite distinct patient populations, and there were few, if any, differences in levels of pain and discomfort observed for the patients in the two plans, it is difficult to avoid the conclusion that hospitalization patterns, whether due to bed availability or to organizational decisions, differed considerably among the two plans in this respect. Whether or not these hospital admissions were medically appropriate and accurately diagnosed will be examined in Chapter 11.

Care Prior to Admission

The extent of ambulatory care received prior to admission is summarized in Table 10.6 in terms of the mean number of physician visits prior to admission by all patients, and of the proportion of patients admitted on a scheduled basis who reported having received medication, treatment, x-rays, and special tests.

Clearly, the number of physician contacts preceding hospitalization differed more across diagnostic categories than among plans, and seems to have been largely influenced by the extent of emergency admissions in each category. The range in both plans was from 1.6 visits to roughly 3.5 visits, with acute conditions below the median and scheduled surgery admissions above it, except in the case of hyperplasia of tonsils and adenoid patients (1.6 visits in BC-BS and 1.9 in GHA). A comparatively large difference between the two plans in the expected direction of more extensive ambulatory physician care under GHA was observed only for uterine fibroid patients; with this exception, the assumption that GHA patients would be seen more often prior to hospital admission was not borne out for the diagnostic categories under study.

On the other hand, there were substantial differences in the extent of services provided in three scheduled surgery categories (gallbladder complaints, breast mass, and uterine fibroids), where the differences in patients reporting x-rays and special tests were statistically significant and, with one exception, indicated that larger volumes of services were provided by GHA. Whether these differences reflect more exhaustive diagnostic work in GHA to rule out invalid diagnoses, or merely the fact that GHA can perform more preoperative tests and procedures on an outpatient basis than physicians in BC-BS is difficult to determine.

LENGTH OF STAY

The examination of time sequences within which patients were admitted to hospital has emphasized the possibility that differences between the two plans in administrative practice and in clinical management may have influenced patterns of care. These may also have affected lengths of hospital stay for the two patient groups, although in Phase I, differences in length of stay were found to be far less frequent, and much smaller, than those observed for admission rates. Lengths of stay are known to be influenced by a range of individual factors, among them severity of illness and the occurrence of complications while in hospital, by administrative factors such as occupancy rates, and by provider attitudes. For the patients in this study, and leaving aside possible differences in levels of clinical severity (a question that will be addressed in Chapter 12), two questions are of interest. First, were overall lengths of stay in each diagnostic category noticeably different between plans? Second, was there a difference in preoperative lengths of stay, indicating that service benefit plan physicians tend to hospitalize patients for diagnostic work-ups prior to surgery?

Table 10.7 summarizes the data relating to these questions in terms of mean lengths of stay under the two plans and of preoperative mean lengths of stay for surgically treated patients. Neither were consistently dissimilar, even in those instances (diabetes mellitus, diseases of the gallbladder and biliary duct, pneumonia, and hyperplasia of the tonsils and adenoids) where plan differences in overall length of stay were statistically significant, a finding that is in accordance with those in Phase I of the study.

While there was some indication from the medical record that lengths of stay tended to cluster within narrower ranges for each group of patients under GHA, suggesting a more uniform approach to clinical management among GHA physicians, this was, of course, also due to the smaller number of physicians attending patients in each diagnostic category in GHA. Stays under BC-BS were distributed over a much wider range, reflecting a greater influence of individual physician (and possibly patient) preferences. The extent to which hospital occupancy rates affected these patterns could not be determined on the basis of the data in the present study.

SUMMARY AND CONCLUSIONS

Patterns of prehospital care and length of stay were reported for a discharged patient sample under two health plans. At the start of the episode of illness leading to hospitalization, GHA patients were somewhat less likely than those in BC-BS to have entered the system through an appointment, and waited longer when appointments were made. Also, for both emergency and scheduled admissions, BC-BS patients were more likely to have seen their regular physicians or been referred by them, while GHA patients were more likely to have been seen by a physician assigned to them. No substantial differences were noted in the time to obtain care for eight of the nine diagnostic categories. Uterine fibroid patients were an exception, with BC-BS patients more likely than GHA patients to have waited more than a week.

Also, there were few important differences in regard to the delay in suggesting hospitalization after the patient had contacted a physician. On the other hand, once hospitalization had been suggested for the elective and scheduled surgical categories studied — breast mass, diseases of the gallbladder and biliary duct, hyperplasia of tonsils and adenoids, and uterine fibroids — GHA patients had to wait longer to be admitted to hospital than BC-BS patients. Whether this is attributable to scheduling delays or to a more conservative approach in patient management among GHA physicians, or both, is not clear. Patient lengths of stay in the different diagnostic categories were similar, confirming the findings in Phase I.

Tentative evidence in support of the hypothesis that differences in patient management between the two health plans might account for lower GHA hospitalization rates was suggested by an examination of patterns of care for patients with uterine fibroids and hyperplasia of tonsils and adenoids.

Significantly higher proportions of GHA than BC-BS patients experienced longer ambulatory care periods prior to admission. Also, employing the criteria of medication, treatment, x-rays, and special tests for three of the surgical categories (breast mass, diseases of the gallbladder and biliary duct, and uterine fibroids), GHA patients were seen to be more likely than BC-BS patients to have received extensive ambulatory care prior to admission.

The precise reasons for these findings cannot be identified from the data at hand, in part because patients with the same diagnoses who were *not* hospitalized under each plan could not be studied. At least two explanations are possible. First, it may be that GHA provides more ambulatory care (more visits and more tests) to *all* its patients with these diagnoses, whether hospitalization is involved or not. Alternatively, ambulatory care patterns could be similar in the two plans for all patients with these diagnoses but, since GHA is more parsimonious in its use of the hospital, only the more severely ill patients within its case mix are available for comparison in this sample. Only a comprehensive follow-up study both of patients who were hospitalized with these conditions and of those who were not could confirm one or the other of these explanations, or suggest more conclusive findings.

Table 10.1 Years from first onset of illness and hospitalizations prior to present admission: Percentage distribution of patients in selected diagnostic categories

Diagnostic category[a]	Plan	Years from first signs of onset				Prior hospitali- zations (percent)
		8+	4–7	2–3	1 or less	
		Percentage distribution				
Breast mass	BC–BS	8	9	7	76	16
	GHA	2	10	17	71	15
Diabetes mellitus	BC–BS	20	17	17	47	30
	GHA	7	20	13	60	47
Gall bladder and biliary duct disease	BC–BS *	6	15	15	62	18
	GHA	5	8	21	67	13
Arteriosclerotic and hypertensive heart disease	BC–BS *	15	21	15	49	44
	GHA	24	24	14	38	33
Myocardial infarction	BC–BS	17	16	8	59	35
	GHA	7	7	14	71	21
Hyperplasia of tonsils and adenoids	BC–BS	10	21	36	33	5
	GHA	14	31	26	29	6
Uterine fibroids	BC–BS *	11	20	22	48	34
	GHA	21	22	24	33	12

[a]Excludes appendicitis and pneumonia.

*P ≤ .05 (4 years or more vs. all others).

Table 10.2 Time sequence in patient care from start of episode to first physician contact: Percentage distribution of patients by diagnostic specific delay periods and mean number of days

	BC-BS	GHA
	%	
Appendicitis		
Less than 24 hours	44	37
1 to 7 days	44	54
7+ days	12	9
Total	100	100
Mean number of days	11	2
Gall bladder and biliary duct disease		
Less than 24 hours	52	49
1 to 7 days	16	15
7+ days	32	36
Total	100	100
Mean number of days	23	21
Pneumonia		
Less than 24 hours	35	31
1 to 7 days	49	54
7+ days	15	15
Total	100	100
Mean number of days	7	7

	BC-BS	GHA
	%	
Breast mass		
Less than 24 hours	49	45
1 to 30 days	20	14
30+ days	31	41
Total	100	100
Mean number of days	13	33
Arteriosclerotic and hypertensive heart disease		
Less than 24 hours	65	71
1 to 7 days	22	19
7+ days	13	10
Total	100	100
Mean number of days	5	5
Hyperplasia of tonsils and adenoids		
Less than 24 hours	67	58
1 to 7 days	10	16
7+ days	23	25
Total	100	100
Mean number of days	10	10

	BC-BS	GHA
	%	
Diabetes mellitus		
Less than 24 hours	48	67
1 to 7 days	19	20
7+ days	33	13
Total	100	100
Mean number of days	18	5
Myocardial infarction		
Less than 24 hours	69	57
1 to 7 days	19	36
7+ days	12	7
Total	100	100
Mean number of days	5	7
Uterine fibroids[a]		
Less than 24 hours	57	64
1 to 30 days	18	24
30+ days	25	12
Total	100	100
Mean number of days	32 *	19

Note: The category "less than 24 hours" includes all emergency admissions.

[a] Excludes patients who did not have a hysterectomy.

*P ≤ .05.

Table 10.3 Time sequence in patient care from first physician contact to date of hospital suggestion: Percentage distribution of patients by diagnostic specific delay periods and mean number of days

	BC-BS %	GHA
Appendicitis		
Less than 24 hours	85	80
1 to 7 days	7	14
7+ days	8	6
Total	100	100
Mean number of days	7	3
Gall bladder and biliary duct disease		
Less than 24 hours	39	41
1 to 14 days	22	15
14+ days	39	44
Total	100	100
Mean number of days	39	29
Pneumonia		
Less than 24 hours	59	77
1 to 7 days	26	15
7+ days	15	8
Total	100	100
Mean number of days	7	2

	BC-BS %	GHA
Breast mass		
Less than 24 hours	41	41
1 to 7 days	14	17
7+ days	45	42
Total	100	100
Mean number of days	30	22
Arteriosclerotic and hypertensive heart disease		
Less than 24 hours	75	71
1 to 7 days	5	10
7+ days	20	19
Total	100	100
Mean number of days	12	21
Hyperplasia of tonsils and adenoids		
Less than 24 hours	59	43
1 to 30 days	11	24
30+ days	31	33
Total	100	100
Mean number of days	41	33

	BC-BS %	GHA
Diabetes mellitus		
Less than 24 hours	67	60
1 to 7 days	12	27
7+ days	21	13
Total	100	100
Mean number of days	16	3
Myocardial infarction		
Less than 24 hours	88	93
1 to 7 days	4	0
7+ days	7	7
Total	100	100
Mean number of days	6	11
Uterine fibroids[a]		
Less than 24 hours	62	63
1 to 30 days	17	19
30+ days	21	19
Total	100	100
Mean number of days	28	21

Note: The category "less than 24 hours" includes all emergency admissions.

[a] Excludes patients who did not have a hysterectomy.

*P ≤ .05.

Table 10.4 Time sequence in patient care from date of hospital suggestion to admission: Percentage distribution of patients by diagnostic specific delay periods and mean number of days

	BC–BS %	GHA
Appendicitis		
Less than 24 hours	88	86
1 to 7 days	10	11
7+ days	2	3
Total	100	100
Mean number of days	1	1
Gall bladder and biliary duct disease		
Less than 24 hours	20	15
1 to 14 days	27	10
14+ days	53	74
Total	100 *	100
Mean number of days	30	31
Pneumonia		
Less than 15 days	81	85
15 to 60 days	18	15
60+ days	1	0
Total	100	100
Mean number of days	1	1

	BC–BS %	GHA
Breast mass		
Less than 15 days	62	41
15 to 30 days	24	33
30+ days	14	26
Total	100 *	100
Mean number of days	19	26
Arteriosclerotic and hypertensive heart disease		
Less than 24 hours	71	76
1 to 7 days	18	19
7+ days	11	5
Total	100	100
Mean number of days	5	3
Hyperplasia of tonsils and adenoids		
Less than 15 days	18	7
15 to 60 days	59	54
60+ days	23	39
Total	100 *	100
Mean number of days	46	54

	BC–BS %	GHA
Diabetes mellitus		
Less than 24 hours	51	73
1 to 14 days	38	20
14+ days	11	7
Total	100	100
Mean number of days	6	2
Myocardial infarction		
Less than 24 hours	87	93
1 to 7 days	6	0
7+ days	6	7
Total	100	100
Mean number of days	1	1
Uterine fibroids[a]		
Less than 15 days	25	8
15 to 90 days	63	61
90+ days	12	31
Total	100 *	100
Mean number of days	45 *	75

Note: The category "less than 24 hours" includes all emergency admissions.

[a]Excludes patients who did not have a hysterectomy.

*$P \leqslant .05$.

Table 10.5 Summary of time sequence in patient care from first physician visit to hospital admission: Percentage distributions of patients by diagnostic specific delay periods and mean number of days

	BC-BS	GHA
		%
Appendicitis		
Less than 24 hours	84	77
1 to 7 days	8	15
7+ days	8	9
Total	100	100
Mean number of days	8	4
Gall bladder and biliary duct disease		
Less than 24 hours	15	15
1 to 30 days	30	26
30+ days	55	59
Total	100	100
Mean number of days	70	60
Pneumonia		
Less than 24 hours	50	69
1 to 7 days	34	23
7+ days	17	8
Total	100	100
Mean number of days	8	2

	BC-BS	GHA
		%
Breast mass		
Less than 15 days	35	24
15 to 30 days	24	24
30+ days	41	52
Total	100	100
Mean number of days	48	48
Arteriosclerotic and hypertensive heart disease		
Less than 24 hours	61	67
1 to 7 days	12	14
7+ days	28	19
Total	100	100
Mean number of days	17	24
Hyperplasia of tonsils and adenoids		
Less than 31 days	26	13
31 to 60 days	30	21
60+ days	44	66
Total	100 *	100
Mean number of days	87	87

	BC-BS	GHA
		%
Diabetes mellitus		
Less than 24 hours	43	47
1 to 14 days	31	47
14+ days	25	7
Total	100	100
Mean number of days	22	5
Myocardial infarction		
Less than 24 hours	87	93
1 to 7 days	2	0
7+ days	11	7
Total	100	100
Mean number of days	6	12
Uterine fibroids[a]		
Less than 15 days	21	3
15 to 90 days	53	56
90+ days	25	41
Total	100 *	100
Mean number of days	73 *	97

Note: The category "less than 24 hours" includes all emergency admissions.
[a]Excludes patients who did not have a hysterectomy.
*P ≤ .05.

Table 10.6 Patterns of prehospital care: Mean number of physician visits and percent of nonemergency patients reporting ambulatory care prior to admission

Diagnostic category	All Physician visits (mean)		Nonemergency patients (percent)							
			Medication		Treatment		X-rays		Tests	
	BC-BS	GHA	BC-BS	GHA	BC-BS	GHA	BC-BS	GHA	BC-BS	GHA
Appendicitis	2.2	2.1	56	50	9	0	82	50	52	37
Breast mass	2.6	2.8	7	9	3	8	43 *	67	20 *	47
Diabetes mellitus	2.2	1.9	68	88	18	38	20	50	62	75
Gall bladder and biliary duct disease	3.4	3.5	53	48	83	91	45 *	76	10 *	0
Arteriosclerotic and hypertensive heart disease	2.0	2.0	74	86	13	43	37	43	49	57
Myocardial infarction	1.9	2.1	83	100	8	0	83	100	75	100
Pneumonia	2.0	1.6	80	50	12	25	56	25	33	75
Hyperplasia of tonsils and adenoids	1.6	1.9	83	76	12	15	6	16	50	47
Uterine fibroids	2.8	3.5	40	51	9	11	28 *	63	39 *	80

*P ≤ .05.

Table 10.7 Length of stay for patients in selected diagnostic categories

Diagnostic category	Total days		Preoperative days	
	BC–BS	GHA	BC–BS	GHA
	Mean			
Appendicitis	6.4	7.5	0.3	0.5
Cystic disease of the breast	2.3	2.1	1.0	1.0
Breast cancer	9.7	9.5	1.1	1.7
Diabetes mellitus[a]	9.4 *	7.1	––	––
Gall bladder and biliary duct disease	9.5 *	9.0	2.0	1.4
Arteriosclerotic and hypertensive heart disease[b]	7.8	7.0	––	––
Myocardial infarction[b]	19.1	16.4	––	––
Pneumonia[c]	7.5 *	5.8	––	––
Hyperplasia of tonsils and adenoids	1.4 *	2.0	0.4	0.8
Uterine fibroids	8.3	7.4	1.1	1.0

[a]Excludes 1 case with a stay of 122 days.

[b]Excludes 3 BC–BS patients with arteriosclerotic and hypertensive heart disease and 6 BC–BS patients with myocardial infarction who died in hospital.

[c]Includes patients with related surgery in BC–BS.

––Not applicable. *P ⩽ .05.

11

Appropriateness of Hospital Admission

Thomas D. Koepsell and Sharon B. Soroko

As discussed in Chapters 1 and 8, a variety of factors have been cited as possible explanations for the lower hospitalization rates observed for members of prepaid group practice plans as compared to those in service benefit plans, and the study reported here is only one of many which have documented this finding (Perkoff, Kahn, and Mackie, 1974; Robertson, 1972; Perrott, 1966; Densen et al., 1960; Anderson and Sheatsley, 1959; Densen, Balamuth, and Shapiro, 1958). These differences have been related to organizational features of prepaid group practices which are thought to affect the process of decision making that allocates hospital resources for the care of certain patients and which suggest greater efficiency of hospital use under prepaid group practice. There is evidence suggesting that the process of medical decision making is indeed different in prepaid group and fee-for-service practice, physicians in the former setting having less propensity to recommend hospitalization in certain clinical situations (Demlo, 1975). One mechanism for achieving this might be the reduction or elimination of admissions which, on medical grounds, are only marginally justifiable or clearly unnecessary. Another might be a conservative approach to the hospitalization of patients who carry diagnoses of questionable accuracy. This chapter explores these issues in relation to BC-BS and GHA, the two health plans under study, by an attempt to test two hypotheses:

- A larger proportion of admissions among patients with comparable diagnoses will be judged medically inappropriate under BC-BS than under GHA.

- Evidence verifying the accuracy of the discharge diagnosis will more often be present in the hospital records of GHA patients.

The general description in Chapter 10 of patient and provider behavior prior to admission to the hospital should be borne in mind in the following evaluation of the appropriateness of the admission.

METHODS OF ANALYSIS

Assessment Criteria

Judgments about the medical appropriateness of admission and the accuracy of diagnoses for the discharged patient sample were based on sets of explicit, disease-specific criteria available from published sources. The criteria for appropriateness of admission specify the clinical situations in which hospitalization is considered justified for each disease, and those for diagnostic accuracy specify objective, confirmatory evidence whose documentation in the medical record verifies the diagnosis listed. Each criteria set was developed by panels of practicing physicians, drawing on the medical literature and on their collective experience in treating patients with the targeted conditions. Thus, to a great extent, the criteria embody professional consensus on which hospital admissions can be considered medically justified and on the evidence that should be available to support the diagnosis in each case. The first set of criteria used in this study was developed by physicians in Hawaii for Payne and Lyons' Episode of Illness Study (Payne and Lyons, 1972). These criteria, which relate to appropriateness of admission only, were developed initially for research purposes, extending earlier work of Fitzpatrick, Riedel, and Payne (1962) on the relationships among physician performance, practice setting, and personal characteristics of the physician. The criteria were subsequently adapted for use in peer review in a variety of other settings, such as the Experimental Medical Care Review Organization program (Decker et al., 1973), demonstrating that their usefulness was not confined to a particular setting. Since these criteria were among the few available when the present study was initiated, they were used extensively in designing the medical record abstract forms used in the study.

The second criteria set used was developed under the auspices of the American Medical Association as technical support for the Professional Standards Review Organization (PSRO) program, a federally mandated network of medical care provider organizations charged with assuring the quality and efficiency of care for beneficiaries of federal health programs. Using input from various medical specialty bodies, the American Medical Association published their *Sample Criteria for Short-Stay Hospital Review* in 1976. They include two types of criteria used in the present study: (1) disease-specific admission review guidelines intended to facilitate the screening of admissions in various disease categories in order to detect medically inappropriate admissions, and (2) diagnostic validation criteria to permit screening for inaccurate diagnoses.

The AMA criteria were chosen because of their broad base of professional opinion and their relatively modest data requirements. In addition, they covered many diagnoses besides those selected in this phase of the study, thus providing admission review criteria for patients admitted with diagnoses that were different from their eventual discharge diagnoses. It should be noted that the AMA criteria were not developed for research purposes; they were designed for screening large numbers of cases in the context of peer review programs, and to single out cases with a relatively high probability of an inappropriate admission or inaccurate diagnosis. In such programs, the final decision about the adequacy of care is left to a reviewing physician. Since a second review stage was not feasible in the present study, cases that met and those that failed the AMA criteria should therefore be considered as reflecting either a low or a high probability of a true deficiency in care.

Space limitations preclude presenting the criteria sets in full detail for all diagnoses. For illustration, the criteria for diseases of the gallbladder and biliary duct are shown below (criteria for the remaining diagnoses may be obtained from the monographs by Payne and Lyons (1972) and by the American Medical Association (1976)):

Payne and Lyons Criteria for Appropriateness of Admission. An admission was classified as appropriate if at least one of the following was documented as having been present on admission:

- Pain, nausea, and vomiting

- Recurrent gallbladder attacks

- Fever

- Jaundice

- Right upper quadrant mass

- Diagnosis of cholelithiasis or cholecystitis, admitted for operation

AMA Criteria for Appropriateness of Admission. An admission was classified as appropriate if at least one of the following was documented as having been present on admission:

- Scheduled for operation, with radiological evidence of a pathological gallbladder or abnormal common bile duct

- Suspicion of gallstones, on the basis of a tender, palpable gallbladder (with or without evidence of peritonitis); or radiological evidence of gallstones

- Jaundice

- Abdominal pain suggesting biliary colic or acute cholecystitis

- Palpable, tender gallbladder

AMA Criteria for Validation of Discharge Diagnosis. At least one of the following must be documented:

— Radiological demonstration of gallstones, mucosal abnormalities, or nonvisualized gallbladder by repeat oral cholecystogram or intravenous cholangiography
— Tender, palpable gallbladder
— Pathology report showing stones or cholecystitis

The use of criteria from external sources implies that the physicians providing care in the two health plans under study had no direct input into the assessment of their performance. Had criteria of admission and diagnostic accuracy been developed by GHA and BC-BS physicians themselves, they might have differed from those actually employed. The extent to which criteria should be subject to adaptation to local standards of care is a subject of considerable debate, and one reason for using two separate sets of criteria in this study was to examine whether, and to what extent, the results would depend on the particular criteria set used.

The Data

Detailed disease-specific abstracts were prepared from the hospital medical records of patients under both plans who were discharged in one of the diagnostic categories chosen for the study. (See Chapter 8 for completion rates and methods used and Chapter 9 for a description of the sample population.) The information abstracted indicated in some detail the complaints and physical status of patients at the time of admission, reasons for admission, information about the results of tests and treatments, and discharge diagnosis. Because patients were included in this analysis only if a complete medical record abstract was available, the sample size for some diagnostic categories differs slightly from those shown in Table 8.2. No attempt was made to gather information from the outpatient medical record.

In keeping with the practice employed in admission certification programs, criteria corresponding to the admitting diagnosis (not the discharge diagnosis) were applied in each case for an assessment of the appropriateness of admissions under each plan. Overall, ten cases (fewer than 1 percent of the total) were excluded from analysis under the AMA criteria because they had been admitted with diagnoses for which no criteria were available. All patients in two of the diagnostic categories (appendicitis and myocardial infarction) plus about 4 percent overall of those in the remaining categories were excluded from analysis by the Payne and Lyons criteria for similar reasons. As some of the relevant criteria became available only after completion of abstracting, a total of 21 cases were excluded from diagnostic validation by the AMA criteria because the medical abstracts did not include the requisite information.

In applying the admissions criteria, there was generally a direct match between the Payne and Lyons criteria and the abstract form, so that requisite data could be coded into machine readable form and the criteria applied to these data. For the AMA criteria as well, there was often a direct match between criteria and data on the form. Where this was not the case, standardized decision rules were developed which operationalized the criteria in terms of the data on the abstract form. These were then uniformly applied to cases in both plans.

Methodological Observations

In interpreting the findings, some features of the assessment method in relation to the study sample should be noted. First, use of the criteria described above places a premium on the level of completeness of the medical record. If a patient has a key physical finding that justifies hospitalization for a specific diagnosis, but that finding is not documented in the medical record, the case does not meet the criteria. Deficiencies in medical recording practices thus have the same effect on the results as do deficiencies in care. However, since very few cases did in fact fail the criteria for appropriateness of admission, this potential limitation does not appear to have been a serious problem. For diagnostic validation as well, a large majority of cases passed the criteria. As the decision on diagnostic accuracy frequently hinged on the documented presence of an abnormality on a single diagnostic test, a case could fail the criteria for either of two reasons: (1) the record contained no indication that the specific test had been performed, or (2) the record indicated that while the test had been performed, its results did not support the diagnosis assigned. Since the relative seriousness of these two types of deficiency differs from one diagnosis to another, an attempt was made in the data that follow to identify which of these two possible reasons for failure to meet the criteria was responsible in each case.

A second point of note is that, in order to meet other study objectives, the sample of hospitalized cases for this phase of the study was drawn according to discharge rather than admitting diagnosis. Despite this sampling method, criteria for assessment of the appropriateness of admission were chosen to correspond to the *admitting* diagnosis in each case, whether or not this was the same as the discharge diagnosis. (This choice was made because the criteria were developed to be used in this manner in peer review programs.) Thus, some cases were considered to have been appropriately admitted even if they entered the hospital with a diagnosis other than that which defines the patient sample. The size of any bias introduced by this method of sampling cases was probably not large and would apply equally to both plans. Overall, 96 percent of the sample (range, 87.5 percent to 100 percent across diagnoses) were discharged with diagnoses that were sufficiently similar to the respective admitting diagnoses that the criteria applied would be the same regardless of which diagnosis were used. This high percentage may be related to the particular diagnostic categories studied, all of which were relatively well defined disease entities. Two recent studies investigating a broader range of diagnoses suggest that, on the average, diagnoses remain the same from admission through discharge in about 60 percent of cases (Burford and Averill, 1979; Institute of Medicine, 1977). Diagnostic crossover aside, however, early findings of the present study (Chapter 2) showed that admission rates under GHA were markedly and pervasively lower for nearly all diagnostic categories. If inappropriate admissions under BC-BS were to account for any substantial fraction of these differences, there should be little difficulty finding inappropriate BC-BS admissions regardless of how the study sample was chosen.

APPROPRIATENESS OF ADMISSION AND
VALIDATION OF DIAGNOSIS

Diagnostic Categories

Appendicitis. The sample in this diagnostic category consisted of 192 BC-BS patients and 30 GHA patients discharged with a diagnosis of appendicitis. While Payne and Lyons did not develop criteria for appendicitis, the relevant AMA admission review criteria regard mere suspicion of appendicitis as sufficient justification for admission, thus equating the diagnosis itself with a need for hospital care. Table 11.1 shows that by far the majority of patients discharged in this category also entered the hospital with a presumptive diagnosis of appendicitis; they were, therefore, appropriate admissions under the AMA criteria. Not more than 10 percent of patients in each plan entered the hospital with other diagnoses, and these constituted justified admissions on the basis of the respective AMA criteria, except for 1 percent of BC-BS cases with nonspecific admitting diagnoses for which no AMA criteria existed.

The AMA criterion for validation of the diagnosis of appendicitis is a positive tissue report if appendectomy is performed, and over three quarters of cases under both plans met this criterion (Table 11.2). However, although all patients were discharged with a diagnosis of appendicitis, 2.6 percent in BC-BS and 3.3 percent in GHA had pathologically normal appendices, and in 5.2 percent of BC-BS cases, the removed tissue, though pathologically abnormal, failed to validate the diagnosis of appendicitis. Twenty percent of GHA cases and 2.6 percent of BC-BS cases were classified as failing the criteria because there were no pathology reports in the hospital medical records.

Breast Mass. The patients in this group fell into two diagnostic categories at discharge, breast cancer and cystic disease of the breast. There were no patients with known metastases who were being treated with radiation or chemotherapy in the sample, so that the cases discussed here (208 in BC-BS and 49 in GHA) consisted entirely of patients undergoing breast biopsy and/or mastectomy. Payne and Lyons did not develop criteria specifically for cystic breast disease, but their admission criteria for breast cancer specify presence of breast tumor or suspected breast carcinoma as an indication for hospitalization. The AMA criteria as well consider the mere existence of a mass in the breast an indication for admission. Since all patients in the sample had a documented mass in the breast at the time of admission, all admissions under both plans were classified as medically appropriate by both criteria sets.

The AMA also has a single set of diagnostic validation criteria for breast mass, whether malignant or not. By these criteria, the diagnosis of breast mass was validated in all cases simply by documentation of the presence of a mass. The diagnosis of either breast cancer or cystic breast disease, on the other hand, must be validated by pathology report. One case in BC-BS had a nonmalignant tumor of the breast but was discharged with a diagnosis of breast cancer, and one case in GHA had malignant neoplasm of the breast yet was discharged with a diagnosis of cystic disease (Table 11.3). For all other cases in both plans, the pathology report confirmed the discharge diagnosis.

Diabetes Mellitus. The Payne and Lyons criteria for diabetes specify ten indications for admission that cover both acute and chronic manifestations. As shown in Table 11.4, all 12 GHA cases met the admission criteria, and of 175 patients in BC-BS admitted for diabetes, only 0.5 percent failed to meet any of the criteria. Appropriateness of admission for the 4.6 percent of BC-BS cases who were admitted with diagnoses other than diabetes cannot be judged in the absence of relevant Payne and Lyons criteria. The AMA criteria deal with the fairly wide range of reasons for which hospitalization of diabetics is indicated by specifying separate criteria for diabetics with coma or precoma, juvenile-onset diabetics admitted for reasons other than coma, diabetics with chronic complications such as kidney or peripheral vascular disease, and diabetics admitted for reasons such as intercurrent infections or to readjust insulin dosages. The overall proportion of cases which clearly met these more detailed criteria was virtually identical in the two plans (92.6 and 91.7, respectively, for BC-BS and GHA; Table 11.4), although slightly lower than for the Payne and Lyons criteria. In BC-BS, 1.1 percent of cases were admitted with nonspecific diagnoses for which no AMA criteria are available, and 6.3 percent in BC-BS and 8.3 percent in GHA were admitted with a diagnosis of diabetes but failed to meet any of the indications for admission in the corresponding AMA criteria set.

The AMA also specifies separate validation criteria for each of the four criteria subsets for diabetes. The 175 BC-BS and 12 GHA cases were matched to the appropriate subset based on the discharge diagnosis, with the results shown in Table 11.5. In all, 1.1 percent of the BC-BS cases failed to meet the applicable validation criteria; the diagnoses were validated in all other cases assessed. It should be noted that a total of 21 cases with discharge diagnoses of diabetes with coma or precoma had to be excluded from analysis because the respective criteria require knowledge of blood pH, pCO_2, or serum osmolarity. These data had not been abstracted because the medical record abstracts for the discharged patient sample had been prepared before the AMA criteria became available. Thus, for those cases in which a diagnosis of diabetes with coma or precoma could not be validated by other means, it was not possible to determine whether the discharge diagnosis was validated in its entirety.

Diseases of the Gallbladder and Biliary Duct. Appropriateness of admission was examined for a total of 234 BC-BS patients and 34 GHA patients with a discharge diagnosis of cholelithiasis and/or cholecystitis. The Payne and Lyons criteria consider an admission for treatment of acute cholecystitis to be indicated in the presence of specific clinical findings substantiating acute illness, and admission for scheduled surgery is always considered appropriate in the presence of a diagnosis of cholelithiasis or acute or chronic cholecystitis. In 93.6 percent of BC-BS cases and 97.1 percent of GHA cases admitted with diagnoses of cholecystitis or cholelithiasis, these criteria were met (Table 11.6). The remaining cases were admitted with other diagnoses for which Payne and Lyons criteria were not available. The AMA criteria for cholecystitis and cholelithiasis also consider admission justified if abdominal pain suggestive of cholecystitis is present or if surgery is scheduled electively. Application of the AMA criteria to the patient sample thus yielded almost identical results to those obtained for the Payne and Lyons criteria in Table 11.6. Again, all cases with admitting diagnoses of cholecystitis or cholelithiasis met the criteria, and of the 16 cases admitted with other diagnoses, all but one BC-BS patient met the criteria for the respective admitting diagnosis, which ranged from abdominal pain of unclear etiology to peptic ulcer. The remaining case (a BC-BS patient admitted for urinary tract infection) failed the criteria.

The discharge diagnosis was validated in a similarly high proportion of cases (Table 11.7), although a total of 5.8 percent of GHA cases and 3.8 percent of BC-BS cases failed to meet any of the AMA diagnostic validation criteria for cholecystitis and cholelithiasis. No x-ray abnormalities were found in 2.1 percent of BC-BS cases, and for the remainder, there was no evidence in the medical record that the required tests had been performed.

Arteriosclerotic and Hypertensive Heart Disease. The Payne and Lyons criteria specify 13 different indications for admission to deal with the range of symptoms in this diagnostic category. Of 163 cases in BC-BS and 16 cases in GHA, 93.8 percent of the former and all of the latter were classified as appropriately admitted (Table 11.8). Only one BC-BS case (0.6 percent) failed the criteria, and in 5.5 percent of BC-BS cases, appropriateness of admission could not be assessed because the patients were admitted with diagnoses for which no Payne and Lyons criteria were available. The AMA criteria do not deal with this diagnostic category as a single entity, but instead provide five separate sets of criteria which apply to subgroups within the broader category of heart disease, i.e., myocardial infarction, arteriosclerotic heart disease, congestive heart failure, hypertension, and atrial fibrillation, the last applying to other cardiac rhythm disturbances as well. This more disaggregated approach to appropriateness of admission for heart disease yielded only slightly different results from those for the Payne and Lyons criteria shown in Table 11.8; 5.5 percent of cases in BC-BS and 6.3 percent in GHA were admitted with diagnoses other than heart disease, and though these were subsequently changed, all must be considered appropriate in the light of corresponding admission review criteria. One case in BC-BS (0.6 percent), although admitted with a diagnosis of heart disease, failed the admission criteria, and 20.2 percent of BC-BS cases were admitted with a diagnosis of suspected myocardial infarction which was found, after further study, not to have been present. There were no such cases under GHA. Demographic differences in the composition of two plans could play a role in explaining the different distributions among diagnostic subcategories. The AMA criteria for validation of the discharge diagnosis were met in 97.5 percent of BC-BS cases and 100 percent of GHA cases (Table 11.9).

Myocardial Infarction. Payne and Lyons did not develop specific criteria for myocardial infarction, and the AMA admission criteria for myocardial infarction are part of the previously described set for heart disease, where admission is considered indicated in the presence of a diagnosis or suspicion of acute myocardial infarction. As with appendicitis, therefore, the mere suspicion of a myocardial infarction is considered tantamount to a need for hospitalization, and admission was thus judged appropriate for all 14 GHA patients in the sample and for 97.7 percent of the 88 BC-BS patients (Table 11.10). Of the two patients in BC-BS who entered with admitting diagnoses other than myocardial infarction, one was initially diagnosed as pulmonary embolism; here the AMA criteria corresponding to the admitting diagnosis were met. The other patient, who suffered a myocardial infarction while in the hospital undergoing diagnostic tests for obstructive uropathy, failed the AMA criteria applicable to his admitting diagnosis.

The AMA diagnostic validation criteria for myocardial infarction, which accept compatible electrocardiographic changes, cardiac enzyme changes, or a classic history as sufficient evidence, were likewise met by nearly all of the cases examined (Table 11.11). Only 2.3 percent in BC-BS failed to meet any of the criteria, the diagnosis in all other cases being validated by at least one criterion.

Pneumonia. The 156 BC-BS cases and 12 GHA cases with discharge diagnoses of pneumonia were divided into subgroups by age, since both criteria sets specify separate admission requirements for adults (aged 18 years and over) and children (aged less than 18 years). The Payne and Lyons criteria for admissions of adults regard mere suspicion of pneumonia as justification for hospitalization. For children, the criteria require in addition the presence of one or more specific findings. All of the GHA cases admitted with a diagnosis of pneumonia, whether adults or children, met the criteria for admission (Table 11.12). Of the BC-BS cases, 12.2 percent were children for whom the criteria for admission were not met. Also, 10.2 percent of cases in BC-BS were admitted with diagnoses other than pneumonia for which Payne and Lyons criteria are not available. Using the AMA criteria, under which the proportion of unclassified cases was reduced to 0.6 percent, all cases in GHA were again judged to have been appropriately admitted. In BC-BS, 5.1 percent failed to meet the criteria, six of them with pneumonia and two admitted with fever of unknown origin.

Validation of a diagnosis of pneumonia in adults by the AMA criteria requires a confirmatory chest x-ray, while the physical finding of rales is considered sufficient evidence of pneumonia in children. Here, 33.3 percent of GHA cases failed the criteria, in each case because there was no documentation in the hospital medical record that a chest x-ray had been taken. By contrast, only 6.4 percent of BC-BS cases failed to meet the diagnostic validation criteria (Table 11.13), chest x-rays having been normal in 2.6 percent and no record of a chest x-ray found in the remaining cases.

Hyperplasia of Tonsils and Adenoids. Appropriateness of admission in this category was assessed for 107 BC-BS patients and 61 GHA patients, all admitted for scheduled tonsillectomy, adenoidectomy, or both procedures. The question of appropriateness of hospitalization here hinges on the medical appropriateness of surgery, and the Payne and Lyons criteria, which specify quite detailed indications for tonsillectomy and adenoidectomy, thus address both aspects of appropriateness for this patient sample.

Several features of the Payne and Lyons criteria are noteworthy for this surgical category. First, they specify that an "indication for removal of one tissue is not an indication for [removal of] both." Since their indications for removal of tonsils and adenoids are different, a separate assessment is necessary of whether the specific surgical procedure performed (tonsillectomy, adenoidectomy, or both) was justified in the circumstances. Second, the criteria specify both absolute indications for tonsillectomy (i.e., surgery is mandatory) and relative indications (i.e., surgery is not usually mandatory but may be chosen as the best form of therapy at the physician's discretion). Since absolute indications were nonexistent in the present sample, tonsillectomy was considered appropriate whenever evidence of a relative indication was present.

Third, Payne and Lyons used two physician panels — pediatricians and otolaryngologists — to establish the criteria, the latter specifying the somewhat more liberal criteria for adenoidectomy which have been employed here. Fourth, the criteria require evidence of three or more episodes of illness within a year. In the present study, hospital medical records were not always sufficiently explicit in this respect and often used descriptions such as "recurrent" or "repeated." Therefore, cases were classified as follows:

- Met criteria: if the record specified that the required number of illness episodes had occurred within a year or if surgery was justified on other grounds

- Questionable: if the record indicated, by use of terms such as "recurrent," "repeated," or "frequent," that at least two illness episodes had occurred, unless available data justified surgery on other grounds

- Failed criteria: if the record failed to indicate that more than one illness episode had occurred, unless available data justified surgery on other grounds

There was a large and equal proportion of cases in both plans (32.7 percent in BC-BS, 36.1 percent in GHA; Table 11.14) which failed these criteria, and a similar proportion of admissions of questionable appropriateness (36.4 percent in BC-BS and 27.9 percent in GHA).

There are two sets of AMA criteria for this diagnostic category, one applicable to those aged less than 18 years and the other to those aged 18 years or over. It was again necessary to define a category for cases in which compliance with the criteria was questionable, i.e., where the record indicated "recurrent" or "repeated" episodes of otitis media or tonsillitis without specifying whether four or more such episodes had occurred in a single year, as required by the AMA criteria. Despite differences between the Payne and Lyons and the AMA sets, quite similar proportions failed to meet the AMA criteria for admission (33.6 percent in BC-BS, 39.3 percent in GHA) or were questionable (37.4 percent in BC-BS, 23 percent in GHA).

The difference between plans was larger with regard to the type of surgery performed. Slightly over half of GHA cases (55.8 percent) underwent tonsillectomy only, whereas 57 percent in BC-BS underwent both procedures (Table 11.15). A closer examination of the appropriateness of the specific type of surgery performed as judged by the Payne and Lyons criteria (also shown in Table 11.15), indicates that a total of 58.3 percent of tonsillectomies in GHA and 41 percent of those under BC-BS failed the respective criteria, while the opposite was found for adenoidectomies, where a third of GHA cases failed the criteria compared to 57.6 percent of BC-BS adenoidectomies. Despite the rather small sample sizes, these differences were all statistically significant. Overall, a rather large proportion of cases failed the Payne and Lyons criteria in both plans. Differences between plans were mainly confined to the type of surgery performed and the degree to which specific procedures were justified according to the criteria.

The AMA criteria for validation of a diagnosis of diseased tonsils and/or adenoids require a pathology report for those aged less than 18 years, while for those aged 18 years or over, the diagnosis is also considered validated if there is documented evidence of large and/or infected tonsils or adenoids on physical examination. In fact, the diagnoses could not be validated in 10.3 percent of cases in BC-BS and 8.2 percent in GHA (Table 11.16). These all refer to patients in the younger age group, who were classified as having failed the criteria because of the lack of pathology reports in their medical records. Considering that no specific pathology finding is required by the AMA criteria to validate the diagnosis, this result may be more a reflection of record completeness than of diagnostic accuracy.

Uterine Fibroids. The Payne and Lyons criteria for appropriateness of admission list ten admission indications for patients with uterine fibroids. Here, 1.9 percent of 162 BC-BS cases and 3.3 percent of 60 GHA cases hospitalized with admitting diagnoses of uterine fibroids failed to meet the criteria (Table 11.17), and 4.9 percent in BC-BS and 1.7 percent in GHA were admitted with diagnoses for which there were no criteria in the Payne and Lyons set. The results of applying the AMA criteria for uterine leiomyoma (essentially a synonym for fibromyoma or fibroids) were in close agreement with those obtained with the Payne and Lyons criteria. Under BC-BS, two cases (1.2 percent) entered with admitting diagnoses of infertility for which data on the abstract form were insufficient for classification, and one GHA patient (1.7 percent) entered the hospital with an admitting diagnosis for which no AMA criteria were available. Application of the AMA criteria for validation of diagnosis (validation by pathology report, surgeon's description in an operative note, or x-ray report) indicated that none of these criteria were met in 3.1 percent of BC-BS cases and 1.7 percent of GHA cases (Table 11.18).

SUMMARY AND CONCLUSIONS

Applying the Payne and Lyons criteria for appropriateness of admission revealed only small differences between plans regarding compliance with the criteria, and in no case were they large enough to be statistically significant (Table 11.19). For six of the eight diagnostic categories for which criteria were available, less than 5 percent of cases in either plan failed to meet the criteria, and only for tonsillectomy/adenoidectomy and, in the case of BC-BS, pneumonia was there an appreciable number of admissions which were inappropriate by the Payne and Lyons criteria. Also, the results in each diagnostic category were in close agreement with those reported by Payne and Lyons from their experience in Hawaii (Payne and Lyons, 1972).

More detailed analysis showed that significantly more BC-BS patients underwent both tonsillectomy and adenoidectomy than either procedure only, so that somewhat more extensive surgery was performed under the service benefit plan patients in this diagnostic category. Also, on the basis of the separate criteria for these two procedures developed by Payne and Lyons, it was found that 57.6 percent of the adenoidectomies performed under BC-BS failed these criteria, versus 33.3 percent under GHA. On the other hand, more tonsillectomies performed under GHA failed the respective criteria than under BC-BS (58.3 percent as compared to 41 percent); both differences were statistically significant.

Similar findings hold for the AMA admissions criteria for all ten diagnostic categories in almost every respect. Again, less than 5 percent of cases in either plan failed the criteria in seven of the ten diagnostic categories; the exceptions were tonsillectomy and adenoidectomy, pneumonia in BC-BS, and diabetes mellitus in both plans (Table 11.20). A somewhat smaller proportion of cases overall remained unclassified under the AMA criteria because of the wider range of diagnostic categories covered.

The AMA diagnostic validation criteria as well failed to demonstrate important differences between the two plans. Although in nearly every diagnostic category there were a few cases which failed the criteria, differences across diagnoses were not consistent (Table 11.21). The major exception was pneumonia, where 33.3 percent of GHA cases (as compared to 6.4 percent in BC-BS) failed the criteria, mainly because the hospital medical record contained no indication that a chest x-ray had been performed. Despite the small sample size in GHA (12 cases), this difference is statistically significant. However, as noted earlier, the study sample was drawn according to discharge rather than admitting diagnosis, and the validation of diagnosis criteria were applied according to discharge diagnosis. Since discharge diagnoses are assigned after diagnostic information obtained in the hospital has become available, discharge diagnoses are likely to be more accurate than admitting diagnoses. Accordingly, the degree of diagnostic inaccuracy present on admission among patients in the two plans is probably underestimated in this analysis. Insufficient information was captured on the abstract forms to apply criteria according to the admitting diagnosis in each case. A comparison of the frequency with which diagnoses were changed from admission to discharge under each plan shows that such changes were relatively rare under both plans (Table 11.22), though there was some suggestion of more frequent changes under BC-BS. A summary chi square test for a consistent difference between plans across diagnoses showed no significant difference at the $P \leq .05$ level, however (Mantel and Haenszel, 1959).

These findings on appropriateness of admissions and diagnostic validity provide little support for the hypothesis that a larger proportion of admissions under the service benefit plan would be classifiable as medically inappropriate. Only in considering the medical justification of adenoidectomy could important differences between plans in the expected direction be documented. This was counterbalanced by the finding that a larger share of tonsillectomies in GHA failed to meet the criteria specifying indications for surgery. Overall, differences between plans with respect to the proportion of cases in which hospital admission was classified as medically appropriate were quite small. Thus, it is doubtful that they would have much practical significance even if they could have been shown to be statistically significant on the basis of larger sample sizes. The results are perhaps most striking because of the small number of cases in either plan which were classified as medically inappropriate admissions by the criteria. Also, the fact that very few patients in either plan were discharged with diagnoses which could not be validated indicates that differences in hospitalization rates for these diagnostic categories cannot be explained by a larger proportion of diagnoses of questionable accuracy in BC-BS. The finding that changes in diagnosis from admission to discharge were rare and fairly evenly split between the plans substantiates this.

One possible explanation for the findings could be that there were, in fact, lower levels of morbidity among GHA enrollees, thus reducing the need for hospital services. This would account for the lower hospitalization rates in GHA reported in Chapter 2, and would be compatible with the finding that a large majority of BC-BS cases warranted hospitalization on medical grounds. However, Phase II (Chapter 5) showed that GHA enrollees reported a greater number of episodes of illness per year after adjusting for differences in racial composition, and suggested that the illness experience of this group was, if anything, worse than that of the BC-BS group. Also against this explanation is the fact that several of the diagnostic categories for which admission rates differed significantly between the two plans correspond to diseases that are not preventable by any known means:

for example, appendicitis, cystic disease of the breast and breast cancer, uterine fibroids, and diseases of the gallbladder and biliary duct.

A second possible explanation for the findings of this study could be that the process of deciding who is to be hospitalized in GHA results in restrictive use of the hospital: that is, there could have been GHA patients in these diagnostic categories for whom hospitalization would have been medically appropriate but who were not hospitalized. This explanation would be compatible with the finding that very few GHA cases were unnecessarily admitted; presumably those who were admitted were those for whom hospitalization was least discretionary. This explanation is also consistent with the finding that few of the BC-BS cases failed the criteria. It has been argued (Greenberg and Rodburg, 1971; Monsma, 1970) that underuse of the hospital is likely to be more visible to, and less tolerated by, the consumer than excessive use. To the extent that such attitudes can potentially be translated into consumer action (e.g., malpractice litigation, changing plan membership) they may act as a deterrent to underuse in both plans. Moreover, medical education inculcates physicians with the belief that it is a more grievous error to fail to treat a treatable disease than to provide diagnostic and therapeutic services which may prove to be unnecessary. This, too, would tend to produce more rather than less use. Perhaps the most conclusive way to confirm or refute this second explanation would be to investigate the outcome of treatment in patients with each disease under both plans, regardless of whether treatment was provided in a hospital or not. Should GHA be inappropriately denying hospitalization to some patients, poorer outcomes under GHA should be apparent. This is an ambitious undertaking which was beyond the scope of this project; however, it may be a fruitful area for future inquiry.

A third possible explanation for the findings reported in this chapter could lie with the criteria themselves and the meaning of certain terms used in conjunction with them. It is tempting to think in terms of two mutually exclusive categories of potential hospital admissions: those which are necessary, appropriate, and justified versus those which are unnecessary, inappropriate, and unjustified. However, it is probably more realistic to assume that the clinical situations presented by patients fall into three occasionally overlapping categories with respect to the medical legitimacy of hospitalization:

— *Mandatory admission*: where there would be a high degree of consensus among physicians that hospitalization is the only reasonable way to manage a specific patient's illness. Among medical peers, failure to admit such a patient would be considered grounds for sanction.

— *Discretionary admission*: where physicians might often disagree among themselves on whether the benefits of hospitalization consistently outweigh its costs and risks. The medical literature often fails to provide a clear answer to the question of which of several alternative treatment methods is the best way to manage a given clinical problem, and such disagreement would be regarded as legitimate differences of opinion among professionals. The choice to admit or not would thus be left to "clinical judgment," and neither admission nor failure to admit in such circumstances would offer grounds for sanction.

— *Unwarranted admission*: where there would be a high degree of consensus among physicians that hospitalization offers no important benefits over outpatient management and represents a waste of resources. Admission in such circumstances might well be considered grounds for sanction.

Clearly, the distribution of patients among these three categories would vary from one diagnostic category to another. But in general, one might expect the terms "necessary," "justified," and "appropriate" to refer to different subsets of admission thus classified. The group of discretionary admissions would occupy the middle ground of a range extending from clearly necessary to clearly unnecessary and would be considered justified and appropriate (no sanction for electing to hospitalize) but not mandatory or necessary (no sanction for electing not to hospitalize).

The criteria used in this study covered appropriateness of admission and justification for admission. The criteria were thus intended to discriminate between clearly unwarranted admissions and all others. This implies that not all cases passing the criteria were necessarily mandatory admissions; rather, they were probably a mix of mandatory and discretionary admissions. Even though the proportion of admissions classified as unjustified by the criteria was small under both plans, substantial differences in admission rates could still have resulted from differences in hospitalization decisions for patients who would be in the discretionary category. In that case, mandatory admissions would still have been hospitalized and unwarranted admissions treated as outpatients; both plans would have performed similarly in terms of compliance with the criteria and would be practicing acceptable medicine in the eyes of their peers, as indicated by the findings.

In order for this explanation to account for the twofold difference in hospitalization rates observed in Phase I of the study, one must postulate a fairly large gray zone of admissions which would be classified as discretionary. Such a view would be consistent with theory on the sociology of professions (Freidson, 1970). Medicine is a profession in which the judgment of the individual practitioner is highly valued and the right to exercise that judgment is closely guarded. When practitioners are asked to establish rules which specify how they and their colleagues are expected to practice, it seems reasonable to expect that those rules might be set sufficiently broad to permit a good deal of room for the exercise of professional discretion.

To the extent that application in this study of explicit criteria for hospital use resembles their application as screening criteria in formal systems of peer review such as PSROs, it is interesting to view the results in another way. One motive for the promotion of both prepaid group practice plans and PSROs has been a desire to enhance the efficiency of hospital use. Perhaps the present data can provide some hint on how these two approaches compare in effectiveness toward achieving that goal.

Note: The criteria sets used for assessing appropriateness of admission and validation of the discharge diagnosis in the following tables were developed by the American Medical Association (American Medical Association. 1976. *Sample Criteria for Short-stay Hospital Review: Screening Criteria to Assist PSROs in Quality Assurance.* Chicago; referred to as AMA criteria) and by Payne and Lyons (Payne, B.C. and Lyons, T. 1972. *Method of Evaluating and Improving Personal Medical Care Quality: Episode of Illness Study.* Ann Arbor: University of Michigan School of Medicine; referred to as Payne and Lyons criteria). Payne and Lyons did not provide diagnostic validation criteria, nor admissions criteria for appendicitis, breast mass, and myocardial infarction.

Table 11.1 Appropriateness of admission assessed by AMA criteria: Percentage distribution of patients with a discharge diagnosis of appendicitis

Classification by admitting diagnosis	BC–BS (%) (n = 192)	GHA (%) (n = 30)
Met criteria		
Appendicitis	95.8	90.0
Other	3.1[b]	10.0[c]
Subtotal	99.0	100.0
Unclassified[a]	1.0[d]	0.0
Total	100.0	100.0

[a]No criteria available.

[b]Abdominal pain (3 cases); acute abdomen (1); pancreatitis (1); ureteral calculi (1).

[c]Abdominal pain (1 case); acute abdomen (1); diverticulitis (1).

[d]Possible tissue disorder (1 case); possible brucellosis (1).

Table 11.2 Validation of diagnosis by AMA criteria: Percentage distribution of patients with a discharge diagnosis of appendicitis

Classification by discharge diagnosis	BC–BS(%) (n = 192)	GHA (%) (n = 30)
Met criteria	89.6	76.7
Failed criteria		
Normal tissue	2.6	3.3
Other pathology finding	5.2	0.0
Missing pathology report	2.6	20.0
Subtotal	10.4	23.3
Total	100.0	100.0

Table 11.3 Validation of diagnosis by pathology report for patients with a discharge diagnosis of breast cancer or cystic breast disease

Classification by discharge diagnosis	BC–BS (%)	GHA (%)
Cancer	(n = 58)	(n = 10)
Validated by pathology	98.3	100.0
Not validated	1.7[a]	0.0
Total	100.0	100.0
Cystic breast disease	(n = 150)	(n = 39)
Validated by pathology	100.0	97.4
Not validated	0.0	2.6[b]
Total	100.0	100.0

[a]Nonmalignant.
[b]Malignant neoplasm.

Table 11.4 Appropriateness of admission assessed by Payne and Lyons and AMA criteria: Percentage distribution of patients with a discharge diagnosis of diabetes mellitus

Classification by admitting diagnosis	BC–BS (%) (n = 175)	GHA (%) (n = 12)
Payne and Lyons		
Met criteria	94.9	100.0
Failed criteria	0.5	0.0
Unclassified[a]	4.6[b]	0.0
Total	100.0	100.0
AMA		
Met criteria		
Diabetes with coma	20.6	33.3
Juvenile diabetes	10.3	16.7
Diabetes with chronic complications	12.0	8.3
Other diabetes	46.3	33.3
Other diagnosis	3.4[c]	0.0
Subtotal	92.6	91.7
Failed criteria		
Other diabetes	6.3	8.3
Unclassified[a]	1.1[d]	0.0
Total	100.0	100.0

[a]No criteria available.

[b]Hypertension (3 cases); acute pancreatitis (1); alcoholism (1); recurrent weakness (1); conversion reaction (1); arteriosclerotic heart disease (1).

[c]Hypertension (3 cases); acute pancreatitis (1); alcoholism (1); arteriosclerotic heart disease (1).

[d]Recurrent weakness (1); conversion reaction (1).

Table 11.5 Validation of diagnosis assessed by AMA criteria: Percentage
distribution of patients with a discharge diagnosis of diabetes
mellitus

Classification by discharge diagnosis	BC–BS (%) (n = 175)	GHA (%) (n = 12)
Met criteria		
Diabetes with coma or precoma	10.3	8.3
Juvenile diabetes	11.4	16.7
Diabetes with chronic complications	12.0	8.3
Other diabetes	54.9	41.7
Subtotal	88.6	75.0
Failed criteria	1.1	0.0
Excluded[a]	10.3	25.0
Total	100.0	100.0

[a]Relevant data not abstracted.

Table 11.6 Appropriateness of admission assessed by Payne and Lyons and AMA criteria: Percentage distribution of patients with a discharge diagnosis of cholecystitis and/or cholelithiasis

Classification by admitting diagnosis	BC–BS (%) (n = 234)	GHA (%) (n = 34)
Payne and Lyons		
Met criteria	93.6	97.1
Unclassified[a]	6.4[b]	2.9[c]
Total	100.0	100.0
AMA		
Met criteria		
Cholecystitis and/or cholelithiasis	93.6	97.1
Other	6.0[d]	2.9[e]
Subtotal	99.6	100.0
Failed criteria		
Urinary tract infection	0.4	0.0
Total	100.0	100.0

[a]No criteria available.

[b]Abdominal pain of unclear etiology (2 cases); intestinal obstruction (2); possible myocardial infarction (2); gastroenteritis (1); acute pancreatitis (1); pulmonary embolism (1); abdominal pain—possible pelvic inflammatory disease (1); pelvic pain of unclear etiology (1); urinary tract infection (1); hypertension of unclear etiology (1); possible kidney stone (1); peptic ulcer (1).

[c]Epigastric pain—rule out myocardial infarction (1 case).

[d]Abdominal pain of unclear etiology (2 cases); intestinal obstruction (2); possible myocardial infarction (2); gastroenteritis (1); pulmonary embolism (1); abdominal pain—possible pelvic pain of unclear etiology (1); hypertension of unclear etiology (1); possible kidney stone (1); peptic ulcer (1).

[e]Epigastric pain—rule out myocardial infarction (1 case).

Table 11.7 Validation of diagnosis by AMA criteria: Percentage distribution of patients with a discharge diagnosis of cholecystitis and/or cholelithiasis

Classification by discharge diagnosis	BC–BS (%) (n = 234)	GHA (%) (n = 34)
Met criteria	96.2	94.2
Failed criteria		
Normal x-rays[a]	2.1	0.0
No documentation that required tests performed	1.7	5.8
Subtotal	3.8	5.8
Total	100.0	100.0

[a]And no documentation that diagnosis validated by other means.

Table 11.8 Appropriateness of admission assessed by Payne and Lyons and AMA criteria: Percentage distribution of patients with a discharge diagnosis of hypertensive or arteriosclerotic heart disease

Classification by admitting diagnosis	BC–BS (%) (n = 163)	(GHA) (n = 16)
Payne and Lyons		
Met criteria	93.8	100.0
Failed criteria	0.6	0.0
Unclassified[a]	5.5[b]	0.0
Total	100.0	100.0
AMA		
Met criteria		
Hypertension, hypertensive heart disease	22.1	18.8
Arteriosclerotic heart disease	33.7	50.0
Congestive heart failure	11.7	18.8
Atrial fibrillation or other arrhythmia	4.9	0.0
Myocardial infarction	20.2	0.0
Other	5.5[c]	6.3[d]
Subtotal	98.2	93.8
Failed criteria	0.6	0.0
Unclassified[e]	1.2[f]	6.3[g]
Total	100.0	100.0

[a]Criteria not available.

[b]Carcinoid syndrome (1 case); probable bronchopneumonia (1); epistaxis (1); anxiety neurosis (1); possible cerebrovascular accident (1); extreme weakness (1); acute and chronic bronchitis (1); epigastric pain (1); coronary artery disease, admitted for revascularization (1).

[c]Suspected pulmonary embolism (2 cases); bronchopneumonia (2); epistaxis (2); acute and chronic bronchitis (1); epigastric pain (1); anxiety neurosis (1).

[d]Suspected pulmonary embolism (1 case).

[e]No criteria available.

[f]Syncope (1 case), carcinoid syndrome (1).

[g]Syncope (1 case).

Table 11.9 Validation of diagnosis by AMA criteria: Percentage distribution of patients with a discharge diagnosis of hypertensive or arteriosclerotic heart disease

Classification by discharge diagnosis	BC–BS (%) (n = 163)	GHA (%) (n = 16)
Met criteria		
Hypertension or hypertensive heart disease	31.9	12.5
Arteriosclerotic heart disease	49.7	68.8
Congestive heart failure	11.0	18.7
Atrial fibrillation or other arrhythmia	4.9	0.0
Subtotal	97.5	100.0
Failed criteria		
Hypertension	1.2	0.0
Arteriosclerotic heart disease	1.2	0.0
Total	100.0	100.0

Table 11.10 Appropriateness of admission assessed by AMA criteria: Percentage distribution of patients with a discharge diagnosis of myocardial infarction

Classification by admitting diagnosis	BC–BS (%) (n = 88)	GHA (%) (n = 14)
Met criteria		
Myocardial infarction	97.7	100.0
Other	1.1[a]	0.0
Subtotal	98.8	100.0
Failed criteria	1.1[b]	0.0
Total	100.0	100.0

[a]Acute pulmonary embolism (1 case). [b]Patient admitted for obstructive uropathy.

Table 11.11 Validation of diagnosis by AMA criteria: Percentage distribution of patients with a discharge diagnosis of myocardial infarction

Classification by discharge diagnosis	BC–BS (%) (n = 88)	GHA (%) (n = 14)
Met criteria	97.7	100.0
Failed criteria	2.3	0.0
Total	100.0	100.0

Table 11.12 Appropriateness of admission assessed by Payne and Lyons and AMA criteria: Percentage distribution of patients with a discharge diagnosis of pneumonia

Classification by admitting diagnosis and age	BC–BS (%) (n = 156)	GHA (%) (n = 12)
Payne and Lyons		
Met criteria		
Aged 18 years or over	41.7	58.3
Aged less than 18 years	35.9	41.7
Subtotal	77.6	100.0
Failed criteria		
Aged less than 18 years	12.2	0.0
Unclassified[a]	10.2[b]	0.0
Total	100.0	100.0
AMA		
Met criteria		
Pneumonia, aged 18 years or over	41.7	58.3
Pneumonia, aged less than 18 years	44.2	41.7
Other	8.3[c]	0.0
Subtotal	94.2	100.0
Failed critera		
Pneumonia, aged less than 18 years	3.8	0.0
Other	1.3[d]	0.0
Subtotal	5.1	0.0
Unclassified[a]	0.6[e]	0.0
Total	100.0	100.0

[a]No criteria available.

[b]Croup/bronchitis/bronchiolitis (5 cases); asthma (2); gastroenteritis (2); acute viral disease (2); fever of unknown origin (2); possible pulmonary embolism (1); possible myocardial infarction (1); cholecystitis (1).

[c]Croup/bronchitis/bronchiolitis (5 cases); asthma (2); gastroenteritis (2); acute viral infection (1); possible pulmonary embolism (1); possible myocardial infarction (1); cholecystitis(1).

[d]Fever of unknown origin (2 cases).

[e]Generalized viral disease (1 case).

Table 11.13 Validation of diagnosis by AMA criteria: Percentage distribution of patients with a discharge diagnosis of pneumonia

Classification by discharge diagnosis and age	BC–BS (%) (n = 156)		GHA (%) (n = 12)
Met criteria			
Aged 18 years or over	40.4		33.3
Aged less than 18 years	53.2		33.3
Subtotal	93.6		66.7
Failed criteria			
Aged 18 years or over			
Chest x-ray normal	2.6		0.0
No documentation of chest x-ray	2.5	*	25.0
Aged less than 18 years			
No documentation of chest x-ray[a]	1.3		8.3
Subtotal	6.4	*	33.3
Total	100.0		100.0

[a]And no documentation of other validating data.

Table 11.14 Appropriateness of admission assessed by Payne and Lyons and AMA criteria: Percentage distribution for patients discharged after tonsillectomy and/or adenoidectomy

Classification by admitting diagnosis	BC–BS (%) (n = 107)	GHA (%) (n = 61)
Payne and Lyons		
Met criteria	30.8	36.1
Questionable[a]	36.4	27.9
Failed criteria[b]	32.7	36.1
Total	100.0	100.0
AMA		
Met criteria	29.0	37.7
Questionable[a]	37.4	23.0
Failed criteria[b]	33.6	39.3
Total	100.0	100.0

[a]No mention in hospital record of specific number of illness episodes within one year and surgery not justified on other grounds.

[b]No documentation of more than one previous illness episode and surgery not justified on other grounds.

Table 11.15 Type of surgery performed and appropriateness of surgery assessed by Payne and Lyons criteria: Percentage distribution of patients discharged after tonsillectomy and/or adenoidectomy

	BC–BS (%) (n = 107)		GHA (%) (n = 61)
Type of surgery			
Tonsillectomy and adenoidectomy	57.0	*	42.6
Tonsillectomy only	36.4	*	55.8
Adenoidectomy only	6.6		1.6
Total	100.0		100.0
Appropriateness of surgery			
Tonsillectomy			
Met criteria	14.0		25.0
Questionable[a]	45.0		16.7
Failed criteria[b]	41.0		58.3
Total	100.0	*	100.0
Adenoidectomy			
Met criteria	31.8		33.3
Questionable[a]	10.6		33.3
Failed criteria[b]	57.6		33.3
Total	100.0	*	100.0

[a]No mention in hospital record of specific number of illness episodes within one year and surgery not justified on other grounds.

[b]No documentation of more than one previous illness episode and surgery not justified on other grounds.

*P ≤ .05.

Table 11.16 Validation of diagnosis by AMA criteria: Percentage distribution of patients discharged after tonsillectomy and/or adenoidectomy

Classification by discharge diagnosis and age	BC–BS (%) (n = 107)	GHA (%) (n = 61)
Met criteria		
Aged 18 years or over	29.0	31.1
Aged less than 18 years	60.7	60.6
Subtotal	89.7	91.8
Failed criteria		
Missing pathology report	10.3	8.2
Total	100.0	100.0

Table 11.17 Appropriateness of admission assessed by Payne and Lyons and AMA criteria: Percentage distribution of patients with a discharge diagnosis of uterine fibroids

Classification by admitting diagnosis	(BC–BS (%) (n = 162)	GHA (%) (n = 60)
Payne and Lyons		
Met criteria	92.0	95.0
Failed criteria	1.9	3.3
Unclassified[a]	4.9[b]	1.7[c]
Total	100.0	100.0
AMA		
Met criteria		
Uterine fibroids	93.2	95.0
Other	3.7[d]	0.0
Subtotal	96.9	95.0
Failed criteria		
Uterine fibroids	1.9	3.3
Unclassified[a]	0.0	1.7[e]
Excluded[f]	1.2[g]	0.0
Total	100.0	100.0

[a]No criteria available.
[b]Endometriosis (2 cases); abnormal pap smear (2); ovarian tumor (1); infertility (3).
[c]Right adnexal mass (1 case).
[d]Endometriosis (2 cases); abnormal pap smear (2); ovarian tumor (1); infertility (1).
[e]Right adnexal mass (1 case).
[f]Insufficient data on abstract.
[g]Infertility (2 cases).

Table 11.18 Validation of diagnosis by AMA criteria: Percentage distribution of patients with a discharge diagnosis of uterine fibroids

Classification by discharge diagnosis	BC–BS (%) (n = 162)	GHA (%) (n = 60)
Met criteria	96.9	98.3
Failed criteria[a]	3.1	1.7
Total	100.0	100.0

[a]No documentation of pathology report, surgeon's operative note, or x-ray report.

Table 11.19 Appropriateness of admission assessed by Payne and Lyons criteria: Summary data for patients in selected diagnostic categories

Discharge diagnosis	Admitting diagnosis							
	n		Met (%)		Failed (%)		Unclassified (%)[a]	
	BC–BS	GHA	BC–BS	GHA	BC–BS	GHA	BC–BS	GHA
Breast cancer	58	10	100.0	100.0	0.0	0.0	0.0	0.0
Cystic breast disease	150	39	100.0	100.0	0.0	0.0	0.0	0.0
Diabetes mellitus	175	12	94.9	100.0	0.5	0.0	4.6	0.0
Diseases of gall bladder and biliary duct	234	34	93.6	97.1	0.0	0.0	6.4	2.9
Arteriosclerotic and hypertensive heart disease	163	16	93.8	100.0	0.6	0.0	5.5	0.0
Pneumonia	156	12	77.6	100.0	12.2	0.0	10.2	0.0
Hyperplasia of tonsils and adenoids	107	61	67.2[b]	64.0[b]	32.7	36.1	0.0	0.0
Uterine fibroids	162	60	9.32	95.0	1.9	3.3	3.7	1.7
Range			69.2–100	64.0–100	0–32.7	0–36.1	0–10.2	0–2.9

[a]No criteria available for admitting diagnosis.

[b]Includes cases classified as questionable in Table 11.14.

Table 11.20 Appropriateness of admission assessed by AMA criteria: Summary data for patients in selected diagnostic categories

| Discharge diagnosis | n | | Admitting diagnosis | | | | | |
| | | | Met (%) | | Failed (%) | | Unclassified (%)[a] | |
	BC-BS	GHA	BC-BS	GHA	BC-BS	GHA	BC-BS	GHA
Appendicitis	192	30	99.0	100.0	0.0	0.0	1.0	0.0
Breast cancer	58	10	100.0	100.0	0.0	0.0	0.0	0.0
Cystic breast disease	150	39	100.0	100.0	0.0	0.0	0.0	0.0
Diabetes mellitus	175	12	92.6	91.7	6.3	8.3	1.1	0.0
Diseases of gall bladder and biliary duct	234	34	99.6	100.0	0.4	0.0	0.0	0.0
Arteriosclerotic and hypertensive heart disease	163	16	98.2	93.8	0.6	0.0	1.2	6.3
Myocardial infarction	88	14	98.8	100.0	1.1	0.0	0.0	0.0
Pneumonia	156	12	94.2	100.0	5.1	0.0	0.6	0.0
Hyperplasia of tonsils and adenoids	107	61	66.4[b]	60.7[b]	33.6	39.3	0.0	0.0
Uterine fibroids	162	60	96.9	95.0	1.9	3.3	1.2[c]	1.7
Range			66.4-100	60.7-100	0-33.6	0-39.3	0-1.2	0-6.3

[a] No criteria available for admitting diagnosis.

[b] Includes cases classified as questionable in Table 11.14.

[c] Insufficient data on abstract.

Table 11.21 Validation of discharge diagnosis by AMA criteria: Summary data for patients in selected diagnostic categories

Discharge diagnosis	n		Discharge diagnosis					
			Met (%)		Failed (%)			
					Documented[a]		Not documented[b]	
	BC-BS	GHA	BC-BS	GHA	BC-BS	GHA	BC-BS	GHA
Appendicitis	192	30	89.6	76.7	7.8	3.3	2.6	20.0
Breast cancer	58	10	98.3	100.0	1.7	0.0	0.0	0.0
Cystic breast disease	150	39	100.0	97.4	0.0	2.6	0.0	0.0
Diabetes mellitus[c]	175	12	88.6	75.0	1.1	0.0	0.0	0.0
Diseases of gall bladder and biliary duct	234	34	96.2	94.2	2.1	0.0	1.7	5.8
Arteriosclerotic and hypertensive heart disease	163	16	97.5	100.0	2.4	0.0	0.0	0.0
Myocardial infarction	88	14	97.7	100.0	2.3	0.0	0.0	0.0
Pneumonia	156	12	93.6	66.7	2.6	0.0	3.8 *	33.3
Hyperplasia of tonsils and adenoids	107	61	89.7	91.8	0.0	0.0	10.3	8.2
Uterine fibroids	162	60	96.9	98.3	0.0	0.0	3.1	1.7
Range			88.6-100	66.7-100	0-7.8	0-3.3	0-10.3	0-33.3

[a]Required tests documented, but results failed to validate diagnosis.

[b]No documentation that tests required to validate diagnosis were performed.

[c]Relevant data not abstracted from medical record in 10.3 percent of BC–BS cases, 25 percent of GHA cases.

Table 11.22 Frequency of changes in diagnosis from admission to discharge for selected diagnostic dategories

Diagnostic category	BC–BS		GHA	
	n	% with change	n	% with change
Appendicitis	192	4.2	30	10.0
Breast cancer[a]	58	0.0	10	0.0
Cystic breast disease[a]	150	0.0	39	0.0
Diabetes mellitus	175	4.6	12	0.0
Diseases of gall bladder and biliary duct	234	6.4	34	2.9
Arteriosclerotic and hypertensive heart disease	163	4.9	16	0.0
Myocardial infarction	88	2.3	14	0.0
Pneumonia	156	10.3	12	0.0
Hyperplasia of tonsils and adenoids	107	0.0	61	0.0
Uterine fibroids	162	4.9	60	1.7

[a]Admitted with diagnosis of breast mass.

12

Severity of Illness

Thomas D. Koepsell and Sharon B. Soroko

The findings in Chapter 11 suggest that, at least for the diagnostic categories studied, there were relatively few inappropriate admissions or invalid
discharge diagnoses among patients hospitalized under BC-BS or GHA.
However, it was noted that the criteria used to judge the medical appropriateness of admissions appear to allow the physician considerable latitude in
allocating hospital resources to patients with varying degrees of illness.
Thus, although a large majority of cases in both plans passed these criteria,
it is entirely possible that the kinds of patients eventually hospitalized under
the two plans were quite different with regard to severity of illness. In the
context of the present study, this possibility is of interest because it might
suggest that physicians in the two plans implicitly used different definitions
of what constitutes need for hospital care. This, in turn, might indicate that
lower hospitalization rates under GHA are in part due to the use of more
restrictive admission criteria by physicians in prepaid group practice as
compared both to those used by their fee-for-service counterparts and those
used in peer review. Among the organizational differences between plans
noted in Chapters 1 and 8, three are of special interest in this respect:

- *Extensiveness and integration of ambulatory care arrangements*. The
  referral of patients for consultation or specialized services is facili-
  tated under prepaid group practice because providers practice in the
  same facilities and share a common medical record system. Econo-
  mies of scale also make feasible the provision of a wider range of
  diagnostic and therapeutic services than the individual fee-for-
  service practitioner can provide (Broida et al., 1975; Roemer and
  Shonick, 1973; Greenberg and Rodburg, 1971).

- *Financial incentives*. Under salaried prepaid group practice, there is
  no financial reward for hospitalizing patients; often, an explicit
  financial disincentive exists. In fee-for-service practice, the patient is
  usually charged for each hospital visit by the physician, resulting in

several charges in a short period of time. Also, if complex or specialized physician services necessitating hospitalization are required, the physician collects an additional fee for providing them (Monsma, 1970; Klarman, 1963).

— *Bed supply constraints.* Although these were probably not an important factor in the present setting, limited access to hospital beds in other prepaid group practice settings has been held as important in keeping hospitalization rates low (Wersinger et al., 1976; Perkoff, Kahn, and Mackie, 1974; Klarman, 1963).

Clearly, the degree to which these or similar factors influenced admission decisions will have varied from patient to patient. In caring for patients with an illness that cannot be managed without hospital technology and personnel, physicians in both plans can be expected to have recommended hospitalization. But where hospitalization was more of a discretionary decision, prepaid group practice physicians should more frequently seek alternatives to hospitalization than those in fee-for-service practice. For example, they should be less inclined to hospitalize for diagnostic purposes if the requisite tests can be done on an outpatient basis. By the same token, in chronic diseases which may or may not eventually require hospitalization (e.g., uterine fibroids, gallbladder disease), we might expect the prepaid group practice physician to be more likely to adopt a "wait-and-see" attitude unless exacerbation of the disease demands more immediate action.

Two factors which should affect the degree to which hospitalization is in fact discretionary would be the diagnosis itself and the severity of illness. Certain diagnoses such as myocardial infarction or appendicitis (or even the suspicion thereof) are generally felt to require hospitalization in every case, and variations in severity would be less important in these cases. For certain other diagnoses, admission is not considered necessary in every case, and here the level of illness severity should become a major factor in the physician's decision whether or not to hospitalize the patient. Accordingly, to the extent that physicians in prepaid group practice indeed use more restrictive hospitalization criteria than fee-for-service physicians, observed differences in severity of illness on admission should be most pronounced for this second group of diseases, where a fairly large proportion of admissions are discretionary.

In view of the criteria for appropriateness of admission by Payne and Lyons (1972) and the AMA (1976) applied in this study and described in Chapter 11, the extent to which hospitalization was mandatory or discretionary in this sense can be summarized as follows:

—*Appendicitis*: usually mandatory and on an emergency basis

—*Breast mass* (both breast cancer and cystic disease of the breast): usually mandatory, but generally as scheduled admissions

—*Diabetes mellitus*: mixture of mandatory emergency and discretionary scheduled admissions

—*Diseases of the gallbladder and biliary duct*: mixture of mandatory emergency and discretionary scheduled admissions

—*Arteriosclerotic and hypertensive heart disease*: mixture of mandatory emergency and discretionary scheduled admissions

—*Myocardial infarction*: usually mandatory and on an emergency basis

—*Pneumonia*: mixture of mandatory and discretionary admissions, very few of which can be scheduled in advance

—*Hyperplasia of tonsils and adenoids*: usually discretionary and can be scheduled well in advance or delayed if necessary

—*Uterine fibroids*: usually discretionary and can often be scheduled well in advance or delayed if necessary

METHODS AND VARIABLES

Four indicators of disease severity were employed to determine whether different types of evidence pointed to the same conclusion.

Urgency of Hospitalization. First, the proportion of all cases under each plan who were emergency or unscheduled admissions was calculated as the percentage of cases admitted on the same day on which the physician recommended admission. Second, the necessity of hospitalization was assessed in terms of the proportion of cases in which the recommending physician stated that hospitalization was "absolutely necessary." It should be noted that while both of these measures would be expected to rise and fall with disease severity, they might also be affected by organizational differences or by consistent attitudinal differences between physicians in the two plans.

Perceived Severity of Symptoms. Levels of awareness and pain or discomfort at the time of hospitalization were established for all patients admitted on an emergency basis. Answers to the respective questions in the patient interview were combined into a three-step scale of increasing symptom severity: (1) conscious, with no pain or discomfort; or (2) conscious, with quite a bit of pain or discomfort; or (3) conscious, with much pain or discomfort, too sick to remember, or unconscious. For the present purposes, the comparison between plans is restricted to level 3.

Stages of Illness. For six of the diagnostic categories, a system of disease staging described by Gonnella and Goran (1975) was applied. The system defines discrete levels of severity according to the presence or absence of certain complications or objective findings. Staging criteria were adapted to fit the data available on the disease-specific medical record abstracts. Two or three ordinal levels of severity were specified for each diagnostic category, using the operational definitions shown in Table 12.1.

Disease-Specific Clinical Parameters. For four of the diagnostic categories, key physical findings or laboratory values, when available in the medical record abstracts, provided additional objective indicators of severity as follows:

- *Cystic disease of the breast*: size of breast mass as estimated by the examining physician
- *Breast cancer*: presence or absence of malignant involvement of axillary lymph nodes on pathological examination
- *Uterine fibroids*: largest diameter of uterus on pathological examination if a hysterectomy was performed
- *Diabetes mellitus*: blood glucose level for patients with poorly controlled diabetes or diabetic acidosis

The patient sample examined here consisted of persons discharged from the hospital under BC-BS and GHA in selected diagnostic categories (see Chapters 8 and 9 for sampling methods and demographic characteristics). Data were obtained from three sources: a structured interview with the patient (or suitable proxy) after discharge; a detailed, disease-specific abstract of the hospital medical record; and an interview with the physician recommending hospitalization. Due to differences in completion rates for the various survey instruments, the number of patients for whom specific indicator data were available was less than the entire sample, as noted in Table 8.2. Subsets of the patients in certain diagnostic categories of special interest were analyzed in greater detail than the full sample.

INDICATORS OF SEVERITY

Urgency of Hospitalization. As observed in Chapter 10, there was little if any difference between the two plans in the proportion of patients in each diagnostic category who were emergency admissions (that is, who were admitted on the day on which hospitalization was recommended). This was found even in those diagnostic categories which commonly include a mixture of emergency and scheduled admissions (diabetes mellitus, gallbladder and biliary duct disease, and arteriosclerotic and hypertensive heart disease;

Use of Health Care Resources

KEY: Figures 12.1 – 12.3

AP - Appendicitis
CD - Cystic Breast Disease
BC - Breast Cancer
DM - Diabetes Mellitus
GB - Diseases of Gallbladder and
    Biliary Duct

AS - Arteriosclerotic and Hypertensive
    Heart Disease
MI - Myocardial Infarction
PN - Pneumonia
TA - Hyperplasia of Tonsils and Adenoids
UF - Uterine Fibroids

Figure 12.1   Percent of emergency admissions in selected
                diagnostic categories

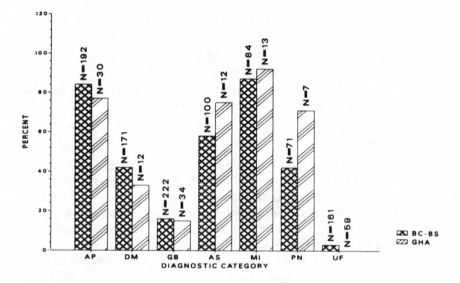

Figure 12.1). The pattern was slightly more variable in respect of the proportion of admissions in each diagnostic category which, in a retrospective interview, were considered absolutely necessary by the physician recommending hospitalization. Here GHA admissions were considered clearly necessary more often than those in BC-BS in three of the diagnostic categories (cystic disease of the breast, arteriosclerotic and hypertensive heart disease, and pneumonia; Figure 12.2). In contrast, fully a quarter of BC-BS admissions for tonsillectomy/adenoidectomy were considered absolutely necessary by the physician recommending hospitalization, as compared to 3.4 percent in GHA, a statistically significant difference; also, among women with uterine fibroids, despite the fact that a much larger proportion underwent hysterectomy under GHA (98 percent) than under BC-BS (78

Figure 12.2 Percent of hospital admissions subsequently confirmed as absolutely necessary by the physician, for selected diagnostic categories (p ≤ .05, tonsillectomy/adenoidectomy)

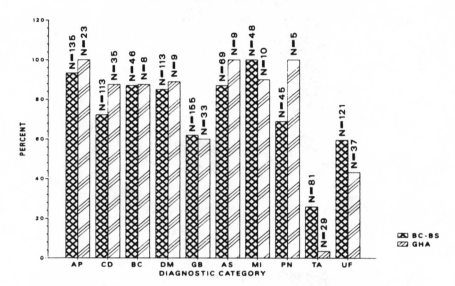

Figure 12.3 Percent of emergency admissions unconscious or conscious but with much pain or discomfort, by selected diagnostic categories (p ≤ .05, appendicitis)

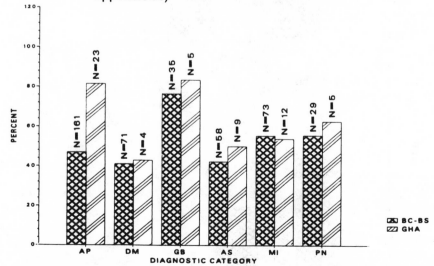

Figure 12.4 Percent of patients by illness stage at hospitalization for selected diagnostic categories

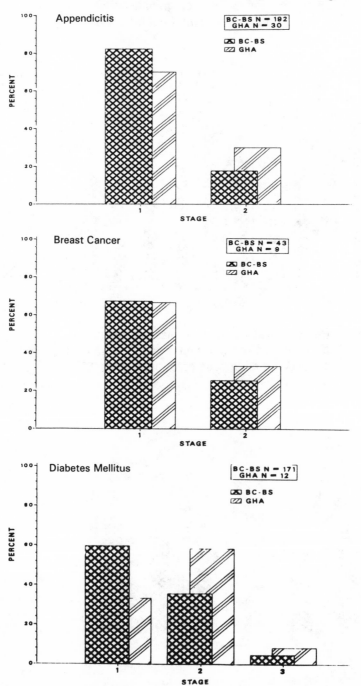

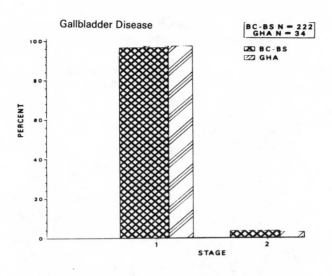

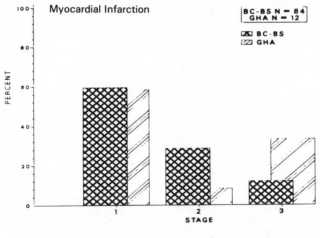

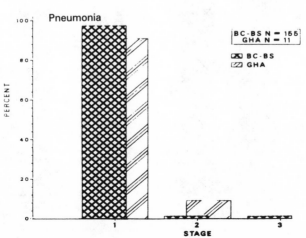

Figure 12.5   Laboratory and pathology findings for patients in selected diagnostic categories (p ≤ .05 for uterine fibroids)

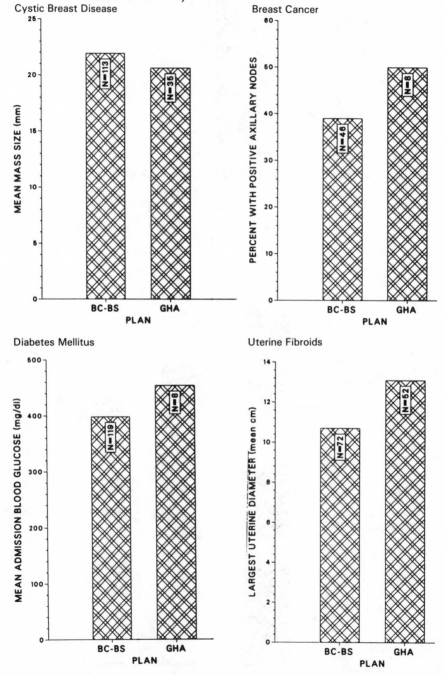

percent), GHA physicians still considered a smaller proportion of these admissions to have been absolutely necessary. Overall, however, no consistent pattern of differences between plans emerged even for those disease categories consisting of a mixture of mandatory and discretionary admissions.

Perceived Severity at Admission. Comparison of the two plans with regard to the proportion of patients who were unconscious or conscious but with much pain and discomfort on admission, as reported in a postdischarge interview by patients hospitalized on an emergency basis, indicated that GHA patients reported more severe symptoms at the time of admission than BC-BS patients only for appendicitis (Figure 12.3). For the other five diagnostic categories examined, the differences between plans were statistically indistinguishable. Four diagnoses were omitted because at least one plan had no same-day admissions in these categories (breast cancer, cystic disease, tonsillectomy/adenoidectomy, and uterine fibroids).

Clinical Findings. Clinical data for subsets of the discharged patient sample were examined based on available evidence from the hospital medical record. For six diagnostic categories, staging criteria developed by Gonnella and Goran (1975) were available, and for four categories, laboratory and pathological findings complement this information.

With regard to the stage of illness of patients at the time of admission (see Table 12.1 for the definition of each stage, where the severity of illness is lowest in Stage 1 and highest in Stage 3), there was a suggestion of more advanced disease among GHA patients with appendicitis and diabetes mellitus (Figure 12.4). Sample sizes were small, however, and yielded no statistically significant differences between plans.

The pathology and laboratory findings as well remained inconclusive, with one exception (Figure 12.5). There was a statistically significant finding of more advanced disease under GHA for uterine fibroids, where an increase in size accounts for some of the most frequent presenting symptoms. For women in this sample who underwent hysterectomy, the largest dimension of the removed uterus was used as an indication of how far the fibroid had progressed prior to removal. In those cases where the necessary data were available (72 in BC-BS and 52 in GHA), the mean size of the removed uterus was greater for GHA women than for BC-BS women. This suggestion of more advanced disease under GHA is consistent with the fact that 98 percent of the total GHA sample in this diagnostic category underwent a hysterectomy, compared to 78 percent of the BC-BS sample.

For cystic disease of the breast, which is typically characterized by a slowly growing mass (or masses) whose size is one indicator of disease progress at the time of admission, there was little difference in mean mass size on admission between those patients of the two plans for whom the required information was available in the medical record (113 in BC-BS, 35 in GHA, or 77 percent and 91 percent of the number of cases in the respective plans). Also, at the time of surgery for breast cancer, the difference in malignant involvement of axillary lymph nodes, an indication of how extensively the disease has progressed, was not statistically significant. However, 50 percent of the 8 GHA patients for whom information was available in the medical record had lymph nodes positive for malignancy, versus 39 percent of 46 cases under BC-BS.

Of the diabetic patients hospitalized, 8 in GHA (67 percent) and 119 in BC-BS (71 percent) were admitted for poorly controlled diabetes or for diabetic acidosis, a condition in which the blood sugar level can serve as a useful indicator of severity. Poor control of blood glucose levels can, in the extreme, result in serious metabolic disturbances and coma. Again, while the mean blood glucose level was higher among GHA patients than among BC-BS patients, the difference was not statistically significant.

SUMMARY AND CONCLUSIONS

An examination of possible differences in severity of illness at the time of hospital admission was undertaken for GHA and BC-BS patients in selected diagnostic categories. In view of the presence of several organizational factors which should encourage selectivity in use of the hospital by GHA physicians, it was expected that patients hospitalized under GHA might manifest more severe illness on admission than BC-BS patients in the same diagnostic categories. Several indicators of severity were employed to take into account perceptions of the patient and of the physician recommending hospitalization as well as objective clinical data.

The most convincing and consistent body of data in support of this expectation was seen for patients with a discharge diagnosis of uterine fibroids. A larger proportion of GHA patients was admitted for hysterectomy, a major surgical procedure. In addition, GHA patients undergoing hysterectomies had evidence of more advanced disease, on the average, than did BC-BS patients undergoing hysterectomies, as evidenced by the mean size of the fibroid uterus. These findings correlate well with those in Chapter 10, which showed that, at least for the illness episode resulting in the hospital admission studied, the average GHA patient with uterine fibroids was treated as an outpatient much longer than her BC-BS counterpart.

Suggestive additional evidence was found for patients with a discharge diagnosis of appendicitis. Among patients admitted on an emergency basis (a large majority of the total sample under both plans), GHA patients reported significantly higher levels of pain or discomfort on the day of admission than did comparable patients under BC-BS. A higher percentage also fell into the Stage 2 category by the staging criteria developed by Gonnella and Goran, although this difference was not statistically significant for this sample size. Diabetes patients under GHA also tended to be somewhat more severely ill on admission; however, the GHA sample in the diabetes group was small, which again limits the conclusions that can be drawn in this respect. On the other hand, the data in Chapter 10 did not show any important differences between plans in terms of delays in seeking care for these diagnoses or in arranging for hospitalization once the first physician visit was made.

For the other diagnoses, there was little evidence of consistent, statistically significant differences between plans. Obviously, the number of GHA cases in several diagnostic categories was quite small and the criterion of statistical significance may thus be unrealistic as a basis of comparison. On the other hand, most of the differences between plans were not particularly large, and there was no consistent indication of more severe disease in GHA patients across diagnoses. The differences observed, with the exception of uterine fibroids, thus do not seem to follow a pattern of higher levels of severity under GHA in those diagnostic categories where there is generally a mix of mandatory and discretionary admissions. For example, the smallest difference between plans was found in gallbladder and biliary duct patients, where this mix should be most obvious.

One explanation for the lack of conclusive findings for most of the diagnoses could be inadequacy of the methods used to reveal a true difference between plans. The staging criteria for gallbladder and biliary duct disease and for pneumonia, for example, resulted in rather skewed distributions in which most cases were classified as uncomplicated. Also, since this analysis was necessarily limited to variables which had been captured on a medical record abstract designed chiefly for other purposes, there were undoubtedly aspects of disease severity which could not be taken into account by the indicators used, such as comorbidity and rate of progression of the underlying disease process. Nonetheless, the failure of multiple indicators to reveal sizeable variance between plans decreases the likelihood that large and pervasive differences were missed.

Another factor which may explain the lack of marked differences between plans is that differences in disease severity within diagnostic categories may be less prominent than shifts among diagnostic categories. Thus, it is possible that the overall mix of patients hospitalized under GHA consisted of greater numbers of cases with relatively serious disorders in which hospitalization is more likely to be mandatory; in contrast, BC-BS physicians may have admitted a mix of patients with diseases which are not as serious and in which hospitalization is more likely to be elective or discretionary. If this was the case, then the largest differences between plans in terms of disease specific admission rates would be expected for diseases which are seldom life-threatening and often involve discretionary admissions. Some of the data from Phase I suggest this (cf. Chapter 2), inasmuch as the four diseases for which the ratio of BC-BS to GHA admission rates was largest were diseases of the oral cavity, salivary glands, and jaw; disorders of menstruation; acute respiratory infections (not including pneumonia); and hypertrophy of the tonsils and adenoids and chronic tonsillitis. This suggestion is at best tentative, however, and its confirmation must await the development of more sophisticated methods for assessing case-mix differences.

Table 12.1 Operational definitions of disease stages[a]

Diagnostic category	Definition
Appendicitis	Stage 1— Appendicitis without evidence of perforation
	Stage 2— Appendicitis with perforation of appendix, as evidenced by at least one of the following: Postoperative or discharge diagnosis of ruptured appendix; pathology report indicating perforated appendix; description of perforated appendix or pus in peritoneal cavity in operative findings
Breast cancer	Stage 1— Discharge diagnosis of breast cancer with none of the features of stage 2 or 3
	Stage 2— Breast cancer with notation of palpably enlarged axillary lymph nodes, but with none of the features of stage 3.
	Stage 3— Breast cancer with notation of at least one of the following: Extensive edema (if quantified, over at least 1/3 of breast); fixation of mass to underlying musculature or chest wall; skin ulceration; palpably enlarged supraclavicular or parasternal node enlargement on x-ray; edema of arm
Diabetes mellitus	Stage 1— Discharge diagnosis of diabetes mellitus with none of the features of stage 2 or 3
	Stage 2— Diabetes mellitus plus at least one of the following (in absence of features of stage 3): Infection, indicated by reason for admission or fever (temperature over $100°$ F) and positive culture; septicemia (positive blood culture); acidosis, as indicated by reason for admission, discharge diagnosis, or serum CO_2 less than 18 mEq/l, without coma; retinopathy, as indicated by discharge diagnosis or reason for admission; glomerulosclerosis, as indicated by discharge diagnosis or reason for admission; neuropathy, as indicated by discharge diagnosis of reason for admission; peripheral vascular complications (e.g., foot ulcers), as indicated by discharge diagnosis or reason for admission
	Stage 3— Diabetes mellitus plus at least one of the following: Acidosis, as indicated by discharge diagnosis, reason for admission, or serum CO_2 less than 18, plus coma; necrotizing papillitis, as indicated by discharge diagnosis, azotemia, as indicated by discharge diagnosis or BUN over 30 mg/dl or creatinine over 2 mg/dl (persisting after treatment)
Cholecystitis/Cholelithiasis (Diseases of gall bladder and biliary duct)	Stage 1— Discharge diagnosis of cholecystitis and/or cholelithiasis, with none of the features of stage 2 or 3
	Stage 2— Cholecystitis and/or cholelithiasis with at least one of the following (in absence of features of stage 3): Perforation of gall bladder, as indicated by discharge diagnosis, operative findings, or pathology report; empyema or gangrene of gall bladder, as indicated by pathology report; obstructive jaundice, as indicated by one or both of the following: total bilirubin over 2.5 mg/dl or notation of jaundice on physical exam; discharge diagnosis of cholangitis; discharge diagnosis of pancreatitis

Table 12.1 (Continued)

Diagnostic category	Definition
	Stage 3— Cholecystitis and/or cholelithiasis, plus a complication qualifying for stage 2, plus at least one of the following: Septicemia, as indicated by fever (temperature over 100° F) and positive blood culture; shock, as indicated by documented systolic blood pressure less than 90, plus pulse over 100
Myocardial infarction	Stage 1— Discharge diagnosis of myocardial infarction with none of the features of stage 2 or 3
	Stage 3— Discharge diagnosis of myocardial infarction plus one or more of the following: Cerebrovascular accident (stroke), peripheral vascular occlusion, infarction of intestinal tract, infarction of kidney; congestive heart failure indicated by discharge diagnosis, presence of leg edema noted on physical examination, or x-ray showing cardiomegaly or lung congestion; shock indicated by discharge diagnosis or systolic blood pressure less than 90, plus pulse over 100
	Stage 3— Myocardial infarction plus cardiac arrest within first 24 hours
Pneumonia	Stage 1— Discharge diagnosis of pneumonia, with none of the features of stage 2 or 3
	Stage 2— Pneumonia plus at least one of the following: Lung abscess, as indicated by discharge diagnosis, reason for admission, or chest x-ray; empyema, as indicated by discharge diagnosis, reasons for admission, or positive pleural fluid culture; pericarditis, as indicated by discharge diagnosis
	Stage 3— Pneumonia plus at least one of the following: Septic arthritis or osteomyelitis, as indicated by discharge diagnosis or positive joint culture; meningitis, as indicated by discharge diagnosis or positive cerebrospinal fluid culture; endocarditis, as indicated by discharge diagnosis; shock as indicated by reason for admission of systolic blood pressure less than 90, plus pulse over 100

[a]Adapted from Gonnella and Goran (1975) and based on personal communication from J.S. Gonnella.

13

Appropriateness of Inpatient Care

Thomas D. Koepsell and Sharon B. Soroko

An inquiry into how BC-BS and GHA differed in use of the hospital would not be complete without some attention to the type of hospital care provided in terms of content and levels of care. This chapter assesses the *process* of hospital inpatient care for the discharged patient sample under each plan in an attempt to relate differences observed in the care rendered to differences between the two plans in the characteristics of their physicians and hospitals.

First, the frequency of documented compliance with disease specific criteria for good care is examined for patients discharged in selected diagnostic categories. Next, summary performance scores are developed based on relative levels of physician compliance with the criteria, and the plans are compared on the basis of these scores. Several factors suggested *a priori* that GHA medical staff should exhibit higher levels of compliance, primarily because a prepaid group practice plan can exert greater control than a service benefit plan over physician selection and assignment and quality of care within the group. The greater use of teaching hospitals by GHA, which is not usual for prepaid group practice plans, was of additional interest in this respect.

This comparison of clinical performance under the two plans stressed elements which have been identified as essential for, or contributory to, high quality of care for patients with a given clinical problem. In addition to providing a framework for meaningful descriptive comparisons, items selected on this basis should constitute useful indicators of how physicians under a prepaid group practice and a service benefit plan performed in caring for their hospitalized patients. It should be pointed out that this approach centers on the technical process of care, i.e., on specific clinical services which are intended to contribute to correct diagnosis and management of a disease, rather than on aspects of performance such as interpersonal skills of the physician, patient satisfaction, or patient health outcomes, which are no less important but more difficult to measure. Since technical decisions regarding diagnosis and treatment are made almost exclusively by the physician, any plan differences detected by means of specific performance indicators should reflect differences between physicians of the two plans in practice and documentation habits.

BACKGROUND AND THEORETICAL CONSIDERATIONS

Several authors have discussed available evidence on the performance of prepaid group practice in terms of utilization rates, accessibility, and consumer satisfaction (Gaus, Cooper, and Hirschman, 1976; Roemer and Shonick, 1973; Donabedian, 1969). Also, some recent research has focused specifically on the process of care in prepaid group practice and service benefit plans, although most of this has examined patterns of ambulatory care.

Hetherington, Hopkins, and Roemer (1975) have compared ambulatory care quality among six California insurance plans and developed a factor analytic method for comparative evaluation of medical record content. Using empirically derived factors called "prevention," "rationality," "verification," and "continuity," they showed that both of the prepaid group practice plans studied ranked higher than the service benefit plans on "prevention" and "verification" and that one of the prepaid plans ranked first on "rationality" while the other ranked third (of six). These findings were partly accounted for by underlying variations in patient and physician characteristics. Louis and McCord (1974) have reported on compliance with ambulatory care process criteria by five California prepaid health plans and a control group consisting of fee-for-service practice patients. While some of the prepaid group practices showed performance levels above the fee-for-service averages, they found great variability among plans, however, some of which performed below fee-for-service averages. Gaus, Cooper, and Hirschman (1976) examined how frequently preventive services were provided in eight prepaid group practices as compared with control groups. They found little evidence to suggest that a larger proportion of visits under the prepaid group practices were made for preventive care or that a larger percentage of prepaid group practice enrollees had availed themselves of such services.

As part of a multifaceted study of medical care in Hawaii, Payne et al. (1976) examined the effects of practice arrangements on a Physician Performance Index (PPI). The PPI consisted of a weighted average of compliance with explicit, physician specified criteria for hospital care. The average PPI for a large prepaid multispecialty group (79.4) was significantly higher than that for a fee-for-service multispecialty group (74.2) and higher than that for solo practice (69.5). However, these performance differences almost disappeared when care delivered by modal specialists only was compared, i.e., by physicians board certified in a specialty that characteristically cares for the diagnosis studied. Payne et al. concluded that superior performance under the prepaid group practice was explained by its ability to direct each patient to the physician most qualified to deal with the specific problem encountered. LoGerfo et al. (1976) have compared compliance with criteria for good ambulatory care for patients with selected clinical problems under a large prepaid group practice and under a service benefit plan. Using a summary physician performance index similar to Payne's PPI, compliance with criteria was shown to be higher under the prepaid group practice for all of the seven diagnostic categories studied. These differences were not explained by variations in board certification status of the physicians providing care.

Attempts to evaluate prepaid group practice performance on the basis of indicators of the health status of enrollees have also suggested superior performance under prepaid group practice as compared to service benefit plans (Robertson, 1972; Shapiro et al., 1960; Shapiro, Weiner, and Densen, 1958). However, these studies did not investigate whether differences in the process of care were related to these outcome differences. Broadly speaking, prepaid group practice can influence patterns of physician performance by three means. It can affect staff composition by preferentially hiring physicians with certain attributes that are believed to affect performance in desired ways; for example, it can choose to employ only board certified specialists. Second, it can control the types of patients referred to each of its physicians, and third, it can alter the organizational setting in which the physician functions; for example, by instituting formal peer review systems. The literature suggests that all three mechanisms play a role.

Greenberg and Rodburg (1971) have argued that prepaid group practice attracts more highly qualified physicians by offering a form of practice that many find an attractive alternative to solo practice. Given limited vacancies, the prepaid group practice can thus be selective and hire physicians with superior credentials. Also, there is some evidence that formal physician qualifications affect performance as measured by compliance with explicit criteria (Rhee, 1976). Payne et al. (1976) propose that assignment of patients to modal specialists with the most appropriate skills in each case is the major factor accounting for the apparently superior performance of prepaid group practices. Also, several authors (Hetherington, Hopkins, and Roemer, 1975; Roemer and Shonick, 1973; Greenberg and Rodburg, 1971; Donabedian, 1969) have suggested that there are greater opportunities for physicians to review each other's work under group practice arrangements because of more intensive formal and informal peer review.

In the present study, another potential source of performance differences between plans was the relatively large proportion of GHA patients cared for in teaching hospitals during the study period (1973–1974). Care in such hospitals might be expected to have been of superior quality for several reasons, including availability of up-to-date medical technology, the involvement of experts in many aspects of care, and the need to pass more stringent institutional requirements to offer a certified training program. On the other hand, much of the care in teaching hospitals may be delivered by relatively inexperienced physicians. While there is some evidence that, overall, care in teaching hospitals may be better than care provided in other hospitals by both process and outcome assessment methods (Goss, 1970; Roemer, Moustafa, and Hopkins, 1968; Lipworth, Lee, and Morris, 1963; and Lee, Morrison, and Morris, 1960), the extent to which this difference is consistent across diagnoses and hospitals is largely unknown.

Thus, there are several factors suggesting that the technical process of care for hospitalized GHA patients may have been superior to the care provided under BC-BS, at least in terms of the indicators used here. Moreover, the literature has suggested certain mechanisms which may have contributed to this difference in performance, and the strength of several of these mechanisms was tested. In summary, two questions are addressed in this chapter: (1) Was there a difference in physician performance between the two plans in terms of compliance with explicit criteria of good care? and (2) To what extent can performance differences, if any, be explained by differences between the plans in terms of the types of physicians and hospitals providing care in the hospitalizations studied?

METHODS

Performance Criteria

In order to identify elements of care on which to base comparisons of plan performance, two sets of explicit disease specific criteria were assembled: a set of optimal care criteria and a set of critical services criteria.

Criteria for Optimal Care

The optimal care criteria were developed to represent those items whose presence in the medical record was thought to be an important indicator of the delivery of good hospital care for patients with a given condition, in that their documentation reflects a degree of thoroughness indicating the provision of superior and not merely adequate care. These criteria focus on documentation of five components of inpatient care:

   —*History* of a patient's current and past illness, including symptoms and events leading up to the hospitalization under study

—*Physical examination* by the physician during the initial inpatient evaluation

—*Diagnostic tests* providing objective clinical data from the clinical laboratory, x-ray department, or other diagnostic facility at the physician's request

—*Therapy* comprising medications, procedures, and other services ordered by the physician as part of the patient's treatment program

—*Discharge status* in terms of documented achievement of certain milestones in the patient's physical functioning prior to discharge

The optimal care criteria were drawn from the following compilations of explicit disease specific criteria:

—American Medical Association Model Screening Criteria to Assist Professional Standards Review Organizations (American Medical Association, 1976)

—Those developed at various Experimental Medical Care Review Organization (EMCRO) sites, e.g., Albemarle, Georgia, Hawaii, Kaiser, Mississippi, Multnomah, University of California at Los Angeles (Decker et al., 1973)

—Hennepin County Foundation for Medical Care (Metropolitan Health Care Foundation, 1971)

—Hospital Utilization Project (1969)

—Iowa Standards of Care (Schonfeld, Heston, and Falk, 1975)

—On-Site Concurrent Hospital Utilization Review (OSCHUR; Utah Professional Review Organization, 1972)

—Episode of Illness Study (Payne and Lyons, 1972)

—Yale-New Haven Hospital Guidelines for Patient Care Appraisal (1974)

—Quality Review Bulletin (Cohen, Wolpin, and Cohen, 1975)

The criteria from each of these sources had been developed for use in medical care quality assessment, chiefly as part of peer review systems. All were formulated by groups of practicing physicians, many of them recognized experts in the diseases under study. For each study diagnosis, all criteria listed in any of the above sources were combined into a single list. (Not all sources had developed criteria for each diagnosis.) Duplicate items were then eliminated, as were items which required data not available from the medical record abstracts. A few additional items were deleted because they were insufficiently explicit and would have required more complex and subjective judgments than were possible to make from the available data.

Criteria for Critical Services

A subset of the optimal care criteria and a summary of their most important elements, the critical services criteria were intended to represent those items whose documentation in the medical record (or, for contraindicated items, the lack of it) is usually considered essential for the delivery of good care for patients with a given disease. They were selected from the American Medical Association screening criteria for use by Professional Standards Review Organizations (AMA, 1976) and include

> . . . those few key services which have such a critical relationship to outcome for the particular diagnosis or problem that their absence or presence would be sufficient to justify review of a record by a physician (AMA, 1976).

As pointed out in Chapter 11 in examining appropriateness of admissions, the AMA criteria were not developed for research purposes but as screening criteria to identify cases in which the probability of a deficiency in the care process is high enough to warrant further inquiry. As such, they were intended to separate cases into groups with a "low probability of deficiency" and a "higher probability of deficiency." Because of the possibility that in certain circumstances a departure from the criteria may be considered medically justified, the final determination as to quality of care is left to the reviewing physician's judgment when these criteria are used in peer review. For present purposes, this second stage of review was not feasible. Thus, use of compliance with the criteria as an indicator of performance depends on the assumption that the number of medically justifiable departures from the criteria was either fairly evenly distributed between the two plans or too small to make any difference.

Again, a few criteria specified by the AMA were omitted because their data requirements could not be met from the medical record abstracts for this study, which were developed before the criteria became available. Several others were considered impractical for present purposes because they called for a subjective judgment based on intimate knowledge of the circumstances surrounding a particular case. As a result, the list of critical services criteria used here is a somewhat abridged version of that specified by the AMA, although the total number of criteria omitted does not exceed 15 percent across all diagnostic categories.

The use of these two criteria sets was considered useful because in several respects they have complementary advantages and disadvantages. The optimal care criteria are extensive and cover a wide variety of aspects of performance, requiring that results be evaluated in relatively disaggregated form. The critical services criteria, on the other hand, while much more restricted in focus, could be summarized in a single score, which made overall plan differences easier to identify. Parts of the optimal care criteria place a premium on the physician's thoroughness in documenting data; this applies in particular to the history, physical examination, and discharge status components. Some writers have objected to this emphasis on documentation because it may be hard to accept the view that mere recording of a piece of data has any impact on the end result of care (Fessel and Van Brunt, 1972). The critical services criteria, however, mainly involve diagnostic tests and therapy, i.e., components of care for which the determination of compliance or noncompliance is much less dependent on documentation by the physician, since much of their recording is routinely done by other hospital personnel and communicated to the physician via the record.

Data Sources

The sample of cases consisted of patients in both plans who were discharged in selected diagnostic categories during a one-year period (August 1973–July 1974). For a description of the categories and the reasons for their selection, see Chapter 8. Two modifications of these categories for the analyses that follow should be noted. The category "arteriosclerotic and hypertensive heart disease" proved too broad in that few criteria could be found that were equally relevant to both subdiagnoses. For the purposes of the following analysis, patients with the more common subdiagnosis, arteriosclerotic heart disease, were selected for analysis. Also, only adult cases were retained for analysis in the pneumonia category, since most sources of performance criteria specified separate criteria for children and for adults, and only five GHA pediatric cases with pneumonia were hospitalized during the study year.

The data for this chapter were obtained from a detailed, disease-specific abstract of the hospital medical record, which was prepared by a specially trained nurse for each patient in the sample. Because a patient could be included in this analysis only if a complete medical record abstract was available, the sample sizes reported here differ slightly from those shown in Table 8.2. Study constraints precluded any attempt to link the hospital medical records with outpatient records of care received before and after hospitalization. However, when the inpatient record indicated that a particular test or service had been delivered prior to admission, this was regarded as satisfactory evidence of compliance with the criterion requiring that service.

Analytic Approach

The analytic plan employs a three-stage approach. First, an item-by-item comparison of performance was made with regard to compliance with each criterion in the two sets. Second, scores were computed which summarized relative plan performance within specific components of the optimal care criteria set and across the critical services criteria set as a whole. Plan differences in these scores were considered the primary evidence of better or worse performance. Third, differences between plans observed in the summary scores were examined in relation to differences in specific physician and hospital characteristics. Since the individual hospitalized patient was the unit of analysis in all three stages, comments regarding the differences between plans with respect to physician and hospital characteristics are based on data which, in effect, weighted each provider and hospital by the number of patients cared for during the study period by that provider or hospital.

For the first stage, plan performance was compared by a straightforward tabulation of the number of cases in each plan to which each criterion was applicable and the percentage of these in which the criterion was met. Chi-square with Yates' correction was used to perform tests of statistical significance, except when there were 20 or fewer cases in a given table; here Fisher's exact test was substituted. For the second stage, performance scores were computed by counting the number of unmet criteria for each case within each component of the optimal care criteria set and for the critical services criteria set as a whole. The mean number of unmet criteria per case was then computed for each plan. For purposes of comparison, these scores were expressed as the ratio of plan means to indicate relative levels of compliance by physicians under the two plans.

This method of operationalizing performance scores requires comment, in that a simple count of the number of unmet criteria implicitly weights each criterion equally. One reason for accepting uniform weighting was the lack of a sound theoretical or empirical basis for assigning differential weights. Presumably, the best rationale for assigning weights would involve weighting each item according to its demonstrated contribution to patient outcomes. However, most of the evidence needed to assign such weights is unavailable, either because of the lack of studies to demonstrate a relationship with outcomes or because the relative importance of items has not been measured under controlled circumstances. Another reason for accepting equal weighting is that studies comparing the use of differential and equal weights in calculating physician performance scores have shown little difference in terms of the conclusion drawn. Lyons and Payne (1974) found correlations of .80 to .97 between Physician Performance Indexes

(PPIs) calculated using differential weights assigned by physicians setting the criteria and those calculated with equal weights applied to all items.

Comparisons between plans based on performance scores employed Student's *t*, using the equal variance assumption postulated under the null hypothesis, except when an F test of equality of the two sample variances rendered this assumption untenable. Sample sizes for some diagnostic categories were rather small, and the distribution of performance scores was bounded below by zero and thus cannot be normal. It was initially felt that the *t*-test might give erroneous results because of non-normality of the sampling distribution of sample means. Accordingly, many of the comparisons were also tested using a nonparametric test (Kendall's *tau c*). The particular test used made little difference in terms of the P-value obtained, however, so routine use of the latter test was dropped.

The third stage of the analysis used a set of independent variables as indicators of physician and hospital characteristics, i.e., physician training and experience, practice structure and participation in activities related to quality control, and hospital teaching status. In this stage of the analysis, the selected physician and hospital characteristics tested as possible mediators of plan effect were dichotomous variables. Consequently, the sample of cases in each plan was subdivided according to each selected explanatory variable, and the ratios of plan means for the total sample and the corresponding subsample were used to indicate changes in the relative performance of both plans when the explanatory variable was controlled for.

Two additional statistical techniques were used for data analysis but were later discarded. One used factor analysis to identify groups of intercorrelated items within the criteria sets on which to base comparisons between plans. The advantage of such an approach would be that factor scores based on these item groups would be statistically uncorrelated with each other, permitting independent comparisons across several dimensions of performance. In practice, however, the items comprising such groups were often conceptually unrelated to each other, making the results difficult to interpret; application of this method yielded no further insights beyond what could be gleaned from grouping items according to history, physical examination, diagnostic tests, etc.

The second statistical technique was a multiple linear regression model for analysis of summary performance scores, taking into account physician, hospital, and patient characteristics. Use of such a model was expected to help isolate the true effect of plan membership on such summary scores, taking into account other possibly confounding factors. Unfortunately, many cases lacked complete data on one or more of the predictor variables, requiring those cases to be excluded from the analysis. Because there was no assurance that cases with complete data on all variables would be representative of the full sample, this approach was also abandoned in favor of the simpler method reported here.

Since there is a measure of evaluation implied in the results that follow, it is important to acknowledge a number of potential weaknesses in the approach employed. One, as already pointed out in the context of Chapter 11, is the fact that the criteria employed to assess performance were unknown to the physicians in each plan during the study. Had these physicians formulated their own criteria, they might have been somewhat different. Also, if the physicians had known that performance criteria would eventually be used to assess the care provided, their recording habits and other aspects of performance might have been different (Greene, 1976). Nonetheless, we must proceed on the assumption that the process by which the criteria were developed was sound and that they do not represent a radical departure from what was considered good medical practice in Washington, D.C., in 1973–1974. Also, the fact that criteria from different sources could be aggregated into a reasonably consistent set provides some reassurance that diseases and the best available ways of treating them do not vary greatly as a function of local characteristics.

A second potential weakness is that at least some of the performance measures used may be as sensitive to variations in the quality of documentation as they are to variations in actual care rendered. The medical record is not always a complete chronicle of medical data gathering processes, yet the present analysis rests in part on the assumption that information not recorded was also not obtained. It can be argued that good documentation is an integral part of good care and that the conditions which bring about good recording practices are also likely to result in high quality care, an assumption that is now endorsed by accrediting and regulating organizations that monitor medical audit activities. Lyons and Payne (1974) have studied the relationship between recording and actual care performance and have shown that, while the relationship is not perfect, there is a positive and significant association.

A third implicit limitation is the approach to assessing physician performance taken in this study. Clearly, there are important aspects of the care process, such as the physician's caring abilities or level of skill and dexterity in executing a surgical procedure, that cannot be judged adequately from a review of the medical record. In addition, a computation of performance scores that weights all items equally may be unsatisfying to clinical readers whose professional instinct tells them that some of the criteria are more important than others. The use of a separate critical services criteria set, which highlights performance in what are felt to be the most crucial areas of care, is one attempt to deal with this problem.

Finally, as noted in Chapter 8, the number of patients hospitalized under each plan for whom the necessary data were available for this analysis is somewhat less than the total discharged patient sample shown in Table 8.2. Thus, small sample sizes in GHA in several diagnostic categories place a limit on the conclusions that can be drawn.

COMPLIANCE WITH CRITERIA
OF GOOD CARE

Levels of Compliance:
Item-by-Item Comparison

The results of the first stage of analysis, an item-by-item comparison of plan performance for each diagnosis, are summarized in the following.

Appendicitis. Overall compliance with history, therapy, and discharge status items of the optimal care criteria set was similar in the two plans, although the medical records suggested that physical examinations were more exhaustive under GHA. Three of seven physical examination criteria were met at least a third more often under GHA than under BC-BS: auscultation for bowel sounds, pelvic examination in females, and rectal examination. Of these, the rectal examination was also a critical service item. In contrast, compliance by GHA with one of the diagnostic criteria, the chest x-ray required in patients under age 18, was only observed in 18 percent of cases, a third that observed for BC-BS. Compliance with the discharge status and critical services criteria was high and comparable for both plans, except for the rectal examination criterion noted above.

Cystic Disease of the Breast and Breast Cancer. At least part of the criteria used for these two diagnostic categories are identical, as in both cases the typical presenting problem is a mass in the breast which must be biopsied to confirm or rule out malignancy. For cystic breast disease, much of the diagnostic workup is thus aimed at ruling out cancer of the breast, and there are no therapy criteria for this disease. The additional breast cancer criteria refer mainly to the more complex diagnostic and therapeutic services required to stage and treat this disease.

Performance on the history and physical examination criteria for cystic breast disease was generally similar under the two plans. Documentation of vital signs (temperature, pulse, blood pressure) was more frequent for BC-BS patients. In contrast to findings for certain other diagnostic categories, GHA patients were considerably more likely to have received a chest x-ray than BC-BS patients. For the remaining diagnostic test, discharge status, and critical services criteria, however, no pattern of plan differences in compliance was evident.

For breast cancer the small sample size in GHA (ten patients) seriously constrained comparative analysis. Nonetheless, it was noted that frequency of compliance was similar overall and none of the differences between plans were statistically significant.

Diabetes Mellitus. For 14 of the 16 history criteria in this diagnostic category, compliance was noticeably higher under GHA, and despite the small sample size (12 patients in GHA), four of these comparisons were statistically significant, including three of the classic symptoms of uncontrolled diabetes: excessive urination, thirst, and appetite. For the physical examination component, GHA compliance rates were similarly higher on nine of the ten criteria. The results were less clear-cut for diagnostic testing, therapy, and discharge status. Also, the complexity of the critical services criteria for this diagnosis fragmented the small GHA sample even further, and the resulting cell sizes were too small to permit valid conclusions based on an item-by-item comparison.

Diseases of the Gallbladder and Biliary Duct. For history and physical examination criteria, patterns of compliance were almost identical under both plans, with two exceptions: the character of abdominal pain was recorded in about half the cases under GHA (compared to 70 percent in BC-BS), while the reverse was found for levels of documentation of a previous oral cholecystogram (gallbladder x-rays). In contrast, compliance with the diagnostic testing criteria showed higher GHA performance on 11 of 12 criteria and on 6 of these, the difference was statistically significant. As observed in other diagnostic categories, most of the differences were for related procedures; here, blood tests used to gauge the degree of hepatobiliary dysfunction and to screen for other diseases which might complicate treatment. Also, an intraoperative or postoperative cholangiogram (a procedure which is also listed as a critical service) was performed twice as often as for BC-BS patients. Differences in the level of compliance with discharge status and critical services criteria were more variable for both plans and show few important differences apart from those already noted.

Arteriosclerotic Heart Disease. The frequency of compliance with most of the optimal care criteria was quite similar under the two plans. For only 2 of 40 criteria was there a substantial difference: the quality of the first and second heart sounds was described almost three times more frequently under BC-BS, and chest x-rays were recorded for 75 percent of BC-BS patients as compared to 55 percent for GHA.

Myocardial Infarction. Again, similar levels of compliance with most criteria were observed, except for two instances. BC-BS patients were more likely to have received a chest x-ray within two hours of admission and a specific sequence of electrocardiograms as required by the optimal care criteria, in both cases by substantial margins. However, the plans performed similarly and high with regard to the electrocardiogram and chest x-ray requirements of the critical services criteria, which are not as specific with regard to timing.

Pneumonia in Adults. While compliance with history and physical examination criteria was quite similar overall, the character of respirations was recorded for all GHA patients but for only 30 percent in BC-BS. For diagnostic tests, there was considerable variation across individual criteria, but the inpatient record again documented performance of a chest x-ray more often for BC-BS patients by a fairly wide margin. These findings carried over into the critical services criteria as well.

Hyperplasia of Tonsils and Adenoids. Few plan differences emerged for history, therapy, or discharge status criteria, although a wide ranged in compliance with individual items and across care components was noticeable for both plans. For instance, while description of the tympanic membrane (eardrum) was present about twice as often in the records of GHA patients, there was no compliance with this criterion in the majority of cases under both plans, and while a bleeding time was rarely done under BC-BS (14 percent), it was never done under GHA. It is possible, of course, that another screening test for bleeding abnormalities had been performed but was not apparent from the abstracts. It is noteworthy that in this group of pediatric patients, GHA physicians obtained a chest x-ray twice as frequently as did BC-BS physicians.

Uterine Fibroids. Compliance rates under GHA were higher for 17 of the 18 criteria in this diagnostic category, in several instances by a substantial margin. As noted previously, a larger proportion of GHA patients underwent a hysterectomy (98 percent versus 78 percent), which may explain higher levels of compliance on some of the diagnostic tests, e.g., type and cross-match of a blood sample and blood sugar determination, which are commonly done in preparation for surgery. On the other hand, some form of surgery was performed for nearly all cases in both plans, and this factor also would not explain differences in cervical cytology reporting.

Summary Performance Scores

From the item-by-item examination of physician performance under the two plans, summary scores were developed to indicate relative plan performance in each component of the optimal care and critical services criteria sets for the diagnostic categories examined. These scores were computed as the mean number of unmet criteria among GHA cases divided by the mean number of unmet criteria among BC-BS cases. This ratio implies higher levels of compliance under GHA when the ratio of plan means is less than 1.0, there being fewer unmet criteria per case under GHA than under BC-BS. Conversely, BC-BS compliance was superior when the ratio exceeds 1.0. Use of this ratio enables comparisons of plan performance across diagnostic categories, since it depends neither on the number of criteria listed for each nor on absolute levels of compliance. Testing for statistical significance was based on the difference between plan means.

Comparisons of the plans based on the critical services criteria showed a mixed pattern (Table 13.1). The difference between plans achieved statistical significance in two instances, diabetes mellitus and uterine fibroids, in both cases favoring GHA. For diabetes, item-by-item analysis suggested that the differences may stem from more intensive monitoring of serum electrolytes and renal function for hospitalized GHA patients with coma or precoma and of blood and urine glucose in juvenile diabetes, although small sample sizes were noted. For uterine fibroids, GHA compliance was superior for all three critical services items, including a pap smear within a year of admission, x-rays of the chest and urinary tract, and hysterectomy or myomectomy.

On the optimal care criteria, scores for the history component showed greater overall compliance with the criteria under GHA in nine of ten diagnostic categories, again with statistically significant differences for the same two diagnoses. For physical examinations and for diagnostic tests, the pattern was more mixed, although in those instances where plan differences achieved statistical significance, the evidence would seem to favor GHA. In the therapy component, seven of eight ratios indicated better performance by GHA physicians, and despite the variable pattern observed for compliance with criteria for discharge status, where superior BC-BS compliance was particularly apparent for diabetes mellitus, the summary scores again favored GHA in seven out of ten instances, in four of these by statistically significant margins.

Thus, at least for the optimal care criteria, the following pattern emerged:

— Of 48 comparisons, 36 indicated higher levels of compliance by GHA

— In 15 instances, the difference between plans was statistically significant at $P \leq .05$ or better

— Of these 15 instances of a statistically significant difference between plans, 14 favored GHA

This reasoning implicitly gives equal weight to each component and to each diagnosis. Strictly speaking, of course, these comparisons may not be statistically independent, inasmuch as the five component scores within a diagnostic category were computed on the same sample of cases. However, in the optimal care criteria, none of the components share any of the criterion items, so that each is a completely separate indicator of performance. Under the independence assumption, if the plans performed equally in each component, the probability of obtaining a chance series of differences so skewed toward one plan is about .0006; the probability of obtaining at least this many statistically significant differences by chance is less than .0000003; and if statistically significant differences had been obtained solely as a result of performing multiple comparisons in the absence of any true differences between plans, these instances of statistical significance should be equally divided between plans, with the probability of obtaining a split so skewed toward GHA being about .000916.

It appears likely, therefore, that these results reflect real plan differences. The evidence based on the optimal care criteria indicates superior compliance under GHA overall and supports the main hypothesis underlying this analysis. However, there was considerable variability in the relative performance of the two plans as a function of discharge diagnosis and care component.

EFFECTS OF ORGANIZATIONAL CHARACTERISTICS ON COMPLIANCE

The findings described are generally in accord with the hypothesis that the prepaid group practice plan would exhibit superior technical performance in providing services to its hospitalized patients. But the question remains whether the data obtained in this study, particularly with regard to organizational characteristics that are believed to differ between the two health plans, can shed light on the reasons underlying these differences in performance. This possibility was tested by reexamining the summary performance scores on criteria compliance shown in Table 13.1 after controlling for selected physician and hospital characteristics. If performance differences between plans were entirely due to the different proportions of cases in each plan receiving care from providers with specific characteristics deemed likely to contribute to superior care, the ratio of plans means for the subsample of patients treated by such providers should be close to one. The factors selected were variables suggested as distinguishing prepaid group practice from fee-for-service settings and which might be expected to affect physician performance. They were:

— Specialty board certification of the attending physician

— Matching of patients to modal specialists

— Physician participation in formal peer review

— Solo versus other practice arrangements

— Teaching status of the hospital in which care was rendered

As before, use of the ratios of mean number of unmet criteria in GHA divided by those in BC-BS was considered an economical and illustrative way of indicating differences in performance, particularly as the question addressed here is not so much the extent to which the selected physician and hospital characteristics in fact ensured superior performance, but rather whether differences between BC-BS and GHA in compliance were, wholly or in part, attributable to differences in the distribution of these characteristics between the two plans.

Specialty Board Certification
of the Attending Physician

If prepaid group practices are indeed selective in their recruitment of physicians, a more highly qualified staff might be one of the factors contributing to the observed edge in GHA performance levels over BC-BS. One indicator of physician qualifications in this study was whether the attending physician in the hospital had been certified by a medical specialty board. For the sample used in this analysis, however, there was no indication of a preponderance of such specialists in GHA (see also Chapter 9). Rather, for patients in seven diagnostic categories the reverse was observed, with board certification of the attending physician more frequent in BC-BS (Figure 13.1(1)). In only three diagnostic categories (diabetes mellitus, pneumonia, and hyperplasia of tonsils and adenoids) did the comparison favor GHA.

As a result, controlling performance differences for board certification status of the attending physician did not materially affect the overall pattern of ratios of plan means for the optimal care and critical services components (Table 13.2), although there were a few instances in which the plan effect was attenuated or even reversed by controlling for board certification status (e.g., myocardial infarction and appendicitis). It should be noted, although the data are not shown, that about 61 percent of the component and disease specific performance scores did in fact improve (i.e., there were fewer unmet criteria) when only those cases were considered in which the attending physician was a board certified specialist. This suggests that board certified specialists did comply with criteria more frequently than did other physicians.

In critical services, there remained about an even split among diagnostic categories in terms of which plan performed better. For the optimal care criteria, 33 of the 48 comparisons still showed GHA performance to be superior. Since under the null hypothesis, the probability of obtaining results so skewed toward one plan is less than .01, it appears from these findings that the pattern of greater compliance with criteria of good care by GHA is not solely attributable to differences in the specialty status of the physicians involved.

Treatment by Modal Specialists

Payne and coworkers, observing superior compliance with criteria of good care in a large prepaid group practice in Hawaii as compared with fee-for-service care in that state (Payne and Lyons, 1972), attributed this difference to the greater likelihood under the prepaid group practice of being treated by a modal specialist. In the present study, patients were considered as having been treated by a modal specialist if their attending physician in the hospital had completed specialty training (with or without board certification) as indicated in the following:

Diagnostic Category	Modal Specialty
Appendicitis	Surgery
Breast Cancer	Surgery
Cystic Disease of the Breast	Surgery
Diabetes Mellitus	Internal Medicine
Diseases of the Gallbladder and Biliary Duct	Surgery
Arteriosclerotic Heart Disease	Internal Medicine
Myocardial Infarction	Internal Medicine
Pneumonia (Adults)	Internal Medicine
Hyperplasia of Tonsils and Adenoids	Otolaryngology or Pediatrics
Uterine Fibroids	Obstetrics/Gynecology

However, contrary to expectation there were only slight differences in the percentage of patients treated by modal specialists for eight of the diagnostic categories (Figure 13.1(2)). Almost all patients in both plans were attended by modal specialists, the exceptions being diabetes mellitus (fewer in GHA) and pneumonia (fewer in BC-BS), although neither difference was statistically significant.

The effect of modal specialty status on the ratios of performance scores for all patients and for those treated by modal specialists was small (Table 13.3) and did little to alter the pattern of ratios favoring GHA. Again, if differential use of such specialists were indeed the only factor underlying the observed plan differences, there should be little or no difference in performance between plans among the subsamples of patients treated by them. Overall, 31 of the 48 comparisons on the optimal care criteria set and six of the ten comparisons for the critical services criteria still favored GHA, suggesting that the overall pattern of superior compliance under GHA is not adequately explained by differential use of modal specialists under the two plans.

Figure 13.1   Provider characteristics postulated to affect
               compliance with optimal care and critical
               services criteria: Percentages for patients
               discharged in selected diagnostic categories

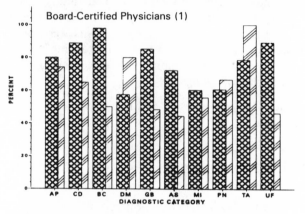

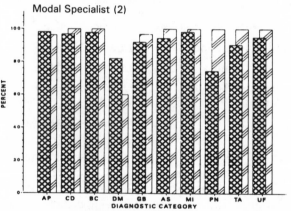

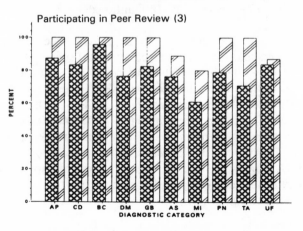

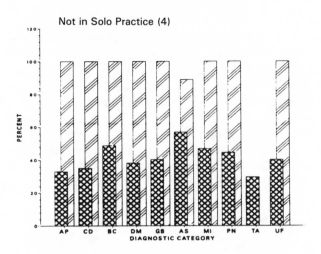

Not in Solo Practice (4)

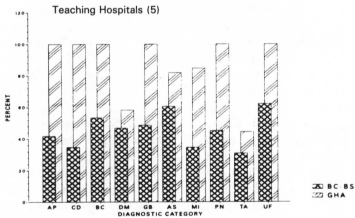

Teaching Hospitals (5)

AP - Appendicitis
CD - Cystic Breast Disease
BC - Breast Cancer
DM - Diabetes Mellitus
GB - Diseases of Gallbladder and
    Biliary Duct

AS - Arteriosclerotic and Hypertensive
    Heart Disease
MI - Myocardial Infarction
PN - Pneumonia
TA - Hyperplasia of Tonsils and Adenoids
UF - Uterine Fibroids

Participation in Formal Peer Review

Another mechanism which is intended to improve the quality and appropriateness of care is participation in formal peer review. Clearly, there should be greater opportunity for, and insistence on, such participation in prepaid group practice. In the present sample, hospitalized GHA patients were indeed somewhat more likely than BC-BS patients to have been treated by a physician who participated in peer review (Figure 13.1(3)). However, the fact that such activities were more customary in GHA did not by itself account for the overall pattern of superior performance under that plan. Despite control for peer review by the physicians involved (Table 13.4), most ratios of plan means remained nearly the same for the subsample of patients and the total sample. There still was a mixed pattern of plan superiority in the critical services criteria; for the optimal care criteria, although the pattern of superior compliance by GHA was muted somewhat in the subsample, 31 of 48 comparisons still favored GHA.

Practice Arrangements

Group practice arrangements are thought to provide another mechanism of quality control in that physicians have more opportunities to review each others' work on a more informal daily basis. Presumably, consistent use of ineffective or harmful practices should be less likely to go undetected. In the present study, patients in the sample were treated by physicians working in practice arrangements varying from solo practice, group practice, and partnership to informal associations and residency training. As it was not feasible to study each of these groups individually because of the small sample sizes, two groups were established according to whether the attending physicians described themselves as being in solo practice or not, as those in practice with at least one other physician should have a greater degree of routine interaction than those entirely in solo practice.

As expected, the vast majority of GHA patients were treated by members of the closed panel of physicians servicing GHA, i.e., by group practitioners, although there were two exceptions (Figure 13.1(4)). Care for GHA patients with hyperplasia of tonsils and adenoids was delivered by physicians who were not on the full-time staff, and this, to a lesser degree, was also true for arteriosclerotic heart disease patients. In contrast, at least half of BC-BS patients in all diagnostic categories were treated by practitioners in solo practice. The practice arrangements of the attending physician seemed to have had only limited effect on most of the compliance scores, however, and there was no clear trend toward better compliance for either plan among patients treated by practitioners not in solo practice. Even after controlling for practice type, GHA compliance was still superior (Table 13.5). Among the optimal care criteria set, while there was a suggestion in the history component that the ratio of plan means was closer to one in the subsample treated by practitioners not in solo practice, no such pattern was apparent elsewhere. Overall, 29 of the 43 subsample comparisons favored GHA, suggesting that differences in plan performance could not be solely attributed to the fact that group practice predominated under GHA.

Hospital Teaching Status

Finally, the status of the hospital to which the patients in the sample were admitted was similarly considered to determine whether teaching status accounted for differences in plan performance. A teaching hospital was defined as one with an active residency training program during the study year in the modal specialty corresponding to the disease of interest. Under this definition, it can be expected that physicians in training would participate to some degree in the care of nearly all study patients in a teaching hospital. Depending on the particular attending physician and resident involved, such participation could range from simply "watching over the shoulder" of the attending physician to assuming major responsibility for care, up to and including the performance of surgery. The involvement of residents might also have increased the completeness of the medical record, in part because the record would become a major instrument of communication among several care providers involved in a given case. Any such effect on completeness of documentation might, in turn, have increased the apparent level of compliance with the criteria used to assess performance.

As noted earlier (see Chapter 9), a large majority of GHA patients were hospitalized in teaching hospitals during the study year. For BC-BS, teaching hospitals were used much less commonly (see Figure 13.1(5)). Fortunately, however, a sufficient number of BC-BS patients were admitted to teaching hospitals to permit a comparison of plans within this setting. Interestingly, within BC-BS a fairly consistent pattern of fewer unmet criteria emerged among the subset treated in teaching hospitals, particularly for history, physical examination, and discharge status. Controlling the relative performance of the two plans for hospital teaching status, however, appeared to have no consistent effect on the ratios of plan means for critical services; the GHA margin was sometimes reversed and sometimes accentuated (Table 13.6). There was suggestive evidence for the optimal care criteria that the plan means were closer in the teaching hospital subsample (the ratio of means was closer to 1.0 in 28 out of 46 comparisons) than in the total sample. But the pattern was hardly uniform, and even after controlling for teaching status, GHA performance remained superior in 32 of 48 comparisons. These results again represented a statistically significant skewing toward GHA.

While some of the differences between plans in compliance with criteria could thus be attributed to differential use of teaching hospitals, there still was a pattern of greater compliance with criteria of good care under GHA even among the subsample of patients treated in teaching hospitals.

Summary

For two out of five factors often cited as a possible reason for superior technical performance of physicians under prepaid group practice, the expected organizational differences between GHA and BC-BS failed to emerge: there was no convincing evidence that GHA used board-certified specialists or modal specialists more consistently than did BC-BS. Furthermore, controlling for these factors did little to abolish the pattern of superior compliance with criteria under GHA. For the remaining three factors, physician participation in formal peer review, practice arrangements, and hospital teaching status, the expected organizational differences between plans were indeed found. However, controlling for each of these three factors individually failed to abolish the statistically significant skewing of results in favor of GHA. Thus, none of the five organizational factors examined here appears, by itself, adequately to explain the pattern of better compliance with criteria of good care under the prepaid group practice plan.

DISCUSSION AND CONCLUSIONS

Comparisons between the two health plans of patterns of medical care received by patients hospitalized in selected diagnostic categories were based on explicit criteria formulated by independent physician groups and specifying data items whose documentation in the hospital medical record is considered an indicator of good care. Before considering differences between plans in compliance with the criteria, an observation about overall compliance levels may be of interest. It was evident in the item-by-item comparisons that compliance with some criteria items was much higher than with others. Part of this pattern may be due to the fact that the criteria were not developed locally and some of them might not have been endorsed by the physicians under study. Certainly, the fact that some of the optimal care criteria were included in multiple published criteria sets, while others were mentioned in only one set, indicates variable degrees of medical consensus. However, an assumption behind use of each criterion for present purposes is that, other things being equal, documented compliance with an item is preferable to no documented compliance with that item. Moreover, since physicians under both plans were part of the same medical community, departures from the criteria due to local idiosyncrasies should be evenly distributed in both plans. Such factors should be much less important for the critical services criteria, which have been endorsed by national medical organizations.

The central question underlying this investigation was whether the plans differed substantially in levels of physician compliance with the criteria. A sampling of the literature in the field indicated that performance, at least in the light of the record-based criteria chosen, would be superior under the prepaid group practice plan, largely because of its control over factors which are thought to affect medical performance: i.e., the selection of physicians providing care and of the hospitals in which care is delivered. From a statistical point of view, and looking at individual comparisons in each diagnostic category for each criterion item or component of care, most of the observed differences between plans could be explicable on the basis of chance alone. However, such determinations of statistical significance are highly dependent on sample sizes, which were often small in the present data set, and we must therefore look as well for patterns evident in the aggregate. Such a pattern would appear to be present if a clear majority of all comparisons collectively suggests greater compliance with the criteria under one of the plans, even if the levels of significance for each individual comparison vary.

Overall, our first question was answered fairly clearly by the data. There appeared to be superior compliance with criteria under GHA in that a substantial majority of comparisons between plans showed better performance by GHA physicians. Even if attention is confined to comparisons for which a statistically significant difference between plans was found, a substantial majority of comparisons favored GHA.

Variations in this pattern by diagnostic category and by type of criteria were evident, however. Consistent differences between plans in terms of compliance with the critical services criteria were less prominent than with the optimal care criteria. This suggests that the most important items of documented care tended to be complied with fairly consistently under both plans, while those items which may be desirable but not critical tended to be more frequently complied with under the prepaid group practice. For three of the selected diagnostic categories (breast cancer, diseases of the gallbladder and biliary duct, and uterine fibroids), compliance under GHA was higher than under BC-BS across all components of the criteria, including critical services. For the remaining seven diagnoses, the pattern was mixed, with superior compliance under GHA for some components of care and superior compliance under BC-BS for others, although there was no diagnostic category in which compliance was superior under BC-BS across all components of care.

Thus, we are left with a second, more difficult question: What was the reason for these apparent differences in performance? Were they due to underlying differences between the plans in terms of the physicians providing care or the hospitals in which care was provided? Five factors were examined which are often considered as possible reasons for superior technical performance under prepaid group practice: physician qualifications, matching of patients to modal specialists, participation in formal peer review, practice organization involving opportunities for informal peer review, and (in the present setting) preferential use of teaching hospitals in the delivery of care. There was no evidence that there were relatively more board certified specialists and modal specialists in GHA treating patients in the sample, so that superior patterns of performance under GHA cannot be attributed to these two factors. However, the plans did differ significantly with respect to the last three factors. In general, GHA patients were more likely to have been attended by physicians who participated in formal peer review and to have been hospitalized in a teaching hospital, and less likely to have been attended by physicians who described themselves as being in solo practice. Notwithstanding these differences, when each of these factors was held constant by considering only patients under each plan to whom the specific factor applied, plan differences in compliance persisted. Thus, even after controlling for each factor individually, a pattern of superior performance under GHA remained evident.

In the final analysis, none of the variables examined provided a satisfactory answer to the question why compliance with criteria of good care differed between the two plans. A number of possible reasons for this conclusion suggest themselves. First, it is possible that while the correct explanatory factors were identified, the measures expressing them were too crude to show their true effect. A good example is board certification status, which is an imperfect measure of physician qualifications at best.

Second, while no single explanatory factor sufficed to account for the observed difference between plans, these factors may have acted jointly to explain the plan effect. Given a larger data set, explanation of this possibility with a more complex multivariate model would be of interest.

Third, differences between plans may relate to a factor or factors not even considered or measured in this study. Clearly, a great deal of variation in the compliance scores is left unexplained by the variables examined. Health care plans such as GHA and BC-BS are complex social organizations which differ from each other in more than enough ways to tax the observational and classificatory powers of any investigator. Perhaps the answer is simply that the additional factors which determine compliance are so inextricably tied to each form of health care organization that there is no possibility of accounting for each separately. If the method of physician reimbursement were such a factor, it would be impossible to examine it independently of plan type. If this is the case, we could safely attribute differences in performance to the implicit organizational differences between prepaid group practice and traditional service benefit health plans.

Table 13.1 Summary measures of relative compliance: Ratios of plan means[a] for optimal care and critical services criteria

Diagnostic category	Critical[b] services	Optimal care criteria[c]				
		History	Physical examinations	Diagnostic tests	Therapy	Discharge status
Appendicitis	1.21	.93	.76*	1.15	1.35	.46*
Cystic disease of the breast	.48	1.02	1.06	.62*	—	.92*
Breast cancer	.92	.92	.86	.61	.00	.91
Diabetes mellitus	.65*	.63*	.72*	.38	.99	1.35*
Diseases of gall bladder and biliary duct	.57	.97	.86	.53*	.50	.83*
Arteriosclerotic heart disease	1.68	.85	1.04	1.61	—	1.25
Myocardial infarction	1.63	.78	1.06	1.32	.31	.87
Pneumonia (adults)	.88	.95	.61*	1.53	.00	1.26
Hyperplasia of tonsils and adenoids	1.04	.98	.98	.95	.84*	.85
Uterine fibroids	.80*	.73*	.70	.53*	.13*	.53*

[a]The ratios are based on the mean number of unfulfilled criteria in each component for all cases (GHA/BC-BS).

[b]Selected from the AMA Screening Criteria for Use by Professional Standards Review Organizations (1976).

[c]These criteria have been drawn from explicit, disease specific criteria developed for use in medical care quality assessment; see AMA, 1976; Cohen, Wolpin, and Cohen, 1975; Decker et al., 1973; Hospital Utilization Project, 1969; Metropolitan Health Care Foundation, 1971; Payne and Lyons, 1972; Schonfeld, Heston, and Falk, 1975; Utah Professional Review Organization, 1972; Yale–New Haven Hospital, 1974.

—No criteria available.   *P ≤ .05.

Table 13.2 Summary measures of relative compliance with optimal care and critical services criteria: Ratios of plan means[a] for total patient sample and for patients treated by board certified specialists

Diagnostic category	Patient group	Optimal care criteria					
		History	Physical examinations	Diagnostic tests	Therapy	Discharge status	Critical services
Appendicitis	All	.93	.76	1.15	1.35	.46	1.21
	With board certified specialist	.87	.76	.98	1.98	.55	.79
Cystic disease of the breast	All	1.02	1.06	.62	—	.92	.48
	With board certified specialist	1.01	.98	.64	—	.91	.43
Breast cancer	All	.92	.86	.61	.00	.91	.92
	With board certified specialist	.81	.93	.12	.00	1.34	.73
Diabetes mellitus	All	.63	.72	.38	.99	1.35	.65
	With board certified specialist	.67	.82	.79	1.04	1.60	.90
Diseases of gall bladder and biliary duct	All	.97	.86	.53	.50	.83	.57
	With board certified specialist	1.30	1.12	.41	1.40	.93	.60
Arteriosclerotic heart disease	All	.85	1.04	1.61	—	1.25	1.68
	With board certified specialist	.60	.82	1.52	—	.99	2.08
Myocardial infarction	All	.78	1.06	1.32	.31	.87	1.63
	With board certified specialist	.70	1.30	1.43	1.08	1.11	5.71
Pneumonia (adults)	All	.95	.61	1.53	.00	1.26	.88
	With board certified specialist	.80	.66	1.14	.00	.91	1.00
Hyperplasia of tonsils and adenoids	All	.98	.98	.95	.84	.85	1.04
	With board certified specialist	.98	.97	.95	.85	.81	1.07
Uterine fibroids	All	.73	.70	.53	.13	.53	.80
	With board certified specialist	.63	.55	.53	.00	.14	.89

[a] The ratios are based on the mean number of unfulfilled criteria in each component for all cases (GHA/BC–BS).

—No criteria available.

Table 13.3 Summary measures of relative compliance with optimal care and critical services criteria: Ratios of plan means[a] for total patient sample and for patients treated by modal specialists

Diagnostic category	Patient group	Optimal care criteria					Critical services
		History	Physical examinations	Diagnostic tests	Therapy	Discharge status	
Appendicitis	All	.93	.76	1.15	1.35	.46	1.21
	With modal specialist	.87	.71	1.07	1.53	.44	.90
Cystic disease of the breast	All	1.02	1.06	.62	—	.92	.48
	With modal specialist	1.03	1.05	.65	—	.89	.49
Breast cancer	All	.92	.86	.61	.00	.91	.92
	With modal specialist	.84	.91	.57	.00	1.13	.88
Diabetes mellitus	All	.63	.72	.38	.99	1.35	.65
	With modal specialist	.69	.73	.30	.83	1.39	.63
Diseases of gall bladder and biliary duct	All	.97	.86	.53	.50	.83	.57
	With modal specialist	1.02	1.11	.51	.75	.88	.59
Arteriosclerotic heart disease	All	.85	1.04	1.61	—	1.25	1.68
	With modal specialist	.94	1.15	1.47	—	1.22	1.30
Myocardial infarction	All	.78	1.06	1.32	.31	.87	1.63
	With modal specialist	.79	1.22	1.40	.49	.93	2.20
Pneumonia (adults)	All	.95	.61	1.53	.00	1.26	.88
	With modal specialist	1.13	.68	1.36	.00	1.04	1.14
Hyperplasia of tonsils and adenoids	All	.98	.98	.95	.84	.85	1.04
	With modal specialist	.98	1.01	.94	.84	.82	1.05
Uterine fibroids	All	.73	.70	.53	.13	.53	.80
	With modal specialist	.76	.97	.54	.00	.55	.84

[a]The ratios are based on the mean number of unfulfilled criteria in each component for all cases (GHA/BC–BS).

—No criteria available.

Table 13.4 Summary measures of relative compliance with optimal care and critical services criteria: Ratios of plan means[a] for total patient sample and for patients treated by a physician participating in peer review

Diagnostic category	Patient group	Optimal care criteria					Critical services
		History	Physical examinations	Diagnostic tests	Therapy	Discharge status	
Appendicitis	All	.93	.76	1.15	1.35	.46	1.21
	With peer review physician	.90	.75	1.09	1.70	.41	.98
Cystic disease of the breast	All	1.02	1.06	.62	—	.92	.48
	With peer review physician	1.04	1.04	.66	—	.88	.49
Breast cancer	All	.92	.86	.61	.00	.91	.92
	With peer review physician	.85	.79	.54	.00	1.07	.85
Diabetes mellitus	All	.63	.72	.38	.99	1.35	.65
	With peer review physician	.61	.76	.61	1.05	1.52	.69
Diseases of gall bladder and biliary duct	All	.97	.86	.53	.50	.83	.57
	With peer review physician	1.04	1.16	.55	.50	.88	.67
Arteriosclerotic heart disease	All	.85	1.04	1.61	—	1.25	1.68
	With peer review physician	.99	1.26	1.53	—	1.23	1.91
Myocardial infarction	All	.78	1.06	1.32	.31	.87	1.63
	With peer review physician	1.03	1.16	1.48	.49	.72	3.33
Pneumonia (adults)	All	.95	.61	1.53	.00	1.26	.88
	With peer review physician	.81	.67	1.47	.00	1.14	1.25
Hyperplasia of tonsils and adenoids	All	.98	.98	.95	.84	.85	1.04
	With peer review physician	.97	.96	.97	.85	.82	1.05
Uterine fibroids	All	.73	.70	.53	.13	.53	.80
	With peer review physician	.73	.85	.51	.00	.46	.82

[a]The ratios are based on the mean number of unfulfilled criteria in each component for all cases (GHA/BC-BS).

—No criteria available.

Table 13.5 Summary measures of relative compliance with optimal care and critical services criteria: Ratios of plan means[a] for total patient sample and for patients treated by a physician not in solo practice

| Diagnostic category | Patient group | History | Physical examinations | Optimal care criteria | | | Critical services |
				Diagnostic tests	Therapy	Discharge status	
Appendicitis	All	.93	.76	1.15	1.35	.46	1.21
	With physician not in solo practice	1.00	.71	.97	1.31	.38	.95
Cystic disease of the breast	All	1.02	1.06	.62	—	.92	.48
	With physician not in solo practice	1.04	.99	.65	—	.91	.48
Breast cancer	All	.92	.86	.61	.00	.91	.92
	With physician not in solo practice	.93	.91	.59	.00	.73	1.01
Diabetes mellitus	All	.63	.72	.38	.99	1.35	.65
	With physician not in solo practice	.64	.80	.87	1.05	1.50	.72
Diseases of gall bladder and biliary duct	All	.97	.86	.53	.50	.83	.57
	With physician not in solo practice	1.02	1.14	.54	.30	.78	.67
Arteriosclerotic heart disease	All	.85	1.04	1.61	—	1.25	1.68
	With physician not in solo practice	.92	1.11	1.73	—	1.21	1.31
Myocardial infarction	All	.78	1.06	1.32	.31	.87	1.63
	With physician not in solo practice	.83	1.13	1.24	.40	.68	2.35
Pneumonia (adults)	All	.95	.61	1.53	.00	1.26	.88
	With physician not in solo practice	1.06	.67	1.32	.00	.83	1.14
Hyperplasia of tonsils and adenoids	All	.98	.98	.95	.84	.85	1.04
	With physician not in solo practice	—	—	—	—	—	—
Uterine fibroids	All	.73	.70	.53	.13	.53	.80
	With physician not in solo practice	.75	.91	.48	.00	.57	.77

[a]The ratios are based on the mean number of unfulfilled criteria in each component for all cases (GHA/BC-BS).

—No criteria available.

——No cases.

Table 13.6 Summary measures of relative compliance with optimal care and critical services criteria: Ratios of plan means[a] for total patient sample and for patients treated in teaching hospitals

Diagnostic category	Patient group	History	Physical examinations	Optimal care criteria		Discharge status	Critical services
				Diagnostic tests	Therapy		
Appendicitis	All	.93	.76	1.15	1.35	.46	1.21
	In teaching hospital	.95	.83	1.11	1.13	.60	1.15
Cystic disease of the breast	All	1.02	1.06	.62	—	.92	.48
	In teaching hospital	1.13	1.18	.56	—	1.01	.46
Breast cancer	All	.92	.86	.61	.00	.91	.92
	In teaching hospital	.93	.79	.77	.00	.92	1.10
Diabetes mellitus	All	.63	.72	.38	.99	1.35	.65
	In teaching hospital	.76	.67	.33	.78	1.27	.62
Diseases of gall bladder and biliary duct	All	.97	.86	.53	.50	.83	.57
	In teaching hospital	1.19	1.22	.59	.50	.91	.67
Arteriosclerotic heart disease	All	.85	1.04	1.61	—	1.25	1.68
	In teaching hospital	.89	1.02	1.56	—	1.32	1.59
Myocardial infarction	All	.78	1.06	1.32	.31	.87	1.63
	In teaching hospital	1.01	1.34	.89	.31	.63	.94
Pneumonia (adults)	All	.95	.61	1.53	.00	1.26	.88
	In teaching hospital	1.02	.62	1.27	.00	1.10	.86
Hyperplasia of tonsils and adenoids	All	.98	.98	.95	.84	.85	1.04
	In teaching hospital	.93	.81	.87	.52	.96	.99
Uterine fibroids	All	.73	.70	.53	.13	.53	.80
	In teaching hospital	.91	.85	.60	.17	.61	.85

[a]The ratios are based on the mean number of unfulfilled criteria in each component for all cases (GHA/BC–BS).

— No criteria available.

14

A Summary of Findings

Donald C. Riedel, Samuel M. Meyers,
Thomas D. Koepsell, and Daniel C. Walden

The study reported in this book was guided by the wish to obtain a more detailed understanding of the nature and magnitude of differences in use of health services in a prepaid group practice plan (GHA) and a service benefit plan (BC-BS), and of the influence of health insurance benefits and subscriber and provider characteristics on variations in both hospital and ambulatory use. The preceding chapters have documented the specific methods employed and the findings in each component of this study of subscribers to the Federal Employees Health Benefit Plan. We shall now summarize these findings and discuss their implications, both in terms of each phase of the study and in the more general terms of the study objectives.

PHASE I: RATES OF HOSPITAL USE
AND LENGTH OF STAY

The first phase of the study, which is described in Chapter 2, was designed to answer these questions:

- Were there differences between the two plans in rates of hospital admissions, average lengths of inpatient stay, and rates of total days of care?
- Were such differences attributable to differences in the age and sex characteristics of the members of the two plans?
- Were there differences in hospital use by discharge diagnosis?
- What were the hospital and physician characteristics associated with differences in hospital use, particularly length of stay?

Methods

Because the local BC plan acted as the fiscal intermediary for GHA at the time of the study, comparable hospital claims were available. Data on hospital admissions and length of stay were obtained from five sources: computerized claims files of the local BC-BS plan; copies of individual claims; tape files from the local Blue Shield plan; abstracts of hospital records; and abstracts of GHA records. Six thousand hospital admissions for the period January 1, 1967 to September 30, 1970, allocated between single and family contracts on the basis of the ratio of total expected single contract claims to total expected family contract claims, were estimated to be required in each plan to perform diagnostic specific analyses. Forty-three diagnostic categories, estimated to represent almost 60 percent of all admissions, were selected for detailed analysis, based on the requirement that the least frequent of these categories would have to contain at least 30 cases, or about 0.5 percent of all admissions for both plans.

For GHA, 11,949 contracts representing 75 percent of total high-option, nonannuitant single and family contracts were sampled for hospital admission as of September 30, 1970 by means of a systematic sampling procedure; for BC-BS 6,974 contracts were sampled in a similar manner. The difference in sample size reflected the known differences in admission rates between the two plans. Demographic data were limited to those found on the plan enrollment form. While GHA files contained current information on residential address, age, and sex of the contract holder and of family members, BC-BS membership files contained such information only as of the time of the enrollment. To obtain current demographic data for BC-BS contracts, a combined mail and telephone survey was conducted. Missing data for those family contract holders who did not respond to this survey were imputed from the experience of responding contract holders.

Characteristics of hospitals in the Washington metropolitan area as obtained from published sources were known from other studies to be associated with length of stay, i.e., accreditation, for-profit status, and presence of teaching programs. Specialty status and years in practice, two physician characteristics known to be related to differential patterns of hospital use, were obtained for the physician with primary responsibility for the care of hospitalized patients in the sample.

Findings

— There were no overall differences in the age and sex composition of the members in the two plans in 1970; however, the mean family size in BC-BS was 3.55 persons and 4.06 persons in GHA, and length of membership in the respective plan was longer in BC-BS than in GHA.

— As expected, a larger percentage of GHA patients were admitted to teaching hospitals, reflecting the pattern of hospital appointments of physicians in the two plans.

— There were no differences in the proportions of patients attended by board certified physicians in the two plans; a somewhat greater percentage of GHA patients were cared for by physicians in practice a shorter length of time.

— Even after correction for the small demographic disparities, differences between the two plans in rates of hospital admission were substantial: 121 admissions per 1,000 membership years for BC-BS and 69 for GHA (admission rates were based on membership years because not all persons sampled as of September 30, 1970 had been covered for the full sample period). Leaving aside obstetrical admissions, females were admitted at a higher rate under BC-BS than males. Under GHA the reverse was observed, although the magnitude of this difference in admission rates between males and females was considerably smaller. Also, the difference in nonobstetrical admission rates between female members of the two plans was greater than for males. In both plans, however, a higher hospital admission rate was observed for members covered under single contracts than for those under family contracts.

— In 39 of the 46 diagnostic categories examined, the BC-BS rate of admissions was higher than under GHA by a statistically significant margin. A higher GHA admission rate was observed in only one category (wounds and burns). The largest of these differences which could not be attributed to differences in the benefit structure of the two plans were for disorders of menstruation, acute respiratory infections, and hypertrophy of tonsils and adenoids and chronic tonsillitis.

— Differences in length of stay between members of the two plans were smaller than for admission rates and, except for three diagnostic categories, stays by BC-BS members were not longer than by GHA members. In fact, GHA lengths of stay exceeded those in BC-BS in eight diagnostic categories.

— There were thus substantial differences in patient day rates between the two plans. Overall, the difference was almost twofold, with 804 patient days per 1,000 membership years in BC-BS and 453 in GHA. Patterns of differences by age, sex, and type of contract were similar for hospital admission rates and patient day rates.

PHASE II: USE OF
AMBULATORY SERVICES

The principal questions addressed in this phase of the study (1972–1974; see Chapters 3 to 7) were the following:

- Were there previously unascertained differences in demographic, attitudinal, and enabling characteristics of the members of the two plans that might be associated with the use of health services?

- To what extent were the members of the two plans similar in reported health status and levels of illness, including chronic complaints and social dysfunction?

- Was there variation between the plans in the extent to which plan members contacted physicians and other health professionals when illness or injury was experienced, and in the time it took to seek and obtain care?

- Did the rates of use of various types of ambulatory health services differ between the plans?

- Were such differences in rates of use associated with any of the variables specified in the preceding, or with various administrative and structural characteristics of the two plans (e.g., length of time necessary to obtain an appointment)?

- Was there any evidence that ambulatory care was being substituted for inpatient care in the prepaid group practice plan?

- Did patterns of care-seeking behavior differ between the members of the plans within discrete episodes of illness?

- How much out-of-plan use was there among members of GHA, what were the reasons for such use, and was there any indication that out-of-plan hospital use might account for some of the differences observed in Phase I?

- What were the differences in total out-of-pocket expenditures for health care by members of the two plans, and were there differences in the components of these expenditures?

Methods

Data were obtained by monthly personal interviews with a sample of GHA and BC-BS households for one year; data collection extended from the fall of 1972 through the spring of 1974. A month was selected as the interval between interviews to decrease problems of recall. The person who appeared most knowledgeable of matters of health pertaining to each household was selected as the main respondent, although others were encouraged to be present and to respond for themselves if they were old enough.

Of 1,335 contracts sampled, 16 percent were ineligible, and 83 percent of eligible contract holders (1,124) completed the initial interview, with similar completion rates in each plan. Ninety percent remained in the study for the entire 12 months. The initial interview established the demographic characteristics of the sample, additional health insurance coverage, perception of health status and chronic health problems, attitudes toward seeking care, satisfaction with care and with the plan, usual source(s) of care, events of illness and injury and of ambulatory and inpatient care in the preceding month, and out-of-pocket expenditures for health care. Subsequent monthly interviews were shorter and contained questions mainly on events of illness and injury and of ambulatory care and on out-of-pocket expenditures.

Analysis of these data and the structuring of variables were based on the model of individual determinants of health services use by Andersen and Newman (1973), with some modifications as described in Chapter 3. A special point of emphasis was specific episodes of illness, defined as all events of illness or injury and use of health services by a person that were associated with a specific health problem. Because not all sample members were in the study for the entire year, items that required a full year of data, such as number of days in bed or of restricted activity and of pain and worry days, number of contacts with services, and household expenditures for care, were weighted up to a full year according to the number of months the person or household has been in the study. The bulk of the analyses performed in Phase II were based on 934 households, 2,691 persons, and 5,740 episodes of illness.

Findings

Predisposing and Enabling Factors

- The racial composition of the two plans was strikingly different, with twice the percentage of black enrollees in GHA as in BC-BS. As a result, differences between the plans in both predisposing and enabling factors tended to be obscured in overall distributions.
- The median age was slightly higher in BC-BS than in GHA, and higher percentages of whites in both plans were among those 45 years and older, particularly in GHA.
- No differences were observed in the sex composition of the two plans.
- Mean family size was slightly higher in GHA.

— Although a somewhat higher percentage of GHA than BC-BS members lived in households where the most highly educated adult had five or more years of college, a greater percentage in BC-BS ranked high on an occupational scale. Whites in both plans ranked higher than blacks on both measures, GHA whites being the most highly educated and professionally ranked single group in the study population.

— Median annual family incomes in the two plans were similar overall, with the highest median income found for GHA whites and the lowest for GHA blacks.

— In both plans nearly all men were employed full time. The percent of women not working full-time was largest in BC-BS and substantially higher among white women in both plans. Three-fourths of white children in both plans were in families with two parents, only one of whom was employed full time; roughly half of black children in both plans were members of households where both parents worked full time and one-fifth lived with one parent.

— In GHA, two-fifths were members of families where the contract holder reported a high tendency to use physician services, as compared to one-third in BC-BS; blacks in both plans ranked relatively high on this scale. Also, almost all GHA members favored an annual physical examination in the absence of illness as compared to four-fifths in BC-BS. GHA members were more likely to have had a physical examination within the past two years.

— Measures of satisfaction with a wide variety of aspects of care indicated higher satisfaction in BC-BS and by the two white groups.

— Three-quarters of BC-BS members lived in households that had been enrolled with BC-BS for more than six years, as compared to half of members in GHA. A substantially higher percentage of blacks in GHA lived in families that had joined that plan within three years of the survey than was found for BC-BS blacks.

— Twice as many GHA members ranked high in knowledge of the benefits provided by their plan than members of BC-BS, with the white group in GHA most knowledgeable by far.

— Four-fifths in both plans reported having a regular source of medical care, although in GHA only half of these reported having a personal physician, i.e., a physician usually called upon when ill.

— There were major differences between the plans in access to care as measured by appointment waiting times and time to obtain care, with appointment visits in BC-BS requiring shorter waiting times than in GHA. While about three-fourths of all patient initiated visits (including walk-in visits) for diagnosis and treatment were made within 24 hours of the patient's decision to seek care, substantially fewer visits for check-ups and routine physical examinations in GHA occurred within this time than in BC-BS, and at least twice the percentage of GHA visits of this type occurred two weeks or more after the decision to seek medical care. On all these measures of access, however, visits by blacks in either plan occurred more swiftly than visits by the white groups, and in GHA a somewhat higher proportion of visits by the black group were by appointment. Reported office waiting times, on the other hand, were similar for both plans but tended to be shorter for both white groups.

Levels of Perceived Illness

— Overall, no differences were observed for reported health status at the beginning of the survey year.

— Slightly more chronic health problems were reported by GHA members in both race groups than in BC-BS, while members of the latter plan reported more bed and restricted activity days. Whites reported somewhat more illness on this measure in both plans, and this was also observed for days of pain and worry.

— No statistically significant difference was observed between the plans in the race adjusted percent of persons with at least one episode of illness, but both the mean volume of episodes and the number of episodes per person was higher in GHA. Whites in both plans again reported substantially more illness than blacks on this measure. On the other hand, the types of episodes, their length, and the kind of health problem (acute or chronic) associated with each were substantially the same in each plan.

Variations in Use of Ambulatory Services

— Race adjusted rates of use of services were moderately higher under GHA in terms of the percentage of persons using ambulatory services during the survey year and in volume of use (mean number of contacts and mean number of contacts per person).

— GHA members were also more likely to have had an ambulatory visit for a new health problem (entry visit), and for three out of five types of preventive care, the margin of difference was in favor of greater use in GHA.

— On all these measures, both black groups ranked substantially below the white groups in both plans.

—Within episodes of illness, on the other hand, no plan differences were observed in the percent of episodes with medical contact and the volume of contacts within each episode; here, black members of GHA were substantially more likely than all others to seek care within an episode of illness and substantially less likely to experience episodes involving disability days only.

—The moderately greater use of services by GHA members was observed for both likelihood and volume of contacts for most types of services. Statistically significant differences were most pronounced for visits to a physician's office, clinic, or laboratory, particularly for preventive services; telephone calls to a physician's office; and visits to mental health practitioners. An exception to this pattern were visits to an emergency room.

Correlates of Use

—Use of services in both plans tended to be most frequent in the youngest and oldest age groupings, and females in both plans made more use of services than did males.

—The educational and occupational level of the household was positively related to the likelihood of contact, but its relation to volume of use was not as obvious. However, an increase in likelihood and volume of use was observed with rising income levels in both plans, particularly in GHA.

—The tendency to consult a physician in the presence of illness and favorable attitudes toward a routine physical examination were positively associated with use.

—The relationship of length of plan membership to use was strongest in GHA for members of long standing, while the reverse was observed in BC-BS. In both plans, however, knowledge of plan benefits was positively related to likelihood and volume of use.

—Members of both plans with personal physicians were more likely to have had at least one medical contact and to have had greater volume of use.

—All measures of illness (perceived health status, number of chronic health problems, and number of bed days, restricted activity days, and pain and worry days) were positively related to use of ambulatory services, but the differential in use between plans was maintained for volume of contacts.

—The differential between the black and white groups in each plan was maintained when predisposing, enabling and illness factors were taken into account, although it was reduced in GHA.

— Multivariate analyses of the relative importance of independent variables in explaining ambulatory use overall, and visits for diagnosis and treatment and entry visits in particular, demonstrated that this set of variables accounted for 21, 38, and 33 percent of total variance, respectively. In all three analyses, measures of illness explained over 60 percent of this variation. Plan membership considered as a distinct variable had no effect on total ambulatory use or on visits for treatment and diagnosis, and a miniscule effect on entry visits. Race accounted for less than 10 percent of variance for ambulatory medical visits, and for less than 2 percent for treatment and diagnostic visits and entry visits.

Out-of-Plan Use by GHA Members

— Out-of-plan use of hospitals was negligible (4 percent of all admissions) but overall, 14 percent of all health care contacts were out-of-plan, with the highest rate of such contacts occurring in the emergency room and with mental health and other nonphysician practitioners. Twenty percent of all GHA members had at least one out-of-plan contact during the survey year.

— Preference was stated most frequently as a reason for out-of-plan use, followed by care at work or school, distance from facilities, dissatisfaction, lack of coverage of specific services, legal referrals, miscellaneous other reasons, out-of-area care, and emergencies. While dissatisfaction with the plan was not a significant factor in whether or not a person had any out-of-plan use, among the black groups this was frequently given as a reason for such use.

Out-of-Pocket Expenditures

— Annual net out-of-pocket expenditures (including premiums) of GHA families were 14 percent higher than for BC-BS families when adjusted for race and type of contract.

— Little difference was observed in expenditures of single contract holders; for family contracts, expenditures in GHA were 18 percent higher than in BC-BS.

— Out-of-pocket expenditures for services (not counting premiums) were, as expected, 38 percent lower for GHA but expenses connected with out-of-plan use and for services not covered by the plan tended to increase these expenditures.

— The contract adjusted premium in GHA was 48 percent higher than in BC-BS, although it was noted that the actuarial methods for calculating this premium were dissimilar; the GHA premium was community based and the FEHBP BC-BS premium was experience based among all federal employees who selected this option.

PHASE III: HOSPITAL EPISODES
AND PATTERNS OF CARE

The final phase of the study focused on the patterns of patient and physician behavior associated with a specific episode of illness resulting in hospitalization. Specifically, four sets of questions were addressed:

— Were there plan differences in the appropriateness of admission to the hospital and of the services rendered during the course of the hospital stay? Were there differences in the relative proportions of patients for whom the principal diagnosis changed between the time of admission and discharge, indicating differences in the use of the inpatient facilities for diagnostic purposes? Were any of these differences associated with characteristics of the providers of care?

— Were there differences in the severity of the illnesses of the patients in each plan at the time of hospitalization, possibly indicating differences in discretionary use of the hospital by physicians?

— How did the patterns of medical care sought and received by hospitalized members of each plan differ? Were differences found mainly in the prehospital stage or in the in-hospital stage? Was there evidence that specific patient or provider characteristics accounted for these differences?

Methods

Samples of patients in each plan were chosen who were hospitalized with one of several primary diagnoses during the study period (1973–1974). The diagnostic categories were selected according to several criteria: observed differences in admission rates in Phase I; availability of acceptable protocols for evaluation of the appropriateness of care; expected differences between plans in patterns of ambulatory and inpatient care; and the probable involvement of a range of medical specialties in the care of patients with the particular disorder.

Thirteen categories were initially selected for intensive study:

— Appendicitis

— Cystic disease of the breast

— Nonmetastatic malignant neoplasms of the breast

— Diabetes mellitus

- Diseases of gallbladder and biliary duct
- Arteriosclerotic and hypertensive heart disease
- Acute myocardial infarction
- Pneumonia
- Hyperplasia of tonsils and adenoids
- Uterine fibroids
- Disorders of menstruation
- Urinary tract infections
- Benign prostatic hypertrophy and prostatitis

Several pairs of categories were chosen because the presenting symptoms are often the same and the correct diagnosis can only be made after extensive testing. Urinary tract infections and benign prostatic hypertrophy and prostatitis were subsequently eliminated from analysis because of the small numbers of hospitalized cases appearing in GHA during the study period. Disorders of menstruation were considered unsuitable for analysis because the extent to which outpatient surgery facilities were used for this complaint was known for GHA only, but not for the fee-for-service plan.

Cases were selected concurrently for the sample as claims for hospitalizations were received from the hospitals for payment. Because of the low frequency of occurrence, all GHA cases were included in the study; BC-BS patients were selected by probability sample techniques to yield sufficient numbers for analysis. Five sources of data were employed to obtain comprehensive information on the process of care seeking behavior by patients in response to perceived illness, decisions by physicians concerning patient management, clinical details on the patients' conditions and treatment, characteristics of the patients and providers, and circumstances surrounding admission to and discharge from the hospital: (1) interviews with patients after hospital internment; (2) hospital medical records for the sampled stays; (3) personal interviews with the physicians who had suggested hospitalization, with those responsible for actual admission, and with those primarily responsible for the inpatient care; (4) published sources for characteristics of those physicians who could not be interviewed; and (5) published sources for characteristics of the hospitals used.

The completion rates for each component of the fieldwork were high, with nine out of ten sampled patients in each plan interviewed, and 91 percent of these granting permission to have their hospital medical records abstracted. Response rates for the physician interviews were somewhat lower, with approximately 85 percent of the physicians approached in each plan granting an interview concerning the hospitalization and associated ambulatory care.

It is emphasized again that the categories chosen and analyses conducted were to determine patterns of similarity and difference in patient behavior and provider management, and not to produce estimates of *total* appropriate or inappropriate care in the two plans; the findings in Chapters 10–13 and their interpretation should be examined in light of the selective inclusion of a fraction of the patients cared for in each plan.

Findings

Patient Characteristics

- In general, the demographic composition of the discharged patient samples reflected the characteristic pattern of occurrence of each disease according to age, sex, and race. Thus, the arteriosclerotic heart disease and myocardial infarction samples consisted of older adults and contained more men than women. The gallbladder disease sample contained more women than men. The uterine fibroid sample contained proportionately more blacks than did the enrolled population of each plan.

- The discharged patient samples in GHA contained more blacks than whites, while the reverse was true in BC-BS. This difference is, however, adequately explained by corresponding differences in the respective enrollee populations.

Physician Characteristics

- There was no consistent difference in the level of training of physicians providing care to patients discharged under the two plans. However, GHA patients tended to be cared for by physicians with fewer years of practice and with shorter work weeks, especially in the surgical diagnoses.

- Participation in teaching activities was similar for physicians providing care to discharged patients in the two plans. In general, BC-BS physicians had admitting privileges at a larger number of hospitals in the area than did GHA physicians.

- With regard to the question whether GHA or BC-BS patients were cared for more often by physicians who were initiators of referrals to other physicians and recipients of referrals, the findings showed plan differences for several diagnostic categories but these were not consistent across diagnoses. Since many patients in the sample were cared for by the same physicians, the findings are difficult to interpret.

- GHA patients were cared for by physicians who were more frequent participants in certain educational activities (grand rounds, teaching rounds, professional meetings) and in patient care review and evaluation than their BC-BS counterparts, but participation in formal continuing medical education did not differ significantly between GHA physicians and BC-BS physicians providing care to the discharged patients.

Hospital Characteristics

— GHA patients tended to be admitted to larger hospitals—i.e., with more than 500 beds—while BC-BS patients were distributed among hospitals of various sizes, mostly medium-sized hospitals of about 250–500 beds.

— GHA hospitalized most of its patients in university affiliated teaching hospitals during the study period; BC-BS also used these hospitals to some extent, but a significantly larger proportion of its discharged patients were hospitalized in institutions which had no university affiliation.

Patterns of Prehospital Ambulatory Care and Length of Hospital Stay

— In general, the length of the entire prehospitalization phase (including events prior to the current illness episode) was comparable for both plans; but for two diagnostic categories (arteriosclerotic heart disease and uterine fibroids), the data suggest longer durations of illness overall under GHA.

— Promptness of seeking care as reported by the patients was not consistently different between the plans.

— A larger proportion of BC-BS patients who were ultimately hospitalized were first seen via scheduled appointments; in GHA, many more patients were first seen without an appointment. This suggests that the walk-in clinic was a frequent point of first contact for GHA patients who were subsequently hospitalized. GHA patients were also less likely to be seen by their regular physician at the start of the illness episode; instead, they saw the clinic physician on call.

— For uterine fibroids, even considering only patients who ultimately underwent hysterectomy, delays between the onset of symptoms and the first visit were longer under BC-BS than under GHA. For other diagnoses, this component of the preadmission phase did not differ between plans.

— The delay between the suggestion to hospitalize and actual admission was longer under GHA for elective surgeries. For other diagnoses, this delay was similar for the plans. But since this component of the prehospitalization period was relatively short, the overall length of the preadmission period was comparable for the plans, even among elective surgical diagnoses.

- For elective surgeries, patients were likely to undergo more tests under GHA.
- Lengths of stay were comparable for each diagnostic category, and preoperative lengths of stay did not differ importantly between the plans for surgical diagnoses. Hence, there is no evidence that failure to do preadmission tests under BC-BS resulted in longer stays because these tests were done on an inpatient basis.

Severity of Illness

- The perceived severity of illness at the start of each episode was comparable for the two plans.
- There were no differences between plans in the proportion of cases in each diagnosis which were emergency admissions.
- Physicians judged some admissions to be "absolutely necessary" in retrospect, but the proportion of admissions so judged showed no consistent difference between the plans.
- There were, however, a few instances in which the findings suggested that GHA patients had more severe or advanced disease at admission than their BC-BS counterparts:

  Patients with appendicitis reported their symptoms to be somewhat more severe on admission under GHA than under BC-BS and more patients admitted with uterine fibroids underwent hysterectomy under GHA than under BC-BS. Moreover, the fibroid uteri removed under GHA were significantly larger than those removed under BC-BS, suggesting that the disease had been allowed to advance for a longer time.

Appropriateness of Admission

- A large majority of cases in both plans passed two sets of criteria for appropriateness of admission. Departures from these criteria were rare and occurred with about equal frequency under the two plans.
- An exception was tonsillectomies and adenoidectomies, where about one-third of the cases in each plan failed criteria for appropriateness of admission. Since these criteria required documentation of a specific number of antecedent respiratory infections prior to hospitalization, failure to meet the criteria may reflect incomplete documen-

tation of such infections and not true deficiencies in admitting practices.

— A few unverified discharge diagnoses were found in each plan in several diagnostic categories, but their frequency was similar in the two plans and the differences were relatively small. Again, failure to meet these criteria may reflect incomplete documentation of all the evidence gathered in each case.

— For the sample studied (which was chosen by discharge diagnosis), a large majority of cases in all diagnostic categories entered the hospital with the same admitting diagnosis as their discharge diagnosis. The admitting diagnosis differed from the discharge diagnosis for a slightly higher percentage of BC-BS than GHA patients in most categories but, given the small numbers of patients in both plans, these differences were not statistically significant.

Patterns of Inpatient Care

— Subject to sample size constraints and certain limitations inherent in the methods employed, a pattern of greater compliance with criteria for appropriate care under GHA was apparent. This pattern was more apparent for the "optimal care" criteria than for the "critical services" criteria and there was no apparent clustering of plan differences in certain diagnoses.

— Hospitalized patients in GHA were no more likely to be cared for by a board certified physician or by a modal specialist than were BC-BS patients. Hence this factor cannot be invoked to explain the pattern of superior compliance with criteria under GHA.

— GHA patients were indeed more likely to be cared for in the hospital by a physician who participated in formal peer review and who was not in solo practice. However, even when only patients cared for by such physicians were examined under both plans, a pattern of superior compliance under GHA was apparent. Hence these factors alone are insufficient to explain the observed differences.

— GHA admitted a significantly greater proportion of its patients in hospitals with an active residency program in the specialty corresponding to each diagnosis. However, some BC-BS patients were also admitted to such hospitals, permitting a comparison of plan differences after controlling for hospital teaching status. Such an analysis showed a persistent difference between plans, with a pattern of greater compliance with the criteria under GHA.

CONCLUSIONS AND IMPLICATIONS

Patterns of Use of Ambulatory
and Hospital Resources

In general, these findings provide at least partial answers to the questions raised in this study. Phase I confirmed the patterns of differences in use of the hospital by members of prepaid group practice plans compared with that of members of more traditional, fee-for-service plans found in previous studies. Simultaneous consideration of the variation in salient member characteristics as well as plan benefit structure was insufficient to diminish the disparity in rates of admission and days of care.

Findings based on the more comprehensive household survey data collected in Phase II validated the relationships among independent, intervening, and dependent variables posited in the model of use described in Chapter 3 and proved vital to an understanding of some of the intricacies and complexities of these relationships. Findings on membership characteristics and levels of illness, though indicating some differences between the two plans, were mixed with respect to their possible impact on hospitalization rates and were certainly not of sufficient magnitude to account for the large differences in these rates found in Phase I. Similarly, though providing new insights into the ways in which ambulatory services are used by members and providers in two types of health insurance plans, the data in Phase II do not allow a definite assessment of the possible substitution of such services for diagnosis and/or treatment on an inpatient basis, though the magnitude of the differences in ambulatory use did not indicate that substitution was likely to be great, if it occurred at all. Neither was there evidence of any large effect of the differential provision of preventive services in the two plans which could account for the observed rates of hospital admissions. The findings on propensity to seek care in times of illness and attitudes toward regular physical examinations helped explain some of the differences in ambulatory utilization behavior but provided insufficient evidence to allow interpretation of their combined effect on hospital admissions. Furthermore, it was unclear whether these attitudinal differences were the product of plan membership or were antecedent to, and perhaps responsible for, the enrollment in the particular plan.

Findings of particular importance in addressing these questions were provided by the multivariate analyses of ambulatory use. As expected, perceived health status and various measures of illness were the most important determinants of variations in use. In spite of differences observed in the univariate analysis of ambulatory use, race was a relatively weak predictor of use in the multivariate analysis. Plan membership as a variable had a miniscule effect. Again, we are left with an unanswered question of plan impact on the "facts" of health status perception and definition of illness. There is a strong suggestion, especially in the analyses of episodes of illness, that the variation in use between BC-BS and GHA is indeed a plan artifact, perhaps a composite effect of health and illness behavior and access to care. This was particularly true for black members of GHA in comparison with black members of BC-BS. The discrepancy in findings from the analyses using episodes versus those using contacts has important bearing on future research. It was also obvious from the Phase II findings that out-of-plan hospital use by GHA members was not of sufficient magnitude to account for differences in admission rates.

A comparison in Phase III of the demographic characteristics of discharged patients under the two plans (within diagnostic categories) provided no additional clues to possible reasons for the difference in admission rates. In general, contrasting findings between the GHA and BC-BS patient samples were adequately explained by corresponding differences in the populations at risk for admission under each plan. In short, whatever factors caused higher admission rates under BC-BS appear to operate across the board, affecting all segments of the enrolled population.

Examination of patient experiences under each plan before being hospitalized, however, suggested that there may be important differences among diagnostic categories as to the factors contributing to different admission rates. For patients with uterine fibroids — and, to a lesser extent, patients with other conditions involving elective surgery — contrasts in the preadmission experience suggest a more conservative and time consuming approach to these diseases by GHA physicians. Prolongation of the preadmission phase under GHA seems also to be fostered by certain aspects of how the care system is organized. In particular, the typical GHA patient with fibroids

— Had had her disease for a longer time before being hospitalized

— Had to wait longer to be hospitalized once her physician suggested it might be necessary

— Underwent more special tests and x-rays as an outpatient before admission than did comparable BC-BS patients

— Was almost certain to undergo hysterectomy, a more extensive surgical procedure, in comparison with a BC-BS woman with uterine fibroids

— Would be found to have more advanced fibroids than the typical BC-BS woman undergoing hysterectomy for the same disease, as indicated by the physical size of her uterus when removed

These observations, taken together, suggest a reasonably consistent strategy of postponing hospitalization under GHA, possibly in an attempt to substitute outpatient management of a woman's problem for inpatient surgery. For the women under study, of course, this strategy was ultimately unsuccessful, in that these women eventually *were* hospitalized to undergo major gynecologic surgery; for other GHA women, the strategy may have kept them outside the hospital.

The pattern of preadmission care for certain other diagnoses, chiefly those involving elective surgery, had some elements in common with the pattern for uterine fibroids. Once the suggestion was made that hospitalization might be necessary, GHA patients scheduled for elective surgery usually had longer to wait before hospitalization actually occurred than did BC-BS patients. In the meantime, they were more likely to undergo special tests or x-rays on an ambulatory basis. However, there was little evidence of a difference in the severity or extent of disease once patients from the two plans were hospitalized. Moreover, the patterns of preadmission care and the status of disease on admission were so comparable for nonsurgical diagnoses as to provide no hints as to why admission rates for these diseases should be different under the two plans.

To the extent that the plans differed in use of the hospital, the data suggested a conservative approach under GHA, reserving hospitalization only for cases in which it was really necessary. But what of hospitalization practices under BC-BS? Were the excess admissions therefore demonstrably unnecessary? The analysis employing explicit criteria for admission appropriateness, drawn from peer review programs, provided no evidence of "feather-bedding" under BC-BS. Although only selected diagnostic categories were studied and were chosen according to discharge diagnosis rather than admitting diagnosis, this analysis suggested that virtually all admissions under both plans would have passed peer scrutiny as justified on medical grounds.

At least two interpretations of the findings on admission appropriateness are possible, however. Perhaps the finding of few medically unjustified admissions under either plan, in conjunction with the marked differences in admission rates, imply underutilization of the hospital by GHA. Are GHA physicians being overzealous in their attempts to substitute outpatient for inpatient care? A definitive answer to this question would require data beyond the scope of this study; cohorts of patients under each plan with the same chief complaint would have to be followed, whether hospitalized or not, to determine whether differences in outcome correlate with differences in hospital use practices. These aspects would clearly be of interest in future studies. Nonetheless, in general, GHA patients were no more severely ill on admission in most diagnostic categories. Out-of-plan hospital use was rare, suggesting that patients were not driven to seek care elsewhere by a perceived failure to provide care in the face of severe illness.

A second possible explanation for the findings on appropriateness of admission may be that they are, in effect, an artifact of the method used. The criteria used to judge whether an admission was medically appropriate were developed by practicing physicians for use in peer review. As such, it appears that the criteria were designed to accommodate a rather wide range of physician attitudes about when to use hospital resources. The modal practice pattern in most areas of the United States is fee-for-service practice; criteria intended for general use would hardly be designed to declare the practice patterns of a large segment of the medical community inappropriate. Instead, they appear to be designed to detect only rather flagrant abuses. These proved rare indeed. But those cases which passed the criteria may still consist of a mix of discretionary and mandatory admissions, with relatively more discretionary admissions under BC-BS. There is evidence to suggest that prepaid group practice physicians do have somewhat more conservative views than their fee-for-service counterparts on the clinical situations in which hospitalization is medically necessary (Demlo, 1975). Perhaps criteria which would be more sensitive to these possible if subtle attitudinal differences are necessary to demonstrate their effect on practice patterns.

From a broader perspective, perhaps one impression created by this study's findings is that there is no simple explanation for the observed difference in hospitalization rates in terms of uncounted out-of-plan use, demographic characteristics, or the overall illness experience of the enrolled populations. The difference is not confined to a few diagnostic categories, nor is it easily explained by frequent absence of accepted indications for admission in the fee-for-service plan. In part by process of exclusion, such findings tend to focus greater attention on differences in the process of medical decisions about who does and who does not need to be hospitalized. Although this process is undoubtedly dependent on objective medical considerations in each case, there is evidence that it is also sensitive to various incentives and disincentives acting on the medical decision maker. This impression is substantiated by the fact that while hospital use differed markedly in the two settings, this was less pronounced for ambulatory care use. Patients themselves can initiate an outpatient encounter; the physician is the gatekeeper to the hospital. Moreover, Luft (1981, 1978) has observed that Health Maintenance Organization vs. fee-for-service differences in hospital use seem much less pronounced when physicians are not salaried by the HMO and are in predominantly fee-for-service practice.

Thus, future research which seeks to explain why prepaid group practices have lower hospitalization rates might fruitfully explore in greater detail the mechanisms by which such organizations influence the physician's decision to hospitalize. Do these organizations somehow select physicians with conservative philosophies about hospital use to begin with? How do they structure financial and other incentives to influence the hospitalization decisions of member physicians? To what extent do resource constraints imposed by the organization (e.g., limited bed supplies) limit the physician's freedom to admit patients? Finally, to what extent do physicians respond to these organizational influences by changing their views about when hospitalization is medically appropriate?

Quality of Care and Patterns of Delivery of Services

The Phase III findings also permit the identification of certain qualitative differences in the way each plan's patients were managed, even though these differences probably have little to do with the contrast in admission rates. First, it appears that there were some consistent differences between plans in the kind of physician providing care to hospitalized patients. Contrary to experience in other research settings (Payne and Lyons, 1972), there was no evidence that the prepaid group practice physicians were better qualified than the fee-for-service clinicians, or that patients treated under the prepaid practice plan were any more likely to be cared for by a modal specialist. In this setting, physicians under both plans were highly qualified (usually specialty board-certified or eligible). However, patients under GHA were more likely to be cared for by a physician with fewer years in practice (especially patients with surgical diagnoses) and by a physician who had a relatively short work week. Perhaps because of the shorter work week, GHA physicians were more likely to be participants in certain local teaching activities, including grand and teaching rounds. They also participated to a greater extent in formal peer review programs and clearly were more likely to be in practice with at least one other physician. Overall, it appeared that GHA physicians worked under circumstances which brought them into frequent contact with each other, sharing knowledge through participation in teaching activities and applying checks and balances to each other's practices through peer review and sharing of responsibility for cases. The BC-BS clinicians, in contrast, reported less participation in local medical education activities, peer review, or group practice arrangements which would expose them to the possibly contrasting medical viewpoints of their colleagues. Instead, the BC-BS physician typically operated more independently and autonomously.

Another important difference in care delivery patterns concerned the kinds of hospitals to which patients were admitted. Confirming the findings of Phase I, analysis of the discharged patient sample in Phase III showed that GHA patients were admitted chiefly to large, university affiliated teaching institutions during the study period; BC-BS patients were admitted to a much wider range of hospitals in the community, with the majority of admissions occurring at smaller community hospitals. The hospitals to which GHA patients were admitted were also more likely to have an active medical residency program in the specialty corresponding to each patient's disease. Although the extent of involvement of house staff in each case was unknown, it seems reasonable to assume that simply because of these differences in institutional settings, the role of house staff was, in general, greater for GHA patients than for BC-BS patients. Again, this difference between plans would operate in such a way as to increase the number of physicians involved in the care of each hospitalized patient.

Phase III also presented the opportunity to examine in some detail the process of care within the hospital for patients with similar diagnoses under the two plans. By using two sets of criteria for what constitutes appropriate care, it was possible to attach some value to the differences observed. As with the assessment of admission appropriateness, analysis of patterns of inpatient care was based on preestablished, explicit criteria which specify desirable elements for each of several components of the care process (history, physical examination, diagnosis, therapy, and discharge status). While there was considerable variation in the direction of findings across diagnoses and components of care, there was the clear impression of superior compliance with the criteria under GHA. The difference was not usually large, but it was reasonably pervasive throughout the sample of cases examined. Moreover, the difference between plans was not readily explained by certain characteristics of the providers of care or of the institutions in which care was provided. The level of physician qualifications and modal specialty status cannot be invoked as explanations, since there was little difference between plans in those factors. Involvement in peer review, in practice arrangements other than solo practice, and use of teaching hospitals did differ between the plans; but none of these factors by itself appeared to account for the observed difference in compliance with the criteria.

Was the hospital care really better under GHA? Again, certain limitations of the methods used to assess hospital care must be acknowledged. The criteria place a premium on completeness of the medical record, equating a failure of documentation with a failure of performance. As noted above, several factors were operative within GHA which would tend to increase the number of providers involved in the care of each hospitalized patient. This would, in turn, place increased demands on the medical record to serve as a communication channel among these various providers. Accordingly, it is plausible that GHA physicians tended to document the information they obtained and the actions they took more completely, even if there were no substantive differences in the way they treated their patients. The fact that plan differences in compliance with the criteria appeared more pronounced for components of care which rely most heavily on physician documentation (e.g., history, physical examination) tends to support this interpretation. Involvement of house staff in the care of some hospitalized patients may also have affected the apparent level of compliance with criteria, since it is generally felt that physicians in training tend to write more exhaustive admission work-ups and progress notes than more seasoned practitioners. Furthermore, the higher proportion of physicians with recent training (i.e., fewer years in practice) perhaps also contributed to the generally higher ratings of care received by GHA patients, as this relationship has been found in other studies employing the preestablished criteria approach to evaluation of care (Riedel and Riedel, 1979; Riedel and Fitzpatrick, 1964). Because the criteria developed at any one point in time usually reflect the current definitions of "good" care, and these definitions are also likely to be an ingredient in current medical education, it is to be expected that the care rendered by recent graduates of medical training programs coincides with the criteria. It is also to be expected that more senior physicians (in terms of years in practice) who maintain an active affiliation with a training program would exhibit patterns of care in congruence with the criteria in vogue.

In addition, there are other reasons why the observed difference in inpatient care performance should be regarded as suggestive but probably not definitive. First, the criteria focus almost exclusively on certain technical aspects of care, ignoring completely the interpersonal skills involved in providing good patient care. Second, even some technical aspects of the care process, such as the skill and precision with which a surgical procedure is executed, cannot readily be measured by such criteria. Finally, the relationship between compliance with criteria and patient outcomes is by no means clear for all diseases (Brook, 1974), which raises questions about the validity of such criteria.

In concert, the findings of this study have provided a fresh understanding of the ways in which manifold variables interact to affect response to illness by patient and provider, and the allocation of resources by practitioners under different organizational modes. However, it must be reiterated that we have made comparisons between one prepaid group practice plan (GHA) and an aggregation of various forms of organization (BC-BS), even though the great majority of physicians under BC-BS were solo practitioners. Furthermore, the study was conducted at one point in time, and many changes have occurred since the data were collected. The promulgation of HMOs, the introduction of massive peer review programs, and the medical profession's response to new opportunities in financing health care, such as various risk-sharing arrangements, will probably lead to some convergence of system differences, resulting in less heterogeneity in patterns of care. This study has at least provided insight into some of the reasons for the large differences between two programs which continue to serve as a focal point in debate on the most efficient organization of medical practice.

References

Aday, L.A. and Eichhorn, R. 1972. *The Utilization of Health Services—Indices and Correlates*. A Research Bibliography. National Center for Health Services Research and Development. Department of Health, Education, and Welfare Publication no. (HSM) 73-3003. Washington, DC: Government Printing Office.

Allen, G.I., Breslow, L., Weissman, A., and Nisselson, H. 1954. Interviewing versus diary keeping in eliciting information in a morbidity survey. *Am J Public Health* 44:919-27.

Alpert, J.J., Kosa, J., and Haggerty, R.J. 1967. A month of illness and health care among low-income families. *Public Health Rep* 82:705-13.

American Hospital Association. 1971. Guide Issue. *Hospitals* 45 (Part 2).

American Hospital Association. 1974. *Guide to the Health Care Field*. Chicago.

American Medical Association. 1967 and 1969. *Directory of Approved Internships and Residencies*. Chicago.

American Medical Association. 1967 and 1969. *Medical Directory*, 24th and 26th eds. Chicago.

American Medical Association. 1974. *Master List of Physicians*. Chicago (processed).

American Medical Association. 1976. *Sample Criteria for Short-Stay Hospital Review: Screening Criteria to Assist PSROs in Quality Assurance*. Chicago.

Andersen, R. 1968. *A Behavioral Model of Families' Use of Health Services*. Health Research series no. 25. Chicago: Center for Health Administration Studies, University of Chicago.

Andersen, R. 1975. Health service distribution and equity. Ch. 2, in *Equity in Health Services: Empirical Analyses in Social Policy*, Andersen, R., Kravits, J. and Anderson, O.W., eds. Cambridge, MA: Ballinger.

Andersen, R. and Newman, J.F. 1973. Societal and individual determinants of medical care utilization in the United States. *Milbank Mem Fund Q* 51(1):95-124.

Anderson, O.W. and Andersen, R. 1970. Pretest questionnaire, "National Survey—Trends in Health Service Utilization and Expenditures." Center for Health Administration Studies, University of Chicago (processed).

Anderson, O.W. and Andersen, R. 1972. Patterns of use of health services. In *Handbook of Medical Sociology*, 2d ed. Freeman, H.E., Levine, S., and Reeder, L.G., eds. Englewood Cliffs, NJ: Prentice-Hall.

Anderson, O.W. and Sheatsley, P.B. 1959. *Comprehensive Medical Insurance—A Study of Costs, Use, and Attitudes Under Two Plans.* Research series no. 9. New York: Health Information Foundation.

Anderson, O.W. and Sheatsley, P.B. 1967. *Hospital Use: A Survey of Patient and Physician Decisions.* Research series no. 24. Chicago: Center for Health Administration Studies, University of Chicago.

Bashshur, R.L., Metzner, C.A., and Worden, C. 1967. Consumer satisfaction with group practice; the CHA case. *Am J Public Health* 57:1991–99.

Blalock, H.M. 1972. *Social Statistics.* New York: McGraw-Hill.

Broida, J.H., Lerner, M., Lohrenz, F.N., and Wenzel, F.J. 1975. Impact of membership in an enrolled, prepaid population on utilization of health services in a group practice. *N Engl J Med* 292:780–83.

Brook, R.H. 1974. *Quality of Care Assessment: A Comparison of Five Methods of Peer Review.* Department of Health, Education, and Welfare Publication no. (HRS) 74-3100. Rockville, MD.

Burford, R. and Averill, R.F. 1979. The relationship between diagnostic information available at admission and discharge for patients in one PSRO setting: Implications for concurrent review. *Med Care* 17:369–81.

Cannell, C.F., Fisher, G., and Baker, T. 1965. *Reporting of Hospitalization in the Health Interview Survey.* National Center for Health Statistics. Vital and Health Statistics, Public Health Service Publication no. 1000, series 2, no. 6. Washington, DC: Government Printing Office.

Cannell, C.F. and Fowler, F.J. 1963. *A Study of the Reporting of Visits to Doctors in the National Health Survey.* Ann Arbor, MI: Survey Research Center, University of Michigan.

Cannell, C.F. and Fowler, F.J. 1965. *Comparison of Hospitalization Reporting in Three Survey Procedures.* National Center for Health Statistics. Vital and Health Statistics, Public Health Service Publication no. 1000, series 2, no. 8. Washington, DC: Government Printing Office.

Cartwright, A. 1964. *Human Relations and Hospital Care.* London: Routledge and Kegan Paul.

Cohen, S., Wolpin, S., and Cohen, B.D. 1975. Clinical basis for combined patient care audit criteria for diabetic ketoacidosis. *Qual Review Bull* 1(May-June-July):26–32.

Darsky, B.J., Sinai, N., and Axelrod, S.J. 1958. *Comprehensive Medical Services Under Voluntary Health Insurance: A Study of Windsor Medical Services.* Cambridge, MA: Harvard University Press.

Decker, B.D., Bonner, P., Israel, E., Kase, S., Kaslen, J., and Werlin, S. 1973. *Experimental Medical Care Review Organization (EMCRO) Programs.* National Center for Health Services Research, Department of Health, Education, and Welfare Publication no. (HSM) 73-3017. Rockville, MD.

Demlo, L.K. 1975. The Relationship of Physician Practice Patterns to Organizational and Personal Characteristics. Yale University, unpublished doctoral dissertation.

Densen, P.M., Balamuth, E., and Shapiro, S. 1958. *Prepaid Medical Care and Hospital Utilization.* Hospital Monograph series no. 3. Chicago: American Hospital Association.

Densen, P.M., Jones, E.W., Balamuth, E., and Shapiro, S. 1960. Prepaid medical care and hospital utilization in a dual choice situation. *Am J Public Health* 50:1720–26.

Diehr, P.K., Richardson, W.C., Drucker, W.L., Shortell, S.M., and LoGerfo, J.P. 1976. Ch. 2, in *The Seattle Prepaid Health Care Project: Comparison of Health Services Delivery*. NTIS no. PB 267490, Springfield, VA.

Donabedian, A. 1965. *A Review of Some Experiences with Prepaid Group Practice*. Research series no. 12. Ann Arbor, MI: Bureau of Public Health Economics, University of Michigan.

Donabedian, A. 1969. An evaluation of prepaid group practice. *Inquiry* 6(3):3–27.

Doyle, D.N. 1966. Accuracy of selected items of Blue Cross claims information. *Inquiry* 3(3):16–27.

Fessel, W.J. and Van Brunt, E.E. 1972. Quality of care and the medical record. *New Engl J Med* 286:134–38.

Fetter, R.B., Shin, Y., Freeman, J., Averill, R., and Thompson, J.D. 1980. Case mix definition by diagnosis-related groups. *Med Care* 18(2): Supplement.

Fink, R. 1969. The measurement of medical care utilization. In *Conceptual Issues in the Analysis of Medical Care Utilization Behavior*, Greenlick, M.R., ed. Health Services and Mental Health Administration. Washington, DC Government Printing Office, pp. 5–32. NTIS No. PB 195-997.

Fitzpatrick, T.B., Riedel, D.C., and Payne, B.C. 1962. Character and effectiveness of hospital use. In *Hospital and Medical Economics*, McNerney, W.J. ed. Chicago: Hospital Research and Educational Trust, vol. 1, pp. 361–591.

Freidson, E. 1961. *Patients' Views of Medical Practice*. New York: Russell Sage Foundation.

Freidson, E. 1970. The clinical mentality. Ch. 8, *Profession of Medicine*, Freidson, E., ed. New York: Harper & Row.

Gaus, C.R., Cooper, B.S., and Hirschman, C.G. 1976. Contrasts in HMO and fee-for-service performance. *Soc Sec Bull* 39 (5):3–14.

Gonnella, S. and Goran, M.J. 1975. Quality of patient care—A measurement of change: The staging concept. *Med Care* 13:467–73.

Goss, M.E.W. 1970. Organizational goals and quality of medical care: Evidence from comparative research on hospitals. *J Health Soc Behav* 11:255–68.

Greenberg, I.G. and Rodburg, M.L. 1971. The role of prepaid group practice in relieving the medical care crisis. *Harvard Law Rev* 84:887–1001.

Greene, R., ed. 1976. *Assuring Quality in Medical Care: The State of the Art*. Cambridge, MA: Ballinger.

Greenlick, M. 1972. The impact of prepaid group practice on American medical care: A critical evaluation. *Ann Am Acad Pol Soc Sc* 399:100–113.

Hastings, J.E.F., Mott, F.D., Barclay, A., and Hewitt, D. 1973. Prepaid group practice in Sault Ste. Marie, Ontario: Part I. Analysis of utilization records. *Med Care* 11:91–103.

Hershey, J.C., Luft, H.S., and Gianaris, J.M. 1975. Making sense of utilization data. *Med Care* 13:838–54.

Hess, I., Riedel, D.C., and Fitzpatrick, T.B. 1975. *Probability Sampling of Hospitals and Patients*, 2d ed. Ann Arbor, MI: University of Michigan Press.

Hetherington, R.W. and Hopkins, C.E. 1969. Symptom sensitivity: Its social and cultural correlates. *Health Serv Res* 4:63–75.

Hetherington, R.W., Hopkins, C.E., and Roemer, M.I. 1975. *Health Insurance Plans: Promise and Performance*. New York: Wiley–Interscience.

Hill, D.B. and Veney, J.E. 1970. Kansas Blue Cross and Blue Shield outpatient benefits experiment. *Med Care* 8:143–58.

Hospital Utilization Project. 1969. *Criteria for Effective Utilization Review*. Pittsburgh.

Institute of Medicine. 1977. *Reliability of Hospital Discharge Abstracts*. Washington: National Academy of Sciences.

Josephson, C.E. 1964. Hospital utilization and covered charges of federal employees under service benefits. *Blue Cross Rep* 2:1–16.

Josephson, C.E. 1966. Family expenditure patterns of federal employees for covered items of health care services. *Inquiry* 3(1):40–54.

Kane, R.L., Gardner, J., Wright, D.D., Woolley, F.R., Snell, G.F., Sundwell, D.N., and Castle, C.H. 1978. Differences in outcomes of acute episodes of care provided by various types of family practitioners. *J Fam Prac* 6:133–38.

Kane, R.L., Olsen, D.M., and Castle, C.H. 1976. Medex and their physician predictors. *JAMA* 236:2509–12.

Kane, R.L., Woolley, F.R., Gardner, J., Snell, G.F., Leight, E.H., and Castle, C.H. 1976. Measuring outcomes of care in an ambulatory primary care population. *J Comm Health* 1:233–40.

Kasl, S.V. and Cobb, S. 1966. Health behavior, illness behavior, and sick role behavior. *Arch Environ Health* 12:246–66, 531–41.

Kelly, D.N. 1965. Experience with a program of coverage for diagnostic procedures provided in physicians' offices and hospital outpatient departments: Maryland Blue Cross and Blue Shield Plan (1957–1964). *Inquiry* 2(3):28–44.

Kessler, L. 1978. Episodes of Psychiatric Care and Medical Utilization in a Prepaid Practice Plan. Johns Hopkins School of Hygiene and Public Health, doctoral dissertation.

Klarman, H.E. 1963. Effect of prepaid group practice on hospital use. *Public Health Rep* 78:955–65.

Kobashigawa, M.A. and Berki, S.J. 1977. Alternative regression approaches to the analysis of medical care survey data. *Med Care* 15:396–408.

Kravits, J. 1975. The relationship of attitudes to discretionary physician and dentist use by race and income. Ch. 5, in *Equity in Health Services: Empirical Analyses in Social Policy*, Andersen, R., Kravits, J., and Anderson, O.W., eds. Cambridge, MA: Ballinger.

Kravits, J. and Schneider, J. 1975. Health care need and actual use by age, race, and income. Ch. 10, in *Equity in Health Services: Empirical Analyses in Social Policy*, Andersen, R., Kravits, J., and Anderson, O.W., eds. Cambridge, MA: Ballinger.

Lasdon, G.S. and Sigman, P. 1977. Evaluating cost-effectiveness using episodes of care. *Med Care* 15:260–64.

Lebow, J.L. 1974. Consumer assessments of the quality of medical care. *Med Care* 12:328–37.

Lee, J.A.H., Morrison, S.L., and Morris, J.H. 1960. Case fatality in teaching and non-teaching hospitals, 1956–1959. *Lancet* i:170–71.

Lerner, M. 1960. *Hospital Use and Charges by Diagnostic Category*. Progress in Health Services, series 11(5). New York: Health Information Foundation.

Lerner, M. 1961. *Hospital Use by Diagnosis: A Comparison of Two Experiences*, Health Information Foundation Research Series no. 19. New York.

Lerner, M. 1963. Group and nongroup hospital utilization and charges. *Blue Cross Rep* 1(1):1–11.

Lipworth, L., Lee, J.H.A., and Morris, J.W. 1963. Case fatality in teaching and non-teaching hospitals, 1956–59. *Med Care* 1:71–76.

LoGerfo, J.P., Efird, R.A., Diehr, P.K., and Richardson, W.C. 1976. Quality of care. Ch. 4, in *The Seattle Prepaid Health Care Project: Comparison of Health Services Delivery*. NTIS No. PB 267-492, Springfield, VA.

Lohr, K.N.W., and Brook, R.H. 1978. Variations in patterns of care for episodes of common ambulatory care. Paper presented at the annual meeting of the American Public Health Association at Los Angeles, CA, October 17.

Louis, D.Z. and McCord, J.J. 1974. Evaluation of California's Prepaid Health Plans. Final report on Department of Health, Education, and Welfare Contract no. HEW 0-73-194. Santa Barbara, CA: General Research Corp.

Luft, H.S. 1978. How do health maintenance organizations achieve their "savings"? *N Eng J Med* 298:1336–43.

Luft, H.S. 1980a. Trends in medical care costs: Do HMOs lower the rate of growth. *Med Care* 18:1–16.

Luft, H.S. 1980b. HMO performance. Current knowledge and questions for the 1980s: A research agenda considered. *Group Health J* 1:34–40.

Luft, H.S. 1981. *Health Maintenance Organizations: Dimensions of Performance*. New York: Wiley-Interscience.

Lyons, T.F., and Payne, B.C. 1974. The relationship of physicians' medical recording performance to their medical care performance. *Med Care* 12:463–69.

McNerney, W.J. and Study Staff of the University of Michigan. 1962. *Hospital and Medical Economics*. 2 volumes. Chicago: Hospital Research and Educational Trust.

Mantel, N. and Haenszel, W. 1959. Statistical aspects of the analysis of data from retrospective studies of disease. *J Natl Cancer Inst* 22:719–48.

Mechanic, D. 1962. The concept of illness behavior. *J Chronic Dis* 15:189–94.

Mechanic, D. 1969. Illness and cure. In *Poverty and Health: A Sociological Analysis*, Kosa, J., Antonovsky, A., and Zola, I.K., eds. Cambridge, MA: Harvard University Press, pp. 191–214.

Metropolitan Health Care Foundation. 1971. *Metropolitan Health Care Foundation: A Basic Tool in the Evaluation of Medical Practice*. Minneapolis, MN.

Metzner, C.A. and Bashshur, R.L. 1967. Factors associated with choice of health care plans. *J Health Soc Behav* 8:291–99.

Meyers, S.M., Hirshfeld, S.B., Walden, D.C., and Riedel, D.C. 1977. Ambulatory medical use by federal employees: Experience of members in a service benefit plan and in a prepaid group practice plan. Paper presented at the 105th Annual Meeting of the American Public Health Association in Washington, DC.

Mills, R., Fetter, R.B., Riedel, D.C., and Averill, R. 1976. AUTOGRP: An interactive computer system for the analysis of health care data. *Med Care* 14:603–15.

Monsma, G.N. 1970. Marginal revenue and demand for physicians' services. In *Empirical Studies in Health Economics*, Klarman, H.E., ed. Baltimore: Johns Hopkins Press, pp. 145–50.

Mooney, H.W. 1962. *Methodology in Two California Health Surveys*. Department of Health, Education, and Welfare, Public Health Monograph no. 70. Washington, DC: Government Printing Office.

Moscovice, I. 1977. A method for analyzing resource use in ambulatory care settings. *Med Care* 15:1024–44.

Mott, H. and Barclay, A.T. 1973. Prepaid group practice in Sault Ste. Marie, Ont.: Part II. Evidence from the household survey. *Med Care* 11:173–88.

Moustafa, A.I., Hopkins, C.E., and Klein, B. 1971. Determinants of choice and change of health insurance plan. *Med Care* 9:32–41.

Muller, C.F., Waybur, A., and Weinerman, E.R. 1952. Methodology of a family health study. *Public Health Rep* 67:1149–56.

National Center for Health Statistics. 1966. *Current Estimates From the Health Interview Survey, United States, July 1966 to June 1967*. Vital and Health Statistics, series 10, no. 43. Washington, DC: Government Printing Office.

National Center for Health Statistics. 1967. *International Classification of Diseases, Adapted for Use in the United States*. Eighth Revision. DHEW Publication no. (PHS) 1693. Washington, DC: Government Printing Office.

National Center for Health Statistics. 1969a. *Differentials in Health Characteristics by Color, United States. July 1965 to June 1967*. Public Health Service Publication no. 1000, series 10, no. 56. Washington, DC: Government Printing Office.

National Center for Health Statistics. 1969b. *Family Use of Health Services, United States. July 1963 to June 1964*. Public Health Service Publication no. 1000, series 10, no. 55. Washington, DC: Government Printing Office.

National Center for Health Statistics. 1970. *Current Estimates From the Health Interview Survey, United States, 1970*. Vital and Health Statistics, series 10, no. 72. Washington, DC: Government Printing Office.

National Opinion Research Center. 1967. Pretest questionnaire prepared for the Blue Cross Association for a proposed study entitled, "Study of Two Medical Service Insurance Plans." University of Chicago (processed).

National Opinion Research Center. 1969. Draft questionnaire for a study entitled, "Patient Flow Pilot Study." University of Chicago (processed).

Newman, J.F. 1975. Age, race and education as predisposing factors in physician and dentist utilization. Ch. 3, in *Equity in Health Services: Empirical Analyses in Social Policy*, Andersen, R., Kravits, J., and Anderson, O.W., eds. Cambridge, MA: Ballinger.

Payne, B.C. and Lyons, T.F. 1972. *Method of Evaluating and Improving Personal Medical Care Quality: Episode of Illness Study*. Ann Arbor, MI: University of Michigan School of Medicine.

Payne, B.C., Lyons, T.F., Dwarshius, L., Kolton, M., and Morris, W. 1976. *The Quality of Medical Care: Evaluation and Improvement*. Health Services Monograph series T40. Chicago: Hospital Research and Educational Trust.

Peart, A.F.W. 1952. Canada's sickness survey: Review of methods. *Can J Public Health* 43:401-14.

Perkoff, G.T., Kahn, L., and Mackie, A. 1974. Medical care utilization in an experimental prepaid group practice model in a university medical center. *Med Care* 12:471-85.

Perrott, G.S. 1966. The Federal Employees Health Benefits Program: III. Utilization of hospital services. *Am J Public Health* 56:57-64.

Perrott, G.S. and Chase, J.C. 1968. The Federal Employees Health Benefits Program. *Group Health and Welfare News* (October):i-viii (Special Supplement).

Remington, R.D. and Schork, M.A. 1970. *Statistics with Applications to the Biological and Health Sciences*. Englewood Cliffs, NJ: Prentice-Hall.

Rhee, S. 1976. Factors determining the quality of physician performance in patient care. *Med Care* 14:733-50.

Richardson, W.C. 1971. Ambulatory Use of Physicians' Services. In *Response to Illness Episodes in a Low-income Neighborhood*. Research series no. 29. Chicago: Center for Health Administration Studies, University of Chicago.

Riedel, D.C. and Fitzpatrick, T.B. 1964. *Patterns of Patient Care: A Study of Hospital Use in Six Diagnoses*. Ann Arbor, MI: University of Michigan.

Riedel, D.C., Walden, D.C., Singsen, A.G., Meyers, S., Krantz, G., and Henderson, M. 1975. *Federal Employees Health Benefits Program Utilization Study*. National Center for Health Services Research. Department of Health, Education, and Welfare Publication no. (HRA) 75-3125. Rockville, MD.

Riedel, R.L. and Riedel, D.C. 1979. *Practice and Performance: An Assessment of Ambulatory Care*. Ann Arbor, MI: Health Administration Press.

Robertson, R.L. 1972. Comparative medical care use under prepaid group practice and free choice plans: A case study. *Inquiry* 9(3):70-76.

Roemer, M.I. 1961a. Bed supply and hospital utilization: A natural experiment. *Hospitals* (Nov 1) 35:36-42.

Roemer, M.I. 1961b. Hospital utilization and the supply of physicians. *JAMA* 178:989-93.

Roemer, M.I., Moustafa, H.T., and Hopkins, C.E. 1968. A proposed hospital quality index: Hospital death rates adjusted for severity. *Health Serv Res* 3:96-118.

Roemer, M.I., and Shonick, W. 1973. HMO performance: The recent evidence. *Milbank Mem Fund Q* 51:271-317.

Roghmann, K.J. and Haggerty, R.J. 1972. The diary as a research instrument in the study of health and illness behavior: Experiences with a random sample of young families. *Med Care* 10:143-63.

Roos, N.P., Henteleff, P.D., and Roos, L.L. 1977. A new audit procedure applied to an old question: Is the frequency of T-and-A justified? *Med Care* 15:1-18.

Roos, N.P., Roos, L.L., Henteleff, P.D. 1977. Elective surgical rates—Do high rates mean lower standards: Tonsillectomy and adenoidectomy in Manitoba. *N Engl J Med* 297:360-65.

Rosenstock, I.M. 1969. Prevention of illness and maintenance of health. In *Poverty and Health: A Sociological Analysis*, Kosa, J., Antonovsky, A., and Zola, I.K., eds. Cambridge, MA: Harvard University Press, pp. 168-90.

Rossiter, L.F. 1980. *Who Initiates Visits to a Physician?* National Health Care Expenditures Study, Data Preview 3. National Center for Health Services Research. Department of Health and Human Services Publication no. (PHS) 80-3278. Hyattsville, MD.

Schonfeld, H.K., Heston, J.F., and Falk, I.S. 1975. *Standards for Good Medical Care.* Social Security Administration, Department of Health, Education, and Welfare Publication no. (SSA) 75-11926.

Scitovsky, A., Benham, L., and McCall, N. 1979. Use of physician services under two prepaid plans. *Med Care* 17:441–60.

Scitovsky, A., Benham, L., and McCall, N. 1981. Out-of-plan use under two prepaid plans. *Med Care* 19:1165–93.

Shapiro, S. 1967. End result measurements of quality of medical care. *Milbank Mem Fund Q* 45(2):7–30.

Shapiro, S., Jacobziner, H., Densen, P.M., and Weiner, L. 1960. Further observations on prematurity and perinatal mortality in a general population and in the population of a prepaid group practice medical care plan. *Am J Public Health* 50:1304–1317.

Shapiro, S., Weiner, L., and Densen, P.M. 1958. Comparison of prematurity and perinatal mortality in a general population and in the population of a prepaid group practice medical care plan. *Am J Public Health* 48:170–85.

Shipman, G.A., Lampman, R.J., and Miyamoto, S.F. 1962. *Medical Service Corporations in the State of Washington.* Cambridge, MA: Harvard University Press.

Sinai, N. and Patton, D.E. 1949. *Hospitalization of the People of Two Counties: A Study of Experience in Hillsdale and Branch Counties, Michigan, 1940–1945.* Research series no. 6. Ann Arbor, MI: Bureau of Public Health Economics, University of Michigan.

Solon, J.A., Feeney, J.J., Jones, S.H., Rigg, R.D., and Sheps, C.G. 1967. Delineating episodes of medical care. *Am J Public Health* 57:401–08.

Theriault, K., Mills, R., and Elia, E. 1976. *The Autogroup Reference Manual.* New Haven, CT: Center for the Study of Health Services, Yale University.

U.S. Civil Service Commission. 1974. *Rate Sheet.* Bureau of Retirement, Insurance and Occupational Health. Washington, DC.

United Steel Workers of America. 1960. Special Study on the Medical Care Program for Steel Workers and Their Families. A report by the Insurance, Pension, and Unemployment Benefits Department. Tenth Constitutional Convention, Atlantic City, September 1960.

Utah Professional Review Organization. 1972. *Quality of Care Guidelines.* Salt Lake City: Utah Professional Review Organization.

Wan, T.T.H. and Soifer, S.J. 1974. Determinants of physician utilization: A causal analysis. *J Health Soc Behav* 15:100–108.

Ware, J.E. 1978. Effects of acquiescent response set on patient satisfaction ratings. *Med Care* 16:327–36.

Weinerman, E. 1962. Medical care in prepaid group practice. *Arch Environ Health* 5:561–73.

Weinerman, E. 1964. Patients' perceptions of group medical care. *Am J Public Health* 54:880-89.

Wersinger, R., Roghmann, K.J., Gavett, J.W., and Wells, S.M. 1976. Inpatient hospital utilization in three prepaid comprehensive health plans compared with a regular Blue Cross plan. *Med Care* 14:721-32.

Williams, S.J., Trussell, R.E., and Elinson, J. 1957. *Health and Medical Care in New York City.* Cambridge, MA: Harvard University Press/Commonwealth Fund.

Williams, J.J., Trussell, R.E., and Elinson, J. 1964. A survey of medical care under three types of health insurance. In *Proceedings of the Symposium on Medical Care Research*, White, K.L., ed. Oxford, England: Pergamon, pp. 155-60.

Wolfman, B. 1961. Medical expenses and a choice of plans: A case study. *Monthly Labor Review* 84:1186-90.

Wolinsky, F.D. 1976. Health services utilization and attitudes toward health maintenance organizations: A theoretical and methodological discussion. *J Health Soc Behav* 17:221-36.

Yale-New Haven Hospital. 1974. *Guidelines for Patient Care Appraisal.* New Haven.

Yaffe, R. and Shapiro, S. 1979. Reporting accuracy of health care utilization and experiments in a household survey as compared with provider records and insurance claims records. Paper presented at the Third Biennial Conference on Health Survey Research and Methods, Reston, Virginia, May 16-18.

Index of Subjects

Editors and Contributors

SARINA B. HIRSHFELD, a sociologist, was Senior Research Analyst at the Bureau of Social Science Research at the time of the study. She is currently with the Research and Statistics Department of the United Mine Workers of America Health and Retirement Funds.

SUSAN S. JACK was a Research Analyst at the Bureau of Social Science Research, Inc. at the time of the study. She is currently a health statistician in the Division of Health Interview Statistics of the National Center for Health Statistics.

THOMAS D. KOEPSELL is a physician who at the time of the study was a researcher at the National Center for Health Services Research. He subsequently completed a fellowship through the Robert Wood Johnson Clinical Scholars Program and is now on the faculty of the Department of Epidemiology, School of Public Health and Community Medicine, University of Washington.

SAMUEL M. MEYERS directed the study component conducted at the Bureau of Social Science Research, Inc. He is currently a Senior Researcher at the National Center for Health Services Research.

THELMA MYINT, formerly a Senior Research Analyst with the Bureau of Social Science Research, has been involved in the design, planning, and analysis of many large studies.

DONALD C. RIEDEL, the principal investigator for this study, was a member of the faculties of the University of Washington, Yale University, and The University of Michigan. He is author and coauthor of numerous publications in the field of health services.

MARY HELEN SHORTRIDGE, formerly a Research Analyst at the Bureau of Social Science Research, Inc., is on the staff of the Comprehensive Plans Division, Insurance Programs, U.S. Office of Personnel Management.

SHARON B. SOROKO, a Research Fellow at the National Center for Health Services Research at the time of the study, is currently a senior technical analyst at Infosystems Technology, Inc.

DANIEL C. WALDEN, the project officer for this study, is a Senior Research Manager at the National Center for Health Services Research and has guided the design and implementation of a number of studies on health services use and expenditures.

RENATE WILSON is Editorial Associate at the National Center for Health Services Research and a Research Associate at the Johns Hopkins School of Hygiene and Public Health.